PENGUIN BOOKS

FAMILY MEMORIES

Dame Rebecca West was born Cicily Isabel Fairfield in London in 1892. She began to appear in print as a journalist and political writer as early as 1911 and was soon active in the causes of feminism and social reform. Her first book, *Henry James*, was published in 1916. Her classic study, *The New Meaning of Treason*, and five novels, *The Thinking Reed*, *The Fountain Overflows*, *This Real Night*, *Cousin Rosamund*, and *Sunflower*, are all available in Penguin. A towering and brilliant figure in English letters for more than seventy years, she was a powerful and distinguished essayist, biographer, journalist, and novelist. Rebecca West was made Dame Commander of the British Empire in 1959; she died in March 1983 at the age of ninety.

FAMILY
MEMORIES

AN AUTOBIOGRAPHICAL JOURNEY

REBECCA WEST

———

EDITED AND INTRODUCED BY
FAITH EVANS

PENGUIN BOOKS

PENGUIN BOOKS
Published by the Penguin Group
Viking Penguin Inc., 40 West 23rd Street,
New York, New York 10010, U.S.A.
Penguin Books Ltd, 27 Wrights Lane,
London W8 5TZ, England
Penguin Books Australia Ltd, Ringwood,
Victoria, Australia
Penguin Books Canada Ltd, 2801 John Street,
Markham, Ontario, Canada L3R 1B4
Penguin Books (N.Z.) Ltd, 182–190 Wairau Road,
Auckland 10, New Zealand

Penguin Books Ltd, Registered Offices:
Harmondsworth, Middlesex, England

First published in Great Britain by Virago Press Limited 1987
First published in the United States of America by
Viking Penguin Inc. 1988
Published in Penguin Books 1989

1   3   5   7   9   10   8   6   4   2

LIBRARY OF CONGRESS CATALOGING IN PUBLICATION DATA
West, Rebecca, Dame, 1892–1983
Family memories/Rebecca West; edited and introduced by Faith
Evans.
p.   cm.
1. West, Rebecca, Dame, 1892–1983—Biography—Family. 2. Authors,
English—20th century—Biography. 3. Mackenzie family.
4. Fairfield family. 5. Great Britain—Social life and
customs—20th century. I. Evans, Faith. II. Title.
PR6045.E8Z464   1989
828′.91209—dc 19
[B]   88-26574
ISBN 0 14 00.9495 4

Printed in the United States of America
Set in Goudy Old Style

CONTENTS

FAMILY
MEMORIES

INTRODUCTION

Family Memories is not only about Rebecca West's ancestors: it is about herself. Always an imposing narrator, she is never more so than when writing about members of her family, and she uses them to express her own feelings and ideas. Indeed, her very identity seems at times to fuse with theirs. Though she died before she could finish the book, *Family Memories* joins her novels *Sunflower* and *Cousin Rosamund*, both now posthumously published, in the category of 'uncompleted but never relinquished'.

Rebecca West was writing *Family Memories* on and off for the last two decades of her life. There were many interruptions: the illness and death of her husband; work on a commissioned book, *1900*, and new editions of her work from Virago; a social life that continued to be very active until her declining sight and hearing made it difficult. But apart from regular reviewing for the *Sunday Telegraph*, this book was her main concern during the very last years. Perhaps she thought that by writing about her family she could assuage her own sense of rootlessness and displacement, feelings that had always been with her but which increased with the years. Certainly she wrote and rewrote the manuscript continually, often in the middle of the night, and the order and form in which she wanted the material to appear fluctuated according to her mood. A detailed account of the editorial history appears at the end of the book.

Family Memories tells the story of three families: Rebecca West's maternal line, the Mackenzies, which she traces back to Highland pipers on one side and wealthy textile manufacturers on the other; her paternal line, the Fairfields, a dispossessed Anglo-Irish Army family with aristocratic connections; and the Maxwell Andrews, her husband's family, an exotic mixture of Lithuanian, Lancastrian and Scottish. (As this third family does not relate directly to Rebecca West's own story, it has been placed as an Appendix at the end of the book, so that it can be read quite separately.)

The history of Rebecca West's family is wide and rich. It travels from Edinburgh to Melbourne to County Kerry to London, and the telling of it involves an overlapping of several consciousnesses over a period of more than a century. The sources are many: conversations between Rebecca West and her mother Isabella before her death in 1921; letters written by uncles and aunts and cousins from all over the world, mainly to the Mackenzie family in Edinburgh; the auto-biography of her uncle Alick, who became President of the Royal Academy of Music; Mackenzie and Fairfield family trees. Rebecca West's last secretary, the novelist Diana Stainforth, remembers her in the early 1980s poring over letters and photographs, reaching for reference books in search of background information (she was particularly fond of Burke's Peerage), recalling and embellishing childhood memories.

Both Rebecca West's parents were much given to the telling and retelling of familiar tales. Her father, Charles Fairfield, in particular was a great talker. 'I cannot remember a time,' she wrote, 'when I had not a rough idea of what was meant by capitalism, socialism, individualism, anarchism, liberalism and conservatism . . . I grew up with a knowledge of politics and economics comparable to the knowledge of religion automatically acquired by children in a churchgoing and Bible-reading household.' All these sources fed into her imagination and formed the fabric upon which she spun her stories.

It was certainly from Charles Fairfield – and at a very early age, since he left home once and for all in 1901, when she was eight, and died five years later – that Rebecca West acquired her passion for abstract ideas and her enquiring view of the world, though she quickly transformed it into a feminist vision which was not his at all. Like her heroine Ellen Melville in The Judge, she was active in the Edinburgh suffrage movement when still only a teenager. And though she later turned away from the movement, her bold and distinctive brand of feminism never wavered. For more than three-quarters of a century of writing she refused to be constrained within traditional boundaries of any kind, as though challenging her sex not to rest with the easy option of personal concerns. An episode which inspired her epic *Black Lamb and Grey Falcon*, the account of her travels in Yugoslavia before the war, illustrates the process. Lying in a London nursing home in 1934 recovering from an operation, Rebecca West is listening to the BBC when she hears an announcement that gives her a premonition of war. She cries out to the nurse, 'A most terrible thing has happened. The King of Yugoslavia has been assassinated.'

'Oh dear!' she replied. 'Did you know him?'

'No,' I said.

'Then why,' she asked, 'do you think it's so terrible?' Rebecca West offers this to her readers as a dangerous example of the narrow 'female' perspective.

Many of Rebecca West's wider concerns are present in *Family Memories*: the struggle between good and evil, light and dark, life and death; the exposure of cant and hypocrisy; the private drama set against the public or historical backdrop; the redemptive power of art, particularly music; the meaning of betrayal and its co-conspirator humiliation. The manner is also very characteristic, moving freely over a wide range of topics and quite resistant to any critical categorization. Journalistic comments drop into the narrative, contemporary observations mix with events that took place a century ago or a continent away; illusion and reality join.

Although many of these tendencies were present in Rebecca West's work from an early age, the emphases naturally vary at different periods, the themes which were most resonant in any given work tending to be those which were currently preoccupying her in life. This is especially true of *Family Memories* because she had the raw material of memory, some of it personal memory, to draw on. It provides one of the very best examples of her instinctive mixing of life and art, of public and private experience.

It is possible, for example, to read into *Family Memories* many signs of Rebecca West's preoccupation with betrayal. At about the time she started writing about her family she had just expanded and reworked her book about 'public' traitors, *The New Meaning of Treason* (1964), and treated the subject in fiction: her Russian book *The Birds Fall Down* (1966). She was more than ever alert to her own susceptibility, to the possibility of betrayal in her private life, and this apprehension is strongly present in *Family Memories*. But male betrayal can be, and often is, accompanied by female strength. Of this phenomenon, too, we have several striking examples in *Family Memories*.

Although it is more like a sequence of inter-related novellas than a verifiable history, and therefore, like so much of Rebecca West's work, only acceptable within its own terms, a degree of narrative continuity is nonetheless offered in the figure of her mother Isabella Mackenzie, whom we are able to follow from childhood to marriage to motherhood and with whom Rebecca West the narrator identifies very closely indeed. Isabella is a talented pianist, and she shadows Clare Aubrey, that interesting, shabby, eagle-like creature who holds the family together in Rebecca West's novel about her childhood, *The Fountain Overflows*. But it is Isabella's mother Janet (whom Rebecca West knew only when she was old and infirm) who performs the holding function here. As we observe Janet struggling to raise six children (plus two extra cousins that a male relative lands on her, rather as Constance and Rosamund are landed on the Aubreys) in the musical traditions that her husband, Musical Director of the Theatre Royal, had begun in his lifetime, she becomes the very spirit of womanly resilience and restraint. Janet is proud, witty and a good businesswoman, but she has to avoid contact with men (so we are told) because of the 'biological tragedy which the human species was forced to enact on a vast scale so long as there was no system of birth control'. As long as she contains herself, and does not break Scottish male codes of behaviour, Janet can survive. Like Ibsen's Mrs Alving, she knows her strengths but, for better or worse, does not flaunt them. Foiling a burglar who tries to snatch her reticule, Janet does not falter and neither does daughter Isabella: 'I would have been lost if she had whimpered.'

But this was still mid-Victorian Edinburgh, the time and the place in which it was 'as if all menfolk were always right and do not know what failure is', and 'the Victorian community refused to contemplate with any glow of warmth a family not headed by a man'. When Janet's eldest son Alick returns home from a musical apprenticeship in Germany, 'the crown and sceptre were his'. That Alick should reject this honour to marry and lead a life of his own is unthinkable.

Yet this is what Alick, unaccountably, does. He 'betrays' his family by leaving it manless. Here Rebecca West's position as, in Michelene Wandor's phrase, 'a bourgeois radical feminist' leads her into serious conflict — with herself, and potentially with her readers too. Because

Rebecca West actually half believed it, because (like the actress in her novel *Sunflower*) she was caught in the historical bind of autonomy versus domestic respectability, she cannot help seeming to collude with Scottish society's conviction that a household without a man is somehow unnatural, and the feeling comes painfully through in her narrative.

Not only Alick but Mary Ironside, the seamstress who takes him away, come in for passionate hostility from Isabella (who has now more or less fused with the narrator). Rebecca West found it hard to forgive traitors whether public or private, a feeling that might have derived from her own sense of having been abandoned – by her father, by H.G. Wells, and others. (When writing about her childhood at the end of *Family Memories*, she shows the same kind of ambivalence towards her father as she does towards Alick, before and after they 'desert'.)

In her excessive scrubbed prettiness, her refusal to 'taste', and in the devious way she is said to have wormed her way into Alick's affections, Mary Ironside reminds us of a sly French *confidante* or a female Uriah Heep. But so overbearing is Rebecca West's (through Isabella's) antagonism – 'She was all stranger' – that she risks failing to draw her readers into her condemnation. It is a typical weakness – or strength. Once Rebecca West has taken up a position, it is absolutely fixed: she will fight to the death, and the reader, unable to match her single-mindedness, is tempted to rebel, to consider the alternative view. In his autobiography Alick, a largely unattractive and self-regarding character who fails to draw attention to the musicality of the rest of his family, gains even so an element of sympathy at his palpable relief at escaping from the Heriot Row household.

It's significant that it should be a woman who comes in for such vitriol. Mary Ironside joins a band of women for whom Rebecca West expressed an uncontrollable dislike: her aunt Sophie, her sister Lettie and H.G. Wells's wife Jane. These detested women entered her imagination and resurfaced in her work: her guide Constantine's crass German wife Gerda in *Black Lamb*; conformist Cordelia in *The Fountain Overflows*. No man ever receives quite such bruising attention.

If Janet Mackenzie's problems are connected with her status as a woman trying to survive in a Victorian community without a husband, her daughter's are more straightforwardly to do with the limitations imposed by gender conventions. Isabella does not have the freedom to move easily in international musical circles; she cannot aspire to the kind of success that has come to her brother Alick. The best she can hope for is a position as a musical governess. Ultimately, her happiness must depend upon finding the right husband, and although she has charm and beauty, she lacks money and a father, so her chances are not good. Yet after Mary has spirited Alick away, Isabella must effectively, though secretly, provide a regenerative force in the manless household.

Now mature enough to take on the burden of the family's humiliations as well as her own, Isabella offers the strength for which her middle-aged mother no longer, since Alick's departure, has the energy or the will. In a strong scene in which Edinburgh burghers foregather to discuss the undiscussable – another brother, Joey, has been involved in a homosexual scandal – Isabella looks at their faces and concludes, 'There must have been some allegation – which almost certainly, considering they were all looking so fatuous, so masculine, must be nonsensical.' Because she is a woman, Isabella must be 'protected' from knowledge of the nature of Joey's 'crime'; but later, when the family fortunes fail, it is Isabella who is asked to leave home rather than her sole remaining brother, an alcoholic. Isabella 'suffers a moment of blinding rage at this offhand disposal of her future', and everything in her cries out at the injustice and impracticability of the plan.

Yet her compassion and strength save her. She cannot blame her mother because she knows (but again it is not discussed) that even though it has meant sending three of her children out into the world, Janet has had to defer to prevailing male standards of morality. In agreeing to be dispatched to a strange family in London, Isabella gains a stature that makes her a sister to Elizabeth Bennett and Jane Eyre.

Isabella must draw private solace from what Rebecca West calls 'sibship', in particular her bonds with cousin Jessie and brother Joey. In the exaggerated goodness of Jessie Watson Campbell we can recognize something of the 'spirituality' of Cousin Rosamund. Even more intriguing as a prototype is Isabella's beloved, doomed brother Joey, the youngest and most beautiful of the six children (in Rebecca West's imagination, though not perhaps in photographs), who has a voice like an angel and who, in spite of his extreme youth, volunteers to become protector of the household after Alick's 'defection'. Isabella cossets Joey as if he were her own child, though she is barely two years his senior: 'He could have her whole life from the minute she knew he wanted it.' Joey is of course Richard Quin(bury), the idealized younger brother Rebecca West never had, who appears in *The Fountain Overflows* and its sequels and is eventually killed in the First World War. It was in Quinbury, Essex, that Rebecca West spent the first year of her life as an unmarried mother, at the beginning of the war, and many years later, in *Heritage*, his scathing novel about his childhood, her son Anthony called his hero-self Richard. But detective games apart, these images of pure goodness, direct counterpoints to the 'evil' represented by Mary Ironside and the chorus of detested women, bear a heavy symbolic significance for Rebecca West. Together they represent her Manichean view of the world, her fundamental belief that we are governed by, and at the mercy of, the forces of light and dark, good and evil.

'What I chiefly want to do when I write,' Rebecca West said in a BBC talk in 1964, 'is to contemplate character either by inventing my own characters in novels and short stories based on my own experience, or by studying characters in history, ancient or, by preference, modern. This is an inborn tendency in me.' Her need to place her characters can occasionally lead her down long and winding paths, which some call snobbery and others a passion for genealogy (the reality, as so often with Rebecca West, lies somewhere in between). She never tired of looking into people's backgrounds as a means of comprehending their behaviour, and it was a tendency that was bound to surface when writing about her own family and, by extension, herself. The personal nature of her subject simultaneously fuelled and legitimized her search.

Rebecca West habitually contemplates private behaviour in the context of public events, and vice versa. In *Family Memories* she uses a version of this approach when she sets individual members of her family against wide historical canvases. Juxtaposed with Uncle Alick's musical sojourn in Sondershausen is a re-creation of student life in mid-nineteenth-century Germany, with its town guilds, its Hof Marschals and its Stadtpfeifers, and its romantic passion for the 'New Music' of Liszt, Schumann and Schubert. Then there are the customs and hypocrisies of mid-Victorian Edinburgh: the social divide between the New and Old Towns, and the entourage of bogus church-going advisers surrounding the 'brave wee lady' at Heriot Row – negligent lawyers, pompous policemen and a memorable Dickensian doctor, 'Tyrian Purple'. Rebecca West's husband Henry is placed against a background which involves Russian double-dealing in the early nineteenth century, the import/export business in Rangoon in the 1890s, and Germany at the outbreak of the First World War, when he was unaccountably interned in a camp which aimed to brainwash Easterners into spying on Britain after a German victory.

In her descriptions of many of these 'placings' Rebecca West could summon up a lifetime of travel and research, drawing on a combination of her journalist's instinct and her novelist's imagination to weave them into a story. But the most intriguing of all the backgrounds in *Family Memories* is the long section on Australia, which provides the context for her parents' marriage and early life together in St Kilda in the early 1880s.

Australia offered a new challenge: to Isabella, dispatched there by the Edinburgh advisers to check up on her brother Johnnie, and to Rebecca West's imaginative powers as well – for this was a country she had never visited. Admitting to the problems posed by the unfamiliar setting, she adapts her prose style to meet the challenge; and though, not surprisingly, she makes simple errors of fact (in her description of the St Kilda foreshore, for example), she succeeds in creating a remarkable picture of life in late nineteenth-century Australia, especially in the mining areas, where the whole lifestyle of the inhabitants was transformed by the gold rush. The writing takes on a dreamlike quality reminiscent of *The Return of the Soldier*: nightmarish journeys are undertaken; kangaroos engage in weird races; a beautiful Pre-Raphaelite woman appears, disappears and finally kills herself; other incidents open but do not close; conversations have several layers of meaning; nothing is quite what it seems. Even the Australian landscape, with its burning sun and its sinister black river and its labyrinthine hotels, is heavy with symbolism.

The memoir has turned into a novel. In a melodramatic scene at

Melbourne docks, as Charles and Isabella leave the ship on which they have met, there is first of all the suspense of waiting for Isabella's brother Johnnie, and then, when he and his gaudy band do turn up, a series of traditional fictional devices. Charles Fairfield takes in Lizzie's 'gamboge hair' and sees at a glance what Isabella must never know, or admit to knowing: that her brother has married a prostitute. Before leaving he hands her, in a gesture worthy of Mr Darcy, a note with the address of his hotel, in case she should ever need it. And it is not Isabella but Lizzie, the golden-hearted prostitute with whom Isabella forms a deep bond, who preserves the note which eventually reunites the rootless British pair. Lizzie too is not quite what she seems.

This scene contains another symbolic incident: when it has seemed as if all were lost, as if Johnnie would never arrive and Isabella's journey from England has been in vain, Isabella is entranced and reassured when she hears the sound of a whistled Jacobite lament by one of Johnnie's friends. (Only serious musicians, Rebecca West tells us, can fully understand the importance of whistling in the musical pecking order: for one thing, 'it enables them to make sensational contributions to parties.') The point here is that art, even 'low' art like whistling, can always be redemptive. As soon as she hears that pure sound, Isabella knows that both music and her brother are near, and her salvation is possible after all.

The ensuing courtship between Isabella and Charles is watched over by a kindly but misguided couple (misguided because of their unthinking acceptance of the authority of the church) who shadow the many innkeepers in Rebecca West's fiction. The Mullins conspire towards the marriage in an almost ritualistic way, as if responsible for ensuring that the relationship is conducted with proper decorum. And when yet another inn-keeping couple enter the story, the O'Briens, the conversations between the two women, replete with innuendo, smooth insult and *double entendre*, reach back to Restoration comedy.

Isabella, who is recuperating from a broken romance in London, drifts through these events as if in a trance, unable or unwilling to control her own destiny. Throughout the Australian chapters, up to the marvellous sketch of the nurse Alice, shamed by her family's convict origins, there is a sense of mystery and uncertainty and expectation. 'It was the other side of the world, where one could break off what was happening to one and start afresh.'

When we move to Rebecca West's own infancy, there is another sharp change of mood. Though she began this section early on – it was mainly written in the 1960s, before she embarked on her family history – she never returned to complete it, so what we have here is a sequence of fragments. Some of them seem to have been written, like their fictional counterpart, from the arrested childhood viewpoint of *The Fountain Overflows*; others reveal quite clearly the stamp of her adult convictions. All in all these fragments seem to represent another effort to come to terms with the conflicting joy and insecurity of her early life: years in which her parents, particularly her mother, were fighting to keep up some semblance of middle-class life with few resources to support it.

It would (and no doubt will) take a psychoanalytic critic to disentangle her 'real' memories from those which entered her adult imagination from family legend or her subconscious, or to probe the significance of her attitude to her parents and sisters as revealed here. (Of Freud, she herself said, in a *Times* profile in 1982, 'He has shown us how awful we really are, forever nursing grudges we felt in childhood.' On another occasion, she attacked the notion of penis envy because 'it presupposes that the unconscious does not tell little girls that they have perfectly good sex organs within themselves.') The only consistency here is in the startling hostility to her elder sister Lettie, 'who never ceased to convey to me that I was a revolting intruder in her home', and her admiration for her mother, with whom, apart from a brief period after the birth of her son, Rebecca West shared a close and loving relationship. As for her father, she worshipped him, but felt threatened by his sexuality and fecklessness.

Her ambivalence towards him is always present. Sometimes, in later life, she would imply that there was nothing unusual about the way in which he left home; at others she would declare that they were '*totally* fatherless'. In *Family Memories* he is presented both as a loving figure, in his 'tobacco-ish warmth' and his willingness to play silly games, and, ultimately, as a tragic one. In some versions of this section, Rebecca West describes her parents' union as 'the marriage of loneliness to loneliness'. In others, she rejoices that they have passed on to her their fundamental, joint belief in the importance of the pleasure principle.

Rebecca West's fragmented memories of her childhood give a lively sense of some of the qualities that the adult woman and writer was to display in such abundance: her intelligent rebelliousness (an episode at Richmond High School in which she routs a religious headmistress) and her trenchant wit (a child's view of gnarled old age: 'Her way of getting old was to turn blue, and there was nothing more to it'). If she had not been over seventy herself when she started *Family Memories*, would she ever have got round to writing the sustained account of her own life with which she originally intended to finish the book? For many reasons, it seems unlikely.

Obviously age and discinclination were contributory factors – 'Somehow I have lost the finishing power,' she told an interviewer in 1980, when she was eighty-seven – but there was more to it than that. Although she was punctilious about deadlines and commissions she was never, even as a young woman, particularly interested in completing her own work, in packaging and presenting it. A clue to her method can be found in 'My Relations with Music'. In seeking to discover what she knew (which she always declared to be the purpose of her writing) she would take off on all kinds of tangents, reverting to the original point only when most people had quite forgotten it. She would not be bound by the structural formulae of literary conventions.

This was a bone of contention with the methodical Wells. Towards the end of their relationship, on holiday together in Amalfi in 1922-23, his writing project was *Outline of History* and hers *The Judge*. She infuriated him with her lack of discipline. 'I pestered her to make a scheme and estimate a length for the great novel she was writing,' he wrote (*H.G. Wells in Love*, 1984). 'She writes like a loom, producing her broad, rich fabric with hardly a thought of how it will make up into a shape . . .' The title stayed, even without the judge, and the book became instead a powerful portrait of a mother's relationship with her illegitimate son.

Rebecca West's wrangles with her own illegitimate son were another reason for her failure to finish: by the time she began to write *Family Memories*, the grotesque public and private battle between them had been raging for some time, and it was to continue up to, and indeed after, her death, when *Heritage* was published in Britain for the first time. Her papers reveal that whenever she tried to account for her later life, as she often did, the picture is clouded with bitterness, not just against Anthony and Wells but against anyone who had committed the most minor offence or breach of trust. The material is often not coherent and it is certainly not intended for public consumption.

Rebecca West had, in any case, her own misgivings about the veracity and value of autobiography. When researching *St Augustine* (1933) she was not surprised to find that his *Confessions* were not altogether faithful to reality. 'It is too subjectively true to be objectively true. There are things in Augustine's life which he could not bear to think of at all, or very much, or without falsification, so the *Confessions* are not without gaps, understatements, and misstatements.' And in *Family Memories*, she writes that the real flaw in the concept of autobiography is that 'people rarely set down on paper pedantically accurate accounts of their humiliations'. This is not of course strictly true: for some people self-exposure is precisely what autobiography is about. But Rebecca West was, and with some reason, even more susceptible to humiliation than most of us. We can only be thankful for what she did succeed in setting down, gaps, misstatements and all.

FAITH EVANS
April 1987

PART ONE

THE
CAMPBELL MACKENZIES

Just before the Second World War, my husband and I bought a house near the borders of Buckinghamshire and Oxfordshire, in the Chiltern Hills. On our journeys we passed through a district unknown to me, though I was forty-seven years old and have spent much of my life in London. It was the northern part of Notting Hill Gate. We came in through the raw new suburbs, hacked out of the countryside and still bleeding, past the great mock-picturesque Ruskin-inspired prison Wormwood Scrubs, and into a curiously enjoyable monotony of nobly planned and ignobly used neo-classical houses built for the merchant classes in the high noon of the Victorian age, and left, as if by a conqueror, where Paddington Railway Junction had its tracks and yards and sent up puffs of smoke by day and flashes of flame by night. We particularly enjoyed driving down a crescent which, though not very long and not very high, was so designed that it might have been the façade of a baroque palace, and we felt disappointment one evening when the road was up and we had to make a detour. But this took us into a dilapidated square that looked worse than shabby, that looked as if it had been devastated by street battles, in the light of a crimson sunset reflected on the scuffed stucco housefronts. The side that faced the sunset was blazing crimson, the one that faced the reflection of the sunset was the colour of a wine-stain on a tablecloth. There was a light ground mist coming in with the evening and we might have been looking at one of Claude Lorraine's pictures of palaces by the sea. We sat in the car and looked at it until the crimson dimmed, and as we drove away my eye fell on the name of the street and I saw that this was the place where I had been born.

I had been born eighteen months earlier than Henry, in December 1892: at the opposite end of the earth from his birthplace, in wholly different circumstances, into a family as peculiar, but in another way.* Henry had come into the Asian light surrounded by a palace; and round his home was a city where architecture raised up pagodas and needle-fine spires, delicate as the anatomy within small flowers or fern bracts, but going up, up into the skies: and surrounding that were the forests and the rivers and the seas and a land-based sea of people wearing bright clothes, people without end. I was born in one of those rows of stucco Victorian houses, remote heirs of the Adam and Nash tradition, which stood solid and ambitious all across Notting Hill, built to be rival to the new Kensington down past the Albert Hall. But the project had been doomed to failure, and it was too far away from the centre of things, so that at the time of my birth it was thirty odd years old and a palpable failure, very shabby for its age. The district was also frequently veiled by the smoke, dense and dark grey and greasy, which hung about the railway lines, emerging from glass-roofed, Crystal-Palace-bred Paddington and Marylebone Stations to cleave the district on their westerly and north-westerly ways.

ALEXANDER MACKENZIE

My family were living in Notting Hill only briefly, and not wholly because of poverty, although they were certainly poor.

To tell the whole story, I must start far earlier than my own life and spend some time describing the rich textures of my mother's ancestry as manufactured by the Scottish tradition. She came of Highland peasant stock on her father's side: her paternal great-grandfather had been born when his parents were on the run after the rebellion of 1745.* When the family settled down, their reaction was apolitical and musical. They looked round for a town band and joined it, and so did their descendants.

Then came my grandfather, Alexander Mackenzie,* whose gifts as a violinist were above the average, and whose precocity brought him at thirteen into the highly regarded orchestra of the Theatre Royal, Edinburgh. (It stood where the Post Office is today.) On his own savings he went to Dresden and studied under the teacher, Lipinski,* and went later to London to learn from Prosper Sainton* of the Royal Academy of Music. He went back to Edinburgh and became the leader of the Theatre Royal Orchestra, and started on a career as a populist song-writer, setting to music the verses of an old friend, James Ballantine, a house-painter who became a painter of some technical achievement and a poet remarkable only for persuasive emotion, chiefly of a political kind.* All his songs had the tear-jerking quality necessary in material designed by the artists for whom they were designed, the street musicians who then sang, or played wind instruments, in the quieter parts of the town as the darkness enclosed them. Up through the blackness between the tall houses, which was hardly dispersed by the primrose light of the old gas lamps at their bases, the sweet, sweet tune rose like a soaring sugar bird; and then there would come the sounds of a window-sash or two being thrown up, and the chink of coins falling light on cobbles or pavement, and lastly, softly shouted thanks and good-nights came up and down slanting lines from ground level and the high windows, and the street was quiet.

That manifestation of my grandfather left survivals on the childish memories of many among us. Street-singers, muffin-men, the 'Sweet Lavender' callers, the 'Ripe Strawberries' men were all about us: we were glad to have a cause for family pride in our street-singing share of the show (which we thought eternal, but it has utterly passed away). But my grandfather had his roots in a more remote period. The manager of the Theatre Royal, Edinburgh, where he was leader of the orchestra, was a greatly admired actor named William Henry Murray: he was married to an Irish actress whose sister was the wife of Tom Moore.* But Murray was also the grandson of the Sir John Murray who had been secretary to Bonnie Prince Charlie and had betrayed the Jacobites after Culloden, and a hundred years afterwards the shame had not been forgotten. When William Henry Murray went to play in other Scottish provincial cities, great was the glory, but there were landladies who would not give him lodgings; and when he stood as godfather to my Uncle William Mackenzie, the christening mug was oddly inscribed 'To William Murray Mackenzie from William H. Murray, Esquire of – what?' The meaning was: his grandfather's beautiful estate at Broughton in Peebleshire had (like his title) been sequestrated.*

There is a pendant to this story. My uncle Willie lived all his life with his mother in Edinburgh, and the time came when they suffered that preliminary taste of death, that first word of the farewell we must say to the things of this earth, called burglary. My grandmother, giving a list of her losses to a policeman, mentioned the christening mug with the tragic inscription, and briefly explained its significance. The policeman took the point at once. He was aware, not in detail but in heavy outline, of the historical issues involved, and though he was civil to my grandmother he said some very rude things about the Murrays. This would be in the 1870s, about ninety years after the death of Bonnie Prince Charlie in Rome.

UNCLE ALICK

The christening mug was one of six needed for the family. There were two daughters, four sons, of whom only one came to special note. This was the eldest, Alick, a gifted violinist and a more gifted composer than is generally allowed, who became President of the Royal Academy of Music in London and held that office from 1888 to 1924; and probably he was the only eminent member of his family because he was the first-born.* His father had time before his death to put the child's feet on the path that would enable him to develop his evident inheritance of the family's musical talent: the little boy was sent at nine to get a general education at Sondershausen, in Thuringia, which was one of the thirty-six separate states comprising the German Federation, and this could ensure him a good musical education, as there was a renowned orchestra at the court of the local Grand Duke.

Rich, rich as a good plum cake was the substance of Europe in that time. How did a penniless musician with a large family contrive this beneficial arrangement for his little boy at a time when there were none of the agencies, grants and scholarships that nurture young talent in our day? It was easy. In those days even obscure musicians wandered over Europe, footloose as medieval scholars, and foreigners often appeared in Edinburgh and did their stint there for a year or two, and this was a two-way arrangement. My grandfather had noted that there was one exceptionally well-trained cellist in the orchestra of the Theatre Royal, Edinburgh, named Gunther Bartel, and found that he was from Sondershausen and that his father was an important member of the Grand Duke's orchestra, as well as being the Town Musician, its *Stadtmusiker*.* This official exercised a marvellous function. He had to pack his house with apprentice performers whom he had to feed and teach, and when they were up to standard pour them out over the town to meet such need for music as was felt there at balls, weddings, christenings, banquets, funerals, and in the streets at Christmas time.

The elder Bartel consented to receive my uncle Alick as a pupil and boarder, though not in his capacity of *Stadtmusiker*, as that office, and the innocent guild which it had controlled, were about to disappear, for the reason that both Frederick the Great and later Napoleon had worked long and hard to transfer their duties to military bands. The nine-year-old was to be taught from the first with an eye on the Grand Duke's orchestra; and by chance he met the Grand Duke almost as soon as he arrived in Sondershausen. His father wrote to his wife in Edinburgh:

We went for a drive the other day to the 'Possen', a hunting lodge, when we came upon a respectable-looking man who turned out to be the Grand Duke of Schwarzburg-Sondershausen. He entered in conversation and showed us about the place and lifted Alick to see the deer.

A few weeks later, back at his home, Alexander Mackenzie died, of some wasting disease not diagnosed.* On that, his son, alone in another country, fell into a deep melancholy and had an experience he was never to forget, that was to strike him again and again when he remembered it, with the awe caused by the original happening. He was walking in the Bartels' garden, in the shadow of the ancient city wall, when he heard his father calling 'Alick, Alick,' from the street outside. He ran out to find him but there was no one there. All his life my uncle was persuaded that he had recognized his father's voice. Some time after that, he woke one morning to find his obsessive gloom gone and a negotiable grief in its place; and during the day he discovered that he could suddenly speak and understand German, though till then he had found great difficulties with the language.

No doubt he was sustained by his musical rapture. Certainly he was able to study in conditions which would break the spirit of most modern pupils. He was to have a late experience of medieval darkness – gas did not come to Sondershausen till he had been there for two years – and of medieval noise. He had been living with the Bartels for a full year before his host and teacher came to the end of his duties as *Stadtmusiker* and could disembarrass himself of the crowd of young guildsmen who practised their art literally all over the house – the flautists in the attic, the clarinettists in the cellar, the double-bass in the wood shed, the trombones in the garden, and violinists all over the place.

But young Alick himself was to have a more immediate and exciting and prolonged contact with that delicious moment in history when neo-classical Maecenases could pelt the descendants of the gods with roses and bid the Ganymedes to fill up the wine-cups, and when there was no shame in patronage because the patrons knew that the gods were worthy of worship as well as the artists they protected, so that the entertainment was sanctified by piety. This dream of life was to be realized under his eyes as he became absorbed into the ducal orchestra, which offered a spectacle surprising to our modern view. This can be judged from the free open-air concerts provided on Sunday afternoons out of the ducal funds, which took place at a little distance from the town, in a wide clearing in the Thuringian woods. The orchestra was placed in a baroque bandstand in the centre of the open space, and was surrounded by the audience, which consisted of the four organized groups of citizens: the large number of officers on the strength of the very small ducal army, the civil servants, the merchants, the townsfolk and villagers. On the stroke of three the Hof Marschal, who bore the incredible name of Hof Marschal von Wurmb, took his stand in front of the orchestra, and the conductor turned to face him. The Hof Marschal then raised his tall gold-knobbed staff and both bowed. It was a signal that the ducal party had arrived at the edge of the clearing, and were descending from their carriage. By a curiously barbaric routine the orchestra then plunged into the first item of the programme, while the Hof Marschal slowly crossed the sword to find his sacred charges, turned about and led them as slowly back. It is not known how the appearance of the family accorded with the great music which so often accompanied them, as my uncle was blind to that. Even when he was not playing his violin his eyes were elsewhere.

For the audience was not wholly indigenous. It often included music critics and musicians from much larger and more important towns, such as Weimar, Leipzig and Berlin, who felt they had to attend, through this meant for all of them a long and uncomfortable journey by stagecoach. The magnet was the remarkable conductor, Kapellmeister to the Duke, Eduard Stein,* who would have been in trouble in Thuringia had he found himself there only eighty years later, but then walked confidently on that and all ground, believing as Jews did at that time that Germany was as friendly to their people as any country in Europe, provided only that they did not try to get into the army. Stein was the quick-witted but profound intellectual who alone can be the perfect conductor; he loved fostering the individual talents of his orchestra; and because he was an intellectual he understood the battle that was being fought for a new kind of music.

Wagner they played in Sondershausen, and Mendelssohn, Schumann, Liszt. It could not have been a more marvellous place and time for the boy. Most of these great men had been composing seriously during the last twenty years; in fact he was, in a sense, not so much younger than they were; he was playing their music, he had a hand in it; and sometimes there was more to it than that.* Liszt had actually visited one of these Sunday afternoon concerts to hear his own *Mazeppa*;* and then Alick had watched him in the interval with adoration not diminished by his sense that the great man was looking slightly ridiculous. He was as romantic in appearance as was reported: slender and upright, with brooding profile and finely cut lips, a mane of prematurely grey hair and a blanched skin. But he was wearing a hat too small for him, and his hands, large as befits a pianist, were crammed into elegant grey kid gloves wrong for him by a size or two. Though my uncle was a small boy he was moved not to mockery, but to a tender and cherishing amusement, which he was often to feel again when, twenty years later, the great man had become his friend. But there was something about Liszt, however intimate they became, which forbade my uncle to ask him why he once went to a ducally sponsored concert at Sondershausen in somebody else's hat and gloves.

Alick's life was to continue on the same level of happiness he had reached at Sondershausen. He was a master of the theory and practice of music, and in those days there was a network of music-lovers all over Europe which could be approached on the spur of the moment and would welcome them according to their capacity (except where, as in the Paris Opera House, politics had entrenched themselves or where there was furious warfare between the Old and the New music). He took full advantage of that easy situation, finding colleagues, friends, devotees everywhere, and always earning gratitude by his

competence. He was disappointed because he never was recognized as
a composer, and there he had a case: Busoni, though that reserved
being was no close friend of his, admired a piano concerto of his and
played it himself for some years, and taught it to his pupils, as a
neglected and valuable work.* But this neglect was Alick's unique
displeasure, for his unending service to his art gave him everything
else, even personal happiness, since his emotional needs were fully
satisfied by his profession.

Impossible not to respect Alick Mackenzie for these *Studienjahre*. It
looks like a moral triumph. The boy had devoted himself with fervour
to his studies, had accepted hardship so long as it was a condition of
receiving useful tuition, handled his earnings and his poor little
allowance from home with great good sense, did not get himself lost
on long journeys here, there and everywhere by stagecoach, ship and
early train, picked the right teachers, entered himself for the most
convenient scholarships and when he got them, settled in decent
lodgings, finding jobs in theatre orchestras, and presenting himself,
clean and tidy, to fulfil the conditions laid down by all employers and
teachers likely to be useful to him. I would admire him for all these
achievements in any case, and my admiration is the warmer because
such discipline is rare in later generations of my family. Nevertheless I
have to admit that my uncle Alick's independence and fortitude did a
disservice to all his relatives.

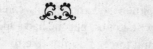

THE HOUSEHOLD AT
HERIOT ROW

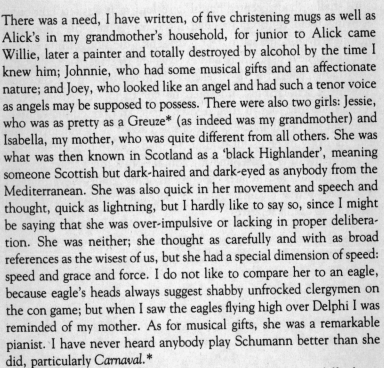

There was a need, I have written, of five christening mugs as well as Alick's in my grandmother's household, for junior to Alick came Willie, later a painter and totally destroyed by alcohol by the time I knew him; Johnnie, who had some musical gifts and an affectionate nature; and Joey, who looked like an angel and had such a tenor voice as angels may be supposed to possess. There were also two girls: Jessie, who was as pretty as a Greuze* (as indeed was my grandmother) and Isabella, my mother, who was quite different from all others. She was what was then known in Scotland as a 'black Highlander', meaning someone Scottish but dark-haired and dark-eyed as anybody from the Mediterranean. She was also quick in her movement and speech and thought, quick as lightning, but I hardly like to say so, since I might be saying that she was over-impulsive or lacking in proper deliberation. She was neither; she thought as carefully and with as broad references as the wisest of us, but she had a special dimension of speed: speed and grace and force. I do not like to compare her to an eagle, because eagle's heads always suggest shabby unfrocked clergymen on the con game; but when I saw the eagles flying high over Delphi I was reminded of my mother. As for musical gifts, she was a remarkable pianist. I have never heard anybody play Schumann better than she did, particularly *Carnaval*.*

My grandmother, Janet Campbell Mackenzie, had some difficulty in providing for this large family, who were between the ages of one year and ten years when her husband died. Her father's decision to reject her because she had married a penniless musician was not softened by her misfortune. I know nothing of this iron man except that he was a Campbell of Gyle (I may be misspelling this name), a family that had edged out of needy aristocracy into industry, that he owned textile mills in the neighbourhood of Galashiels, and that his considerable fortune ultimately found it way to a Society for the Conversion of Jews in Glasgow and the adjoining districts.

Fortunately his daughter, my grandmother, seemed to have her share of iron too. After burying her husband she took a day in bed, but when a friend brought the report that friends had opened a subscription list for her in the Edinburgh Arts Club, she rose and dressed and went down to the Club to close the list and return what money had already been raised, explaining that she was about to set up in business, and expected before long to be providing for herself and her children. This was the madness of grief, the kicking back at the indifferent world. 'What are your plans?' some old man asked. 'To open a shop in George Street,' she replied and quickly left, choked by the lie, which meant nothing except that it had come to her lips.

All the most fashionable shops of Edinburgh lay in that glorious wide trench of the neo-classical running parallel to Princes Street. Going home, she asked herself not what she was to do, but how she was to justify her daft inventions, an embarrassment she was later to confide to her daughters, who perfectly understood. Before she had reached her home in Heriot Row it had occurred to her that she could sell lace. This idea, which would today be the maddest conceivable that could occur to a widow, was then eminently sensible. Hand-made lace was a status symbol: machine-made lace was a social aspiration. Janet Mackenzie understood both sorts. The women of her family had always been fond of lace, and the chests in the house where she had been born were full of old English and Belgian and Venetian lace, which she had been taught to appreciate; and her father had some lace machines working for him in the Border country. It just happened, during the next few days, that one of the smaller shops in George Street fell vacant, and she happened to pass its emptiness: the family lawyer was remarkably kind in furnishing some capital.* My grandmother was pretty and gracious, she chose comely and amiable assistants, she was extremely efficient, she was working feverishly for her children.

She was able to do this only because the care of these six young children had been to a great extent taken off her hands by what was a stroke of good fortune, although it was also a lasting calamity. One day Mr Campbell of Gyle – how I wish the blood of this man did not run in my veins – announced at the breakfast table that my grand-mother had opened a shop, and had thereby disgraced the family a second time; but he wished her no ill, and would pray to the Lord that she might not be punished too harshly for her repeated defiances of the parental authority which the Scriptures had commanded her to obey. At this point one of my grand-aunts rose to her feet and informed him that she was leaving the house for ever. She had never accepted his treatment of her sister, and had insisted on attending the baptism of each of the six children; for which reason my mother was christened Isabella after her. Now she packed a few possessions, made her way to Edinburgh, knocked on my grandmother's door in Heriot Row, and announced that she had come to serve her and her children till the day she died – a promise she kept to the letter. By being an efficient sick-nurse, housekeeper and keeper of accounts she gave the lace shop power to earn her sister and her sister's children an adequate income, and later was to deal with certain grave misfortunes.

It is a beautiful drama of sisterly love, but unfortunately the heroine was badly cast. She was a hunchback, but that could not excuse her: we have all known misshapen people whose well-proportioned natures restored their harmony. But her mind was on the side of her physical deformity. As a child, I once said to my mother after a hateful visit to my grandmother's house, 'I've never once heard Aunt Isa make a pleasant remark,' and my mother said thoughtfully, jettisoning all conventions in the adult-versus-child contest, 'Why, now I come to think of it, neither have I.'

Aunt Isa was eternally critical but made nonsense of criticism, for with her the process never led to praise. There was no alternative but blame. No phenomenon could be analysed and valued; each and all were prisoners in the dock, and guilty. I once drew her attention to a relative of the nasturtium, but more ambitious in its climbing, that was making its way up the garden wall inside the back door. Even as a child I was appalled by the folly of her answer, and the ingratitude of its sullenness. She gave the name of weed to this lovely plant, which anybody would be glad to find in his garden (it is difficult to establish in many districts). She complained of the amounts of money she had to pay a jobbing gardener who had now shown his negligence by suffering this weed to grow. It was hinted vaguely (had she been more explicit she would have got herself into difficulties) that what made her specially resentful of this wasted outlay was the charity she showed to my mother and her family. She had shown none. But I did not hold this sad fiction against her. Through my experience as the child of a nearly destitute widow, I learned that when prosperous adults contemplated the likes of me they thought that it would be nice to make some financial improvement to my lot, but soon reflected that they could not afford to fulfil this impulse; and then later again adjusted the situation by forming the belief that they had actually spent some money to this generous end; then, much later, made this conviction more gratifying to themselves by increasing the imaginary sum of money to an amount which would indeed have been stunning in its generosity had it existed. This technique Jane Austen has exposed in a famous chapter of *Sense and Sensibility*.* I bore them and bear them no malice. From an early age I recognized that there was something odd about the idea of money which made people talk of it as if it were controllable, like milk, which came from the dairy if one ordered it, whereas it was obviously quite uncontrollable, like the weather.

But my grandmother and my grand-aunt had no reason, on the whole, to think the financial weather bad. It was hard at the beginning, when two of the five children in the flat at Heriot Row were sick for a winter with chest infections, and my aunt and the nursemaid simply could not find time to look after the other three; so my mother's sister, the delicately pretty Jessie, was sent away to a curious educational institution, a boarding-school known as the Merchant Maiden's.* It had been founded long ago to deal with the children of guild members who had fallen into misfortune and I understood even then that the qualifying misfortunes included those which had nothing to do with want, such as the death of a mother; but the little girls were sent to school wearing a curious uniform, a scarcely modified version of the dresses that might have been worn in a Puritan community during the seventeenth century. It was not unbecoming, but it suggested to some minds a charity school, and among her schoolfellows were a few who let it be known that they had received and accepted that suggestion. At the end of the winter Jessie was taken back to Heriot Row by her mother and her aunt, but she had been wounded beyond recovery. I know very little about that period of her life, I am not even sure to within five years or so how old she was. But

I know that later, when I knew her as a middle-aged or old woman, she struck me as intelligent, courageous and witty, but lacking in the instinct for self-preservation which is present in almost any human creature not mentally afflicted. She could not, for most of her life, parry any attack.

But for the rest the household got on very well. The shop was very successful. There was more put in it than honest dealing and sound technical knowledge. An old lady who had been a customer, and who had high standards, a customer of Worth when he was at his glorious noon in Paris, once told me with epicurean delight of a trade trick of my grandmother: when she was showing her more prosperous clients her finer goods, the *berthes** of old French needlepoint and the deep collars of Venetian rosepoint, she spread them over panels of melting, muted blue-violet velvet. True, such successful devices were hardly enough to cope with a further addition to the household, a grotesque example of the relationship of the sexes in the nineteenth century. My grandmother had a cousin, a Campbell, who was establishing himself well in the new textile trade and took as a bride a young girl who had one daughter ten months after marriage and another ten months later, and three years after that died of consumption. Young Mr Campbell, explaining that his heart was broken, arrived at the flat in Heriot Row with the two little girls, and announced that he was going to Australia to see if the long sea voyage would cure his excessive grief, dumped the girls on my grandmother and Aunt Isa, and went down to London to sail for Melbourne. It was understood that he would make the return voyage after a month or two, but he found a better way to arrange the future. He married the daughter of a wealthy Australian, set himself up in the wool business and refrained from sending for his two daughters, then or ever after; and the sums of money he sent my grandmother for their maintenance suggest that he had forgotten the nature of the transaction and thought he had left in her charge a couple of canaries.

It never occurred to my grandmother to treat this situation as anything but a huge joke. Years afterwards, when she was a total invalid, she would lie and shake her bed with laughter if anybody reminded her of a letter that Mr Campbell of Sydney had written to her, explaining his failure to write regularly to his daughters or to send them adequate allowances on the ground that his second wife had four children, all boys, and consequently entitled to all that was going: and, he added, he had to do his duty as a God-fearing man. Actually the situation had been corrected by that letter. A rumour of it reached a lady whose name I have forgotten but who was the most aristocratic relative the Campbells of Gyle could boast; and she left my grandmother and Aunt Isa legacies which were not large but were still useful. In any case, one of the daughters paid for her keep a million times over. To all of us, Jessie Watson Campbell was an image of goodness and love and fortitude, no more to be forgotten than St Francis. But not even her saintly presence could deflect the blow that shattered this brave and happy household.

This blow was delivered in 1865. In this year my Uncle Alick returned to his mother's home at the age of eighteen, after a truly impressive eight years spent in laying the foundations of a musical career in his self-directed sojourn in Germany, France and England. What he found waiting for him was a quietly and confidently happy family. When my mother spoke of her early childhood, she described a world in which the sky was always cloudless. This was, I think, because the children and their Aunt Isa knew that my grandmother could do anything: anything that necessity demanded.

My mother had learned that as a fact one winter evening when she was a little girl of eight or nine, and my grandmother, on her way home from her shop, called to take her home from a children's party in one of the neo-classical streets that pour down the slopes of the New Town and towards the Port of Leith; and they had to pass one corner house, always lightless, with a narrow but high porch, long the source of pleasurable fear to the Mackenzie children, for it was filled with black shadow, and took the shape of a huge empty coffin set upright. It was not empty that evening, for a footpad* had jumped out and grabbed at my grandmother's handbag, which she called her reticule, but she was known for being as quick as a moth, and the crook of her umbrella cracked on his ankle. As he went down on the pavement she snatched back her bag, stuck the point of her umbrella into his stomach, gripped her child's hand and stood quite still, her umbrella held in her hand like a foil, and screamed. Doors opened up and down the street, the light poured out of them in slanting bands across the pavement, gentlemen came out and ran towards them across the road, while the footpad hared through the darkness of the side-street that opened by the lightless house. Some of the gentlemen hurried after him, others gathered sympathetically around my grandmother and my mother, and one was rebuked by my grandmother when he expressed hope that her little girl was not frightened. 'Don't put it into her head,' she said, 'that she might be frightened, she won't think of that if she's left to herself.'

As they walked back towards Heriot Row, the wife of one of the protective gentlemen, peering out from an open door, stepped out on to the doorstep and called, 'Why it's Mrs Mackenzie, and wee Isabella, bring them in for Mercy's sake, and let them sit down,' and another wife cried out, 'Oh Mrs Mackenzie, come in and have a wee drop,' and hospitable cries ricocheted up and down the street. But she refused. It was to be noted that my grandmother was well known to the ladies in the community and not known at all to the gentlemen. This was the result of her own fixed policy. When she had been left a widow she was still in her twenties and remarkably pretty, but she had never allowed herself any but the most temperate friendship with any man. In my youth I thought this a consequence of the great love she had borne her husband, but later on I was to see it as due to the biological tragedy which the human species was forced to enact on a vast scale so long as there was no effective system of birth control. She was, and told her daughters when they had grown up, simply in terror of taking a new husband and having more children. As it was, she had five children to keep, to say nothing of the little Campbells, and she could keep them on the proceeds of her lace shop. But if she married again she would probably have more children and would not be able to engage in that or any other money-making career; and she would have been most unlikely to find a husband who could afford to bring up seven children in addition to any he might beget himself. So she said, 'Thank you, but if you would just see me and Isabella home . . .'

When my grandmother and my mother reached the flat in Heriot Row, she was accompanied by several unknown gentlemen and a number of ladies well or partially known, friends or customers, who were bidden to come in and drink some whisky. Immediately the attempted outrage was blotted out and a party was substituted. Tapers were put to all the lights in the drawing-room chandelier, the best glasses were brought out, the Venetian tablecloth was dropped over the round table, the family ran in and cried silently as they listened and smiled with pride, neighbours whom the story had already reached called to offer sympathy and were swept into the circle and told all the boys that none of them would make as fine a man as their mother, while the girls were told that they were lucky in having a mother to bequeath them such spirit, and good looks beside. My mother could remember the aspect of the room when the guests had all gone, and she and her mother stood on one side of the round table with all her brothers and sisters and the Campbell children stood on the other side of the table, and my grandmother said, 'Well, that's water under the bridge,' and yawned, covered her mouth, but brought her hands down to run them over the shoulders of my mother's party dress. 'I would have been lost if she had whimpered,' she told her other children.

The quality of the compliment was characteristic of the Mackenzie household. If they had had their own crest instead of the clan's it should have consisted of an emblem of the arts and a motto referring to valour. Armed with their own talents, they faced a world which they knew would guarantee their well-being only if they insisted, but this did not perturb them. They had envisaged the problem, although all of them were under seventeen. The only one of them who had no special gifts was Jessie, or rather I should say that we do not know what special gifts were hers, because she had been sealed up in scar tissue by her time at the Merchant Maiden's. For the rest, Willie was going to be a painter, but music owned the others. Johnnie and Joey had the same interest in the whole area of music as Alick had, and Johnnie played the piano as well as Alick played the violin, and Joey hoped to be a singer when his voice broke, and was interested in all opera and was prepared to settle as a conductor if he could not sing. My mother was a brilliant pianist, but she was denied by her sex the understanding of the whole field of music that her brothers had, for the reason that she could not play in an orchestra, or undergo any of the rough-and-tumble training that Alick had got for the asking between the ages of ten and eighteen. Jessie Watson Campbell was a good pianist of the sort (which always seems odd to me) which makes a better teacher than performer. Her sister, Elizabeth Watson Campbell, had a pleasant mezzo-soprano voice.

My grandmother and her sister saw to it that all those children had the best general education that Edinburgh could provide, and that each had the best specialist training of the musical gifts which were hereditary in both the Mackenzie and the Campbell families. They kept all their correspondence and after they were dead we found many letters which showed efforts to keep in touch with the friends of the long dead Alexander Mackenzie, and to make contact with the younger musicians of later time, so that if one of the brood wanted to play the French horn or the double bass, he could go straight to the best teacher and plan his life from there. They were careful too to cultivate the other gene which gave distinction to both the Mackenzie and the Campbell families: Alick, Willie and Joey and my mother, and Jessie Watson Campbell, all had unusual linguistic gifts. Alick had dealt with this problem during his astonishing *Wanderjahre*, and Willie and Joey had to leave it till they finished with the classical austerities of the Edinburgh Academy. But Jessie Watson Campbell and my mother were booked to go to Germany, Jessie to Hamburg, my mother to Düsseldorf, that they might study the German language and the piano. The separation was arranged for a purpose. 'You will talk English to each other if you are together,' my grandmother said, 'and you must speak only German.' Pencilled on the letters which set up these arrangements are calculations of the cost. These papers made no great impression on me at the time I found them among my own mother's papers, but now I feel awe at the memory, as if I had once been in a magical world where orchids tended orchids, lovingly regulating heat and moisture and soil where the young ones grew, in order that the splendour of their species should continue to be splendid.

I have no idea how my Uncle Alick appeared to the eye when he returned to put an end to all that sort of thing. Later he did not look like a Scot. As a middle-aged man he had a broad-beamed, thick-bearded, bluffing-it-out Tudor look, and doctoral robes seemed more natural to him than modern suits. He would have managed to survive in Henry VIII's court, would not have cared much for Sir Thomas More, would have kept on accommodating terms with Cromwell, but would not himself have been all schemer, would have been a loyal ally of the music-makers and poets and players and palace-builders and masque-designers. But the needle on his compass would always have twitched to the safety mark. Not for him the Tower; the Traitor's Gate could get its share of victims from that large class who the Scotch call 'ither folk'. The one obstacle his driving energy could not overcome was so inevitable that it did not count. The leadership of the Theatre Royal, Edinburgh, was vacant and his teachers and employers in London thought he could have filled the post. He was technically a marvel; but he was not yet twenty-one, it was ridiculous.

However, he got everything else he wanted. During the last few years Edinburgh had declined as a musical centre, and now he was welcomed when he organized orchestral concerts, many of which he conducted, and set chamber music on its feet again. Distinguished soloists liked his conducting, the public liked his programmes. He founded 'The Scottish Vocal Association'* and made it sing works by Bach, Beethoven, Schubert and Schumann, most of them not previously heard in Scotland, though now constituent parts of the atmosphere throughout the western hemisphere. He taught music classes in several Ladies' Colleges, according to the bizarre fashion of the place and time: eight schoolgirls sat at eight pianos and played the same Clementi exercise or the same Mozart sonata or the same Schumann Kinderszenen, while the music master circled round them in the gate of their own distress, often abandoning human speech as inadequate for the situation in favour of cries such as might have been emitted by a large wounded bird.

Alick did not discontinue this employment when he found happier employment as choirmaster to St George's Church, which sits firmly on its bottom in Charlotte Square, which itself sits as firmly on its corporate bottom.* The New Town gives its peculiar beauty to the solidity of its forms and the contrasting prismatic grey mists that so often envelop them. This appointment was a challenge, for the organ was still banned as a profane instrument in the Established or Free Churches of Scotland.* It meant that he had a capella choir of twenty-five voices which his passionate vitality could train to the last degree of their powers to sing the old music and the new music, which was to become old so soon that to many it became not just familiar but stale, though little of what came to take its place still later succeeded in achieving familiarity.* But for ten years the time and the place and the loved music were all together; and the sustained glow of the experience can be judged from a remark of my grandmother. One evening she told her family that an old customer of hers had that day come to the shop to give in her housekeeper's immense order for bed linen, and had said before she left, 'I wish I could go to St George's and hear the wonderful things your clever son is doing with the choir. But I'm a Catholic, you know.' My grandmother's comment was: 'I just stopped myself from telling the woman, "Well, your Ladyship, it's a question of putting first things first . . ." '

It is hardly to be believed how much my Uncle Alick's advancement in his profession, fierce as it might be, was controlled by a real regard for his art. His ambition purified itself as it came into action, because the medium in which he was working was music, his religion. To his intense earnestness I was to hear testimony more than forty years later. He had started, with the help of Messrs Paterson,* a famous music shop not far from my grandmother's shop, a series of classical chamber music concerts, which had an instant success. Any Edinburgh citizen who attended them was certified as one of the elite. The string quartet he formed was remarkable, and almost over-rehearsed, but his own perfectionism was never satisfied by any available viola player. It happened that at this time the Sheriff of Dumfries, to whom he owed some local engagements, asked him to find an organist who would also give music lessons for the shire. My uncle's reaction was to write to his friends in Germany asking them to find him a young musician who could play both the organ and the viola and was a teacher: by sifting enquiries he got a young man called Frederick Niecks, whose talent was of such an order that he ended as Professor of Music at the University of Edinburgh.* It happened that when he had long been established in that position he came to my mother's house and I heard him describe to her what it had been like to face my uncle as a humble seeker for employment. 'He was very little older than I was, but I did not think of that till I left the room. The questions he asked! About my teachers. About my repertoire. About my public appearances. And questions about my attitude to the music of the time which seemed to me utterly irrelevant – what did it matter how I felt about Wagner and if I knew the work of the new French composers, if he wanted me to play Schumann in Edinburgh and Beethoven and Spohr in Dumfries. And it was all hostile, as if

I had been a young man who wished to become a monk applying to an unusually unsympathetic Abbot. But from the next day, when he told me he wanted me for Scotland, and at once, it was all different, and that for life.'

But Uncle Alick's feeling for his family was different. They were, of course, not wholly strangers, though he had been so much away from home. While he was a boy in Germany my grandmother had seen to it that he came home every year for some weeks. The first time he was so much of a child that on the first night he shouted out from his room, 'I'm back in my ain bed!' as if it were a famous victory. When he was working in London he had come home less often and for briefer periods, owing to the pressure of the work he obstinately undertook. He certainly had a genuine affection for my mother, and for Jessie Watson Campbell: both made good servants. I do not know what he felt for the rest of the family, since the picture is obscured by the operation of two powerful Scottish conventions. The first was that the Scottish male has a right to take what he wants of the family resources: he must be served first and he has the right to clear the dish. There is a good reason why this convention should have sprung up in Scotland; war has been crueller there, in that savage climate, and so has peace. Women could certainly not have replaced men in the continuous wars of the Highlands or the Border Counties, nor in the fishing fleets or on the hill farms. But the functions of society are so varied and so subject to change that steady judgements of value regarding its human constituents are bound to be fallacious. In Scotland, however, the special usefulness of the male in certain areas has overspilled to cover the whole field of their activities from birth till death; it is as if all menfolk were always right and do not know what failure is, and this absurd supposition engenders yet another. Scotsmen often fail, though no more than Scotswomen or any other human beings, and experience rejection through their failures, which comes hard on them, as they have been brought up on the theory that they never fail and are not rejected but reject. Well, how can one better dispel the consciousness that one is a failure and rejected than by presenting oneself in the disgusting condition of drunkenness, and finding that nobody appears to be disgusted by one, and go on accepting one? That complacence can be produced by any Scotsman who gets drunk. His fellow countrymen are on his side, and most of all he can be sure of

Scotswomen. Hence the phenomenon is repeated again and again, the first convention kept afloat by the second.

These conventions operated in most Scottish homes in the past, and it may be so to a lesser extent in the present. The interests of the fathers and the sons were always considered before the interests of the mothers and the daughters, and while it is true that a woman alone is in any society as handicapped as if she had some slight deformity, it was more so in Scotland. So, when Alick returned to his family as a young man and the eldest male in the house, the crown and sceptre were his, and at first he gave as much as he got. My grandmother, my mother and her sister Jessie were all loving women, forever pleased with any opportunity to love, and so was Jessie Watson Campbell, though her sister Elizabeth was notably colder; and the boys, Willie and Johnnie and Joey, were all delighted by this new big brother, who was soon being talked of up and down the town. There was a sparkle in the air which had not been seen when the house was inhabited by a widow, her unmarried sister, and her young sons and daughters and a couple of young girl cousins.

Now Alick gave the house the look of scattered largesse that it had had when his father was alive. There were new scores lying about, sent by the composers or the music publishers, and foreign newspapers. There were important messages left by the 'Highland Porters', the old men who sat on benches at street corners to deliver letters, aged counterparts of the boys who later performed such services in London as District Messengers. At meals he told his family funny stories of what had happened during the day, and pulled out of his pockets letters from musicians who were coming to play at his concerts, and who would, with luck, be the cause of delicious parties being given, of a kind that had never before been given by the busy and thrifty owner of the lace shop in George Street. The great ladies of the New Town might give grand parties for the celebrities from abroad, to which Alick might be invited, though his mother and sisters rarely were; but the celebrities often stayed an extra night or two in Edinburgh and these they might well spend in the flat in Heriot Row, gorgeously pampered by being spoken to in their own language, whatever that might be, and given food of the kind they liked, rich and nourishing stews of game, and fresh fish up from the Firth of Forth, and too much of everything, and good claret, and on winter nights some punch said to be the best in the New Town.

Then my grandmother blossomed like the rose. She had eloped with her musician in her early twenties, and had been first trapped into bearing a succession of children and then into a gruelling career as provider for those children she had borne. Here now was her reward. The boys liked staying up late, and had their first dress-suits; Alick sometimes helped out with a flute part in a new score being played for the visitors; Johnnie and Joey had their more modest chances, and my mother had her success as an accompanist. These parties were so good the family used to sit for long among the empty glasses, very tired, very happy, eager to talk over the evening, though Alick had prudently gone to bed.

At length the golden glow faded. The festivities were not really what the young boys and girls needed. They missed giving the parties for young people of their own age which their mother had no time to arrange. They wearied of guests who had to be talked to in German (although all had been taught that language well) and French and Italian. And as for what the girls felt, there was a warning given by the sudden disappearance of Elizabeth Campbell, one of the two children abandoned to my grandmother's care by their father, on his departure to Sydney to do his duty to God and man by begetting some sons.

Elizabeth had always been an independent child, at once flamboyant and taciturn, expending considerable care on her appearance but none on developing personal relations. When she was eighteen and dividing her time between training her voice and helping my grandmother in the lace shop, she suddenly severed herself from the Mackenzie family by an action interesting because of the cynical use to which she put the tradition of female chastity. One evening, when the rest of the household were at a concert, she packed all her clothes in a hold-all she had bought and smuggled into the house a few days before, took it downstairs, opened the front door and stood beside the case on the doorstep. In the kitchen the servants heard a cab drive up, stop and drive off; and Elizabeth was never seen by any of her family again. My grandmother found a note on the hall table in which the girl told her that she had for some time been meeting in secret an actor who had been playing at the Theatre Royal, and had said nothing about it because he was a married man, and in a few days she would be leaving with him for America; and she thanked my mother and family in adequate but temperate terms for the kindness and generosity they had shown her.

There was a strange lack of hysteria about my grandmother's reception of this news. Both she and her sister, like many of her social equals and social superiors, spoke with a certain refinement when in company but lapsed into the unconquered vernacular when within doors. So when Elizabeth's sister Jessie Watson Campbell, who was the soul of virtue, begged her to ask Alick to go down and find out the identity of her sister's lover from the manager of the Theatre Royal, my grandmother replied, 'There's a wheen married actors in the Theatre Royal,' and went to bed. In the morning Alick came into his mother's room and suggested that perhaps she ought to inform the girl's father; she sniffed and said, 'Wait to see if her prim sister is tempted to do what Elizabeth's done, and then one stamp will do for them both.' But after two or three months, a letter came from Elizabeth in New York, telling her that she had lied when she had alleged that her lover had a wife, simply because she had thought that if my grandmother thought she had become a bad girl she would not trouble to search for her; and actually they had married as soon as they got to America.

Then my grandmother was furious. 'How could she miscall herself, coming from the home I've given her?' she asked. (It was, I was to learn much later from events of my own life, a reasonable question.) Nor was Jessie Watson Campbell ever to forgive her sister, who was to have a career not at all scandalous but very odd. She and her husband made a name for themselves in a small way singing operatic duets in the beerhalls of German communities all over the States, and formed so few connections anywhere else that, though she was pure Scot and he a Welshman, they became German-Americans by adoption. By the end of their lives they must have spoken in German for far more years then they had spoken their native language. They died in a town near the Great Lakes about 1910, having lived through a very agreeable part of American history.*

The other young women in the household would have been the

better for some of Elizabeth's power of decision. My mother did not get off to Düsseldorf to begin her music education so soon as she had hoped: for one thing, my grandmother found some difficulty in finding the money. Jessie Watson Campbell started off in Hamburg earlier; her fees were paid by a Campbell kinsman, abashed at having by accident found out the amount my grandmother had spent in supporting the daughters of the ungracious Mr Campbell, now an Australian magnate. Jessie was, not of her own free will, to be separated from the Edinburgh household for a long time. This same Campbell kinsman gave her name to a Frenchman and his wife who had a property outside Orléans and needed an English governess to see to the education of their adolescent children. They engaged her at once and she went to them straight from Düsseldorf and stayed with them all through the Franco-Prussian War (she had just missed the German-Danish war when she went to Düsseldorf), and for the next thirty years. She never let a year pass without a visit to as many of the Mackenzies as were visitable.

As for the quiet Jessie, my mother's sister, she was busy at home: all these parties needed a great deal of preparation, and there seemed less money than there had been to pay for help. She of all the family had the poorest of social lives, for as she was not musical she had no part in Alick's glory. There was no analysis of the situation, because it was one that would have been taken for granted under most Scottish roofs. Yet I am not certain that this is quite true. It seems to me extreme that during this period of ten years when Uncle Alick lived under his mother's roof he paid her a pound a week and never a penny more, no matter how the punch and claret flowed, and no matter how much game went into the pies and how rich the ice pudding.

This was so far from being a reasonable arrangement that, in whatever framework it operated, it was bound to break down, and it was indeed very unnatural that the family should have suffered the dissolution that followed. They should have stuck together.

❧❧

To show the unity of the family, I will admit (with some diffidence) that my family is unusually subject to an experience which, though it is obviously not supernatural, has somehow the same atmosphere of having been purveyed to one by a lady in gipsy costume in a curtained shop on a seaside pier. We suffer from coincidences. For example, when my eldest sister* was sent by the British Government to Canada to address a medical congress, the Canadian official who received her took her on her first day to his home to lunch, and, giving her a glass of sherry as she sat beside a first-floor window, said to her, 'Do you know anybody in Canada?'

'No,' she answered, 'I only know one person, a fellow student of mine at Edinburgh University who married and came out here, but I have not her address and I do not know where she lives. But there she is, she is walking up the garden path to your neighbour's front door.'

And that is just what she was doing. I myself, when writing a passage in a novel about a cook and a housemaid finding a hedgehog on a lawn,* have been interrupted by my real cook and housemaid who came to bring me a hedgehog they had found on the lawn; writing the word 'Kerensky' I have been interrupted by being handed a letter which was from Kerensky and the only one he ever wrote me; looking in the library of Chatham House for the records of a minor trial at Nuremberg at which a Deutsche Bank official called Puhl gave evidence,* I have said to a librarian, 'It might be any of these hundreds of volumes that look like the one I've just picked up off this shelf, but I haven't the least idea which,' and the book in my hand fell open at Puhl's evidence.

This phenomenon was present in my family's life in the 1860s. It came about that one of the 'Ladies' Colleges' at which my uncle taught music added to its staff a French master called Monsieur Chantrelle, who had an English wife. All the Mackenzies knew them by sight, and Alick and my mother were on speaking terms with Madame Chantrelle, who was a member of the Congregation of St George's, Charlotte Square; they felt no especial interest in them, yet as time went on a certain tie between them seemed to declare itself. A letter was delivered by the postman at my grandmother's house, though it was addressed to Madame Chantrelle, at her own address, which was in quite another part of Edinburgh. Jessie Watson Campbell, travelling to Perth by rail, found Madame Chantrelle in the same carriage; and did so again when going to Glasgow two months later. Joey dropped a school book in the street, Monsieur Chantrelle picked it up and returned it. Then one Sunday morning Uncle Alick, conducting his choir in St George's, saw that though Madame Chantrelle, a very regular attendant at the services, was not to be seen, her husband was, though he never had appeared there before. What was more remarkable, he was there at the afternoon service too. The next day they met on the Dean Bridge and my uncle said to him, obscurely, it seems to me, but I take it from his own record, 'My friend, you are going to the devil!'. Chantrelle stammered, 'What do you mean?' My uncle said, 'You were *twice* in church yesterday!' Chantrelle said uneasily, 'Well, you will have your joke,' and hurried on. My uncle was never to see him again. Not long afterwards he was arrested on the charge of poisoning his wife, tried, and condemned to death.

It happened some months later that my uncle was bidden to rise early and attend a curious gathering in Princes Street Gardens. Some time after seven he was to stand and be photographed at the forefront of a crowd of schoolgirls, to a number that must have been a multiple of eight, for they comprised the teams of eight to whom he gave mass piano lessons. The tryst was held thus early so that the gardens should be empty and the photographer might have time to dispose the groups to the best advantage; and he ultimately marshalled them to a part which used the splendid, better than the Parthenon, hexagon of the Castle Rock as a backcloth. This left the schoolgirls and their teachers facing an eastward-flowing panorama rising to the splendid neo-classical fantasy of the Calton Jail; on which, as they all smiled towards the morning light, a black flag was hoisted. It was eight o'clock and Chantrelle had just been hanged. My mother was there, for she was already teaching music in the same schools as her brother, and was herself to be photographed among her pupils. She was near enough to him to see him point to the black flag and ask its significance and, when he was told by one of the photographer's assistants, throw his hands forward as if to push away the horror which she well understood; and she knew he must also be resenting a wave of feeling because it was irrational. She attributed her knowledge to the fact that that was the cause of her own distress. Alick and she were feeling the death of this man, whom they barely knew, as if he were of the household in Heriot Row.*

MARY IRONSIDE

The destruction of this unity, which was so strong as to bind two of its members together in such a primitive and useless way (for how could it benefit either the Chantrelles or Alick or my mother?) was effected quite suddenly. One day my grandmother was asked by one of her customers, the wife of a peer who owned a famous estate lying towards the Lammermuir Hills, if she could employ as a needlewoman the daughter of one of her gardeners, and added, with proper timidity, that 'perhaps your clever son would like her for his choir. She has a lovely voice. She gave us a song at our Hallowe'en party two years ago and since then she's been sharing my own daughters' singing lessons, and she's been a fine example to them.' My grandmother said 'Mhm,' which is Scottish for 'I make no promises, and would remind you that you have no right to ask me to promise anything, that I know of, but I've no wish to quarrel,' but at once conceded the first request. Yes, she needed a needlewoman. She was disconcerted when the girl arrived and proved to be extraordinarily lovely, and, she thought, to the same degree unlikeable.

The head assistant brought the new needlewoman into my grand-mother's office, which was small but had some nice things in it: a beautiful desk given her by her godmother, the French wife of a cousin, who had lived in Kelso, because she rightly thought that with its central *place*, it looked like a French town, and some architectural drawings made by the Adam brothers for another of her cousins (and kept solely for that reason) hanging in a rosy maple frame on the wall. The girl seemed puzzled and uneasy and perplexed, and my grand-mother said, when describing this first meeting to my mother, 'I knew well what was ailing the lassie. She was saying to herself, "This woman is no marchioness like my former employer, she is a plain old biddy who keeps a shop, but I seem to be expected to bend the knee as if I was back in the castle." But that was a point that mattered little to me, and she was content to be in Edinburgh, so I took her.'

But before the interview had ended by grandmother had begun to regret her decision. When the two of them were alone, my grandmother looked at the rather too bright perfection of the girl's skin and felt she must make it clear what Edinburgh felt about the female epidermis, which it had made a moral battlefield. 'Will you keep in mind, Miss Mary,' she said, 'that it is not the custom here for young ladies of any degree, from the lowest to the highest, to use powder and rouge?' The girl gaped, blurted out, 'Och, it's a' ma ain,' put her finger in her mouth, rubbed it on her cheek, and held it out so that it stopped just short of my grandmother's stony face, caught her breath, and withdrew her finger. 'I could see her, poor lass,' mourned my grandmother afterwards, 'deciding she had to throw away all the habits she had acquired since the cradle, and start all over again. I thought none the better of her for that. But I'd gone too far to tell her she was not for me.'

It did not occur to my grandmother to deny Miss Ironside* the chance of having an audition for Alick's choir. If competent persons thought her singing was up to that standard, then she had a right to that audition, according to the moral code of the Mackenzie family. She passed that test easily; she had a gentle and smooth soprano voice and absolute pitch* and, given an interpretation, she could grasp it quickly and stick by it. She became aware of other tests and passed them too. She lost her thick country accent and acquired an echo of my grandmother's public accent. Her needlework no longer provoked snubs from the chief assistants and acid comments regarding 'country house linen rooms', and conformed to the standards set by the embroideries bought by my grandmother from Belgian convents. She dyed her clothes black, saying that there had been a death in the family: it must have been a close relative who had gone, for she went about for more than a year looking as if she were not only a beautiful but also a serious young woman, and specially in need of consideration. But those who did not initially like her continued to dislike her. These dissidents made a small minority, as against everybody who watched her in the street, neatly slipping in and out of the slamming doors of the weather-harried New Town, the winds never disadvantaging her trim head and her tippeted bodice, but often trying first this and then that arrangement of her skirts round her docile little ankles. But that minority was strongly represented among the younger members of the Mackenzie household, who grumbled more and more because they perpetually found this stranger seated with unstudied but immovable grace in their home. She was all stranger. She was not of their blood, not of their circle and, in spite of her voice, not of their musical community. Her singing was no more to her than her sewing. But because of Alick's unceasing burden of work, which was largely caused by his unceasing and not quite explicable concern with the choir at St George's, she was far too often at the flat in Heriot Row in the evenings, when the Mackenzies wanted the place to themselves, and they always found her aiming arrows at their essence. Supper ought to be an easy meal; she invaded it with her rejections, mincing through the meal, receiving served helpings with little nods of the head, expressing surprise at their lavishness, refusing an offer of wine with the Edinburgh idiom, a whispered exclamation, 'Oh no, I do not taste!'

Then the study, where the two pianos were, and all the other musical instruments, and the books; well, that belonged to the family. If she got in there, the boys said, it was only a matter of time before they found her in the bath upstairs. But there in the family room she was in no time taking down notes on a score at Alick's dictation, at Grandfather's desk, and if anyone came in, raising her head and saying, 'Och! Can we not go out and work on the wee table on the landing?' And as like as not Willie or Johnnie or Joey would be sent out to get her a cab when she wanted to go home. Well, the boys worked and they too wanted to get their sleep, they said. This was sheer hypocrisy. They never wanted to go to bed. But they were on edge, for they all had their own difficulties, and these were not imaginary.

My mother was now into her early twenties, and had gone to Düsseldorf to take up the musical training which she had had to postpone because my grandmother had for a time been overwhelmed by financial difficulties which had, however, disappeared a year or two afterwards. There my mother did very well, and would have made her mark had she not been struck down by what was probably a typhoid or paratyphoid infection, not mitigated by the hospital treatment she endured for several weeks. Her nurse, a Countess who was a member of a famous religious sisterhood, indignantly refused to mention to the doctor that her patient was suffering from constipation. My mother was happy to get back to Edinburgh, particularly when a man she had always liked, a promising artist a few years older than herself, remarkable for his intelligence and gentleness and humour, began to seek out her company. They got on so well together, he was so obviously fond of her, that she was sure he wanted to marry her. But their pleasant relationship went on without change. He lived with an older sister, and it occurred to my mother that perhaps there was little money in the family, and he had to keep this sister. She went back to her old post as one of the music teachers in a 'Ladies' College', but this was not what she wanted to do.

Her sister Jessie was as unhappy, though she had no specific disappointment. She had always had a duller life than the rest of the family, because she was the unmusical one, and people at a musical party literally could not see anyone who was so antipathetic to the whole idea of performance. It was impossible that any sound should cease to be heard in a hall because of her, and thus none of the musicians perceived that she would have been a perfect drudge for a bull moose bass, or a rogue elephant conductor, or a crocodile composer with open jaws. I feel grateful that none of these sacred monsters had the sense to marry her, but she had not the hindsight I am using. So, one night my mother and Jessie found themselves standing at the sink in the kitchen, at a late hour, washing some glasses used by visitors who had just left. Suddenly my mother said, 'We are both crying.'

Jessie gave the little defensive laugh which was characteristic of her: 'We are that. But it's natural. I don't suppose there's anything worse for a woman than not to be married.'

There is no getting away from it. Through the ages the human species has laboured to manufacture traditions that imposed feelings of shame and humiliation on the most innocent and worthy of its children. But my uncles, Johnnie and Joey, were suffering at the same time from frustration due not to human error, but to the malice not of tradition but of the material of which living matter is constructed.

These were the two boys who in their childhood were so continu-
ously assailed by chest infections that, in order that they should be
properly nursed, my grandmother had had to send away little Jessie to
have her pride broken at the Merchant Maiden's; and, as Jessie herself
said to me in her old age, she felt her suffering to be of no consequence, since they grew into such charming brothers. They were fair-
haired and blue-eyed, and all my mother's family who were of that
colouring had laughing faces. Even when their features were in repose,
there was a half-smile on their lips, and indeed these two had never
been far from cheerfulness, all through their childhood and youth.
This seemed a reasonable reaction to their prospects, for Johnnie was
as gifted a violinist as he needed to be if he were to gratify his first
ambition, which was to become the leader of a theatre orchestra; and
for a time at least, that orchestra had to be the Theatre Royal,
Edinburgh, where his father had held that post. This was not a mean
ambition. The old pantomime scores of such theatres reveal what
minds and memories worked away in the dark orchestra pit, even on
the most light-minded of its occasions: it might be a beautifully apt
quotation from Berlioz or Liszt that brought the Demon King up
through the trap-door.

Joey had a more serious ambition: he had a fair prospect of becoming an operatic tenor. But the plans for both boys had to be put aside
after they went for a walk with some schoolfriends on the Pentlands,
that range of hills which lies south of Edinburgh like a vast breaking
wave, and got drenched by a cloudburst. During the following winter,
they had to take to their beds again and again, their breaths jerking up
and down like a rusty iron rod that had been thrust down through
their bodies, their tempers jerking up and down too, because they
hated their family doctor.

The Heriot Row household suffered much from the Scottish convention which required of Scottish professional men with good
middle-class practices that they should clown their way through their
duties by use of obsolete vernacular and by routines such as are used by
old-fashioned music-hall comedians. The Mackenzies' doctor was
known to his patients as 'Tyrian Purple' because of the colour of his
nose; he wore a huge shepherd's plaid as though he were conducting a
flock of sheep round the New Town, which touched the brim of his
top hat, and was furled round his black suit and white silk neckerchief

of his trade; and his playfulness was sometimes quite balletic. The boys' bedrooms were to the right and left of a staircase that rose at the back of the hall, and it was his habit to stand looking up the steps, with his head bent to the left, and his left hand cupping his left ear, listen, stand up straight and then say, 'Ay, that'll be Joey's hoast.'

Once my grandmother, crazed out of her manners by anxiety, snapped, 'And who's used the word "hoast" with a straight face for a hundred years? Caught with a gun at your head, could ye no say that my sons were coughing?' Old Tyrian Purple replied, going down with his joke, 'You're no a good Scot if good Scots words are too good for you.'

But he had to be believed when he gave warning that what was wrong with the boys was not a matter of drenching; their lungs had been damaged by the chest infections they had suffered as little children. Old Tyrian Purple assured them there was no reason for panic, all they had to do was watch out and not overdo things, not go rambling round at all hours like gipsies, and go easy with the football and the curling and the climbing, and things would be right as rain; counsel they mocked and obeyed. But they were certainly as alarmed as all their family was and sometimes they were as crusty as old men. They were certainly that on the evening when the whole family were sitting at the dinner table, as supper had just been served, and the Highland servant-maid came in and told my grandmother that Miss Ironside had just come to keep her appointment with Mr Alick, but knew she was too early and would gladly wait in the hall.

This accounement fell cold on the occasion. The meal was not just a meal, but again it was nobody's birthday, and yet again it was celebrating something, though in a small way – perhaps somebody had won a prize – and it began with a soup which was always a sign of celebration in the family: Partan Bree, a delicious soup, a concoction of crab-meat, rice, white stock, anchovy, pepper and cream. That dish is the only material object remembered clearly by any of the persons present; they did not know whether the room was dark with winter or light with summer, or exactly who was there, and I think that they held that in mind because they were jobbing backwards from Aunt Isa's profile, which was memorably evident. When she was offended she managed to turn her neck so that nobody in the room, no matter where they were sitting, could see anything of her face except for a pale, high-nosed, dismissive profile. It would certainly have been she who made the Partan Bree, and she would certainly have been furious at the prospect that her soup, carefully brought to the table at a proper temperature, had to cool while a place was laid for an unexpected guest.

But of course that was not the real issue for any of the people in that room, and why Alick waited in vain for his mother to say, 'Go bring Miss Ironside,' and had to tell the little servant-girl, 'Show Miss Ironside into the drawing room and tell her I'll be with her in a moment.' The door closed and the silent company dipped their spoons in the soup. Then the relevant words were spoken. Either Johnnie or Joey, nobody could remember which one of the boys unhinged by long illness it was, stood up and cried out, pointing at Alick, 'What is going on? That girl should wait in the kitchen.' It was unpardonable. He shouted as if he were the older of the two. Alick rose from the table and said to the centre of the table, meeting nobody's eyes, but speaking firmly, as if he were meeting everybody's eyes, 'What is going on is that I am going to marry that girl.' He walked out of the room and banged the door, and the Mackenzie family ceased to be. The knot of human beings that were created when my grandfather married my grandmother dissolved into its parts which were much less than its whole. On that day I, and a number of other people, were deprived of our due means of happiness.

People rarely set down on paper or confide to their friends pedantically accurate accounts of their humiliations. This is the real flaw in the concept of autobiography. I can give no clear pictures of the Mackenzie household after it had been suddenly distracted from its Partan Bree. According to my mother, Isabella, there was never any open discussion of Alick's announcement. After my grandmother had put herself to bed her daughters and her sister went to bid her goodnight, on which she lay back on her pillows and closed her eyes, and from her small, sweet, oval face there proceeded a quasi-military address, making it plain that their relations with Alick must not vary by a hair's breadth from what they had always been.

Aunt Isa, in whom the Scotswoman's desire to placate the male was maniacal, mistook this order for nearer total capitulation than it was, and sniffed into her handkerchief, 'And he might find a worse wife yet.' My grandmother replied, 'Where would he go for that?' and seemed to sleep. Next morning she was up and about early, and asked Johnnie and Joey to apologize to Alick but, as they themselves admitted, put no pressure on them when they refused, and simply asked them to keep out of his way as much as possible, so that he would not be reminded that their mother had not been able to teach his younger brothers decent manners. They had found it easy to comply, for from that time Alick was less and less at home, and rarely asked his mother to give parties for the foreign musicians who came to play at his concerts, even when they had already met her and liked her. Miss Ironside had never reappeared at Heriot Row, though she was still working at the shop.

It must not be imagined that Johnnie and Joey were nasty sprigs of the bourgeoisie sneering at an innocent member of the proletariat: there was none of that sort of thing in the Mackenzie household. My grandmother had made her assault on the class system when she married, and she had stayed by her victory; her kin had always had to make the first move towards any meeting. What had inflamed Johnnie and Joey was, I think, a consideration peculiarly Scottish, and historical in nature rather than political. It is the Scots' destiny to have to make good their losses, time and again. The rain and the wind and the Northern Seas eroded their land and nagged at all shelter; tribal warfare was inevitable in a land with these contours and such soil, and Irish and English aggression all brought down hammer-blows on man and beast, pasture and tilth and forest. When the Stuarts buckled under the weight of their destiny, and the Scots had to learn to live under the Hanoverians, a massive engineering job had to be done; and it was then, I have always thought, that Scotland developed its special idea of self-improvement.

This is not the same as the doctrine of Self-help, and the difference can be grasped if one considers how an inventor of that recipe for pulling oneself up by one's own boot-straps, Samuel Smiles,* counselled young men not to spend money on buying newspapers, since these chronicled world events, which were not yet, and might never be, their business; and in any case they should have all their faculties focused on the shops, the factories, or the offices, where they were earning their bread. The Scottish doctrine of self-improvement would have laid it down that young men should read their newspapers every day and with the greatest care, since they must know the pattern traced by world events if they were to understand the uses of the work that they were doing in shop, factory or office, and nourish hopes of ultimately owning these. If one is packing peppercorns, the doctrine of Self-help leaves one packing peppercorns, perhaps at a higher wage, but the doctrine of self-improvement leaves the packer of peppercorns with the hope that possibly his eyes will open and see that in this occupation are involved the basking whale and the further satellites and possibly half the choir of angels.

Everybody in the Mackenzie household (as in many, one might even say most Scottish households) was playing musical instruments, selling lace, making Partan Bree, painting pictures, in the unspoken and never distinctly envisioned belief that these performances, provided they improved – that was the point – would by sympathetic magic tame the universe so that it was no longer cruel. But Miss Ironside's loneliness did not suggest that her ambitions were so oblique. Not self-improvement, but Self-help was her rule of life, and though it had not led her to do anything dishonourable – why should she not have married Alick? – there was a feeling in all the family that her hopes were too finite. Whatever it was they hoped was going to happen to all of us and to everything might not happen at all, because of her small, tight intentions.

But so many weeks went by with no discussion of the situation that it was not unreasonable to hope it was fading out. One Sunday morning, my grandmother and her sister were waiting in the hall, face to the front door, ready to lead the family procession to St George's, Charlotte Square, when Jessie and my mother came up behind them, unseen. Therefore they heard my grandmother sigh, but not in sadness, 'It may never happen, ay, it may never happen,' and Aunt Isa respond, 'Ay, he may just have spoken that way on the spur of the moment.' They then realized that they were no longer alone, enquired whether the boys were coming to church and, on hearing that they were not, forebore to lift their voices and call them, but shrugged their shoulders, opened the door, and set forth to lead the depleted, wholly female group. Jessie tugged at my mother's hand to get her to fall further behind, and looked up at her with the smile which was to be one of her great charms when she was an old lady, a smile at once babyish and cynical, candid yet layered with mockery upon mockery. 'That's what the two of them'll be praying for,' she said in her vague little voice, 'That it'll never happen. I pity the poor Lord. On a Sunday He's enough to do with prayers *en gros* to have the time for prayers *en détail*.'

This is not so odd a remark as might be supposed in one sense. *En gros* and *en détail* were printed on the letter-heads of some French firms with which my grandmother had dealings, which sometimes got back to the house because the French commercial printing was so ornate and pretty. But it is more difficult to account for its slightly sacrilegious flavour. I doubt if my mother, much the freer spirit, would have ventured to make such a daring joke. Nobody in that flat was not a believing Christian; and I doubt if there were many inhabitants of Heriot Row, except for a few heretics (Irvingites and the like),* who did not hold the faith to the letter.

At mid-day dinner my grandmother showed how near assurance she had allowed herself to drift. 'I thought Alick looked fine in the kirk,' she said, across the table, and after a minute Johnnie and Joey received her message and asked what anthems had been sung. On the following evening she returned from her business and was sitting in the drawing room, drinking tea, when Alick came in and sat down beside her. She poured him out a cup, and it seemed all as it used to be. They had often, if he had a leisurely programme, sat together at that hour, drinking tea, sometimes right up to the moment when supper was served. But now he had come for business, which he settled quickly. He drank his cup of tea and put it down, stood up and said, 'Mary and I have found a house that suits us. It is in good condition. It hardly requires anything done to it. So we will be getting married in two months' time.'

My grandmother answered, 'Well, I hope you'll be very happy and I'm truly glad for you that you've found a home you like so easily, for that's often hard to do.' She was in fact deeply shocked by the announcement. It seemed to her that if he stayed in her house when there was a disagreement between them, it should have been because he hoped to convince her in time that right was on his side. But he had made no attempt to do that. Had he ever told her by what acts and words Mary Ironside had made him feel that she was the woman he wished to live and die beside, she would have softened to him; she had after all an elopement to her credit. He had simply used her house as a base from which he could, with the least inconvenience, search for the home which he was going to share with a woman whom he knew she detested, for all her qualities, even to the admirable quality of her needlework. I blush to say my grandmother was afterwards to utter what was for her the lethal opinion that Mary Ironside's hand-sewing looked like machine work.

But she knew she must do something, say something. As things had fallen out, the situation was too ungracious. She rose and said, 'Wait here a minute.' Alick objected that he must leave, he could not stay to supper, he was host at a club to some visiting foreigner. She said, 'I'll no be a minute. You must wait.' She went up to the boys' three bedrooms, which had been hacked out of a large room built out at the back of the house by a previous owner who had been a professor of some physical science, as a laboratory. She knocked on the door of Willie, the youngest son, still a student at the School of Art, who was dark, heavy, taciturn and slow-moving, unlike any of the others. The springs of his bed creaked as he got off it. He opened the door but not far; she saw over his shoulder a slice of the usual disorder of easel, skeleton, mannequin, palette, paint tubes, sketchbooks spread on a table and stacked about the table legs. 'I dinna have to ask my way,' said my grandmother, 'I've found my road to Prince Pig's Palace. Willie, did you no show me a framed watercolour you'd done of Traprain Law that wasna so bad?'

'Ay, Maw,' said Willie. He and Johnnie and Joey all addressed their mother 'Maw', which was what the Keelie boys in the slums of the Canongate and the Cowgate called their mothers, just to annoy her.*

'Oh, Willie lad,' his mother said, 'will you do what I want you to do for once in your life?'

'What ails you, for goodness sake?' he asked in sudden anxiety.

She said, 'I want you to comb your hair and take that watercolour downstairs to your brother Alick and give it to him, and we'll make a ploy of it, and you shall say you want to gi'e it to Mary Ironside and him as their first wedding present.'

The young man stared at her out of a grimace. He said, 'For Christ's sake! Mother! That woman!'

My grandmother said, 'You misheard me. And no blasphemy, or

it'll be you'll have to go, too. I've no asked you to marry Miss Ironside, it is your brother Alick who is going to marry Miss Ironside. Neither you nor I can dae anything about it, nor should we wish to if we could. What I'm asking you is to comb your hair and go down to the drawing room and give that watercolour to your brother Alick, who is also the head of this house till he leaves it. And I hope you'll think of an agreeable message to send to Mary.'

Willie muttered and went behind the door and came back with his hair combed and the watercolour under his arm. Halfway down the stairs he stopped and buried his laughing face against her hair. 'What sort of sweet, sweet, barley-sugar sweet message are you going to send Mary Ironside?'

She pushed him away so that he had to see her distress. 'Wheesht,' she whispered. 'Do you no see that we every one of us know this isn't as it should be, not as it might have been if your father had lived? And all the same we may all of us be wrong about Mary Ironside.'

Because of the disinclination of human beings to record their humiliations in full, which I have mentioned, I know little (and no other living person can know as much) about the feelings of my grandmother and her family during the next few years, and I cannot guarantee that I can set in proper sequence the events which my mother and my aunts and some old friends of the family described to me many years ago. But I know some things for certain, and certainly my grandmother continued to detest Mary Ironside, and her accusation against her was not that she was stupid or unkind or unscrupulous, but that she was wicked, that it was her aim, and even her enjoyed aim, to take away from innocent people what was theirs, and use it for her own pleasure, regardless of what suffering that might cause. But my grandmother was well aware that she had not a grain of evidence to justify this unqualified condemnation; and she certainly pointed this out to her family lest they fall into the same error, and indeed they needed such a warning, for Alick and his wife were not tactful. They had acquired a house which was attractive and not cheap; but the price could hardly have mattered to Alick, who had lived with his mother for the previous ten years, from 1865 to 1874, and had launched the social side of his career from her dining room. Even in the currency of the time the arrangement did too much credit to his thrift. But that was not mentioned. It was how my grandmother had chosen it to be, and it was taken for granted that all sorts of ripe and bursting benefits were conferred on the male and not on the female; and the Mackenzies were not given to nursing grudges.

But there were causes for regret hard to ignore. The new house was only a few minutes' walk from Heriot Row and that was perhaps tactless, as Alick and Mary rarely visited the family and entertained them even less frequently. Many years later my mother, speaking of this stark rejection, made a wry mouth and sighed the Scots word for 'sour' – 'wairsh'. The estrangement meant a special loss for her because she and Alick had both great musical gifts, and these united by what I can only call by its Scottish name, 'sibship', which comes from the same root as 'sibling' and signifies the bond between brothers and sisters, and so suggests emotions deeper and more variable than those implied by the term 'kinship'. The musical sibship of Alick and my mother was manifest in their devotion to Schumann, whom they served with equal force in their different ways. Alick rehearsed his idol's chamber music with a pious scruple that was sometimes furious and agonized; he was married to the master, there was a community of goods between them: those arabesques and that iridescence leaked into his own compositions. As for my mother, *Kinderszenen* and *Carnaval* were maps of different and distant areas in her imagination. She had not to learn to interpret them, it was only the technical problems she had to study; but she was properly humble if Alick entrusted her with the parts in the Quartets and the Quintets:* it was a delightful indulgence to do it. This particular item in their musical sibship was of service to their personal sibship, for they lived to work and then to shine, and be praised for the strength of the light they were shedding, when they were looking their best in rooms lit by chandeliers.

These satisfactions all vanished overnight, destroyed by this hostility which spared nothing, penetrated every place, even to routines which one would think unalterably not perilous. My mother and Alick had been well contented that they both taught the schoolgirls whom they were standing amongst in Princes Street Gardens when the black flag was hoisted above the Calton Jail and they knew that

Chantrelle was dead. It happened that on the two or three days they taught in the week their timetables called each to go from one classroom to another, and that the positions of those four classrooms meant that at a certain hour they met when walking in opposite directions along a corridor which was usually empty. Before the alienation, though they were living under the same roof, they used this brief contact to give sibship a chance to flower. They exchanged smiles, and waved their hands, and if anything funny had come the way of one or other since breakfast time it was described; it might be that if the steam radiators were in cacophonous voice, as in the schools of that day they always were, they would suggest the name of the composer of organ music or the organist responsible for the grunts and squeaks. But after the marriage my mother no longer met Alick in the corridor. At first she thought that his timetable must have been altered, but a look at a noticeboard told her this was not so. One day she had to vary her own routine at that same hour by going to retrieve a new pupil who had gone to the wrong teacher, and she came on Alick, making his way to his classroom by a less direct route on another floor. The defection had done more than dim the proper brilliance of her life; it even took the commonplace and familiar and made it painful and inexplicable.

Of course, Johnnie (or Joey, whichever it was) should not have said, 'That girl should be waiting in the kitchen,' and not unnaturally that reflection haunted the older members of the smitten household. My grandmother and Aunt Isa would often sigh and tell my mother and Jessie that it was no use pretending, it was just not possible for a woman to bring up boys in a fatherless household. 'Boys need a man's firm hand,' they said. My mother and Jessie protested that all around them were households with a man's firm hand in each of them, and all their boys were busy at far worse things than Johnnie had ever done; but they were speaking some decades too soon for them to shake their female elders' conviction of their own inferiority.

JOHNNIE

But suddenly the issue was of no importance. Johnnie was an object of concern for another reason. The North was hit by a long hard winter, and his health failed. There was no question of continuing his studies; he had perpetual heavy colds, then bronchitis, then asthma. Old Tyrian Purple was a daily visitor, and abandoned his pantomime routine of cupping his ear and deciding 'That's Johnnie's hoast, that's Joey's hoast,' so obvious was it that only Johnnie's hoast was now of consequence. The boy's chest condition was causing the kind of inconvenience rarely suffered since the discovery of antibiotics; his breathing was like a slow form of strangulation. He also had a fever that left him only to return. There was, moreover, a difficulty over nursing; it was not considered genteel in certain circles for the un-married women of the family to look after their menfolk during sickness, and this debarred Aunt Isa (who was by this time over fifty), my mother and Jessie from doing more than sitting with Johnnie when he felt well enough for a gossip or wanted to have the newspaper read to him. Even the servant-maids could only come in and make his bed under the chaperonage of my grandmother. Nurses had to be em-ployed, and as it was not twenty years since Miss Florence Nightingale had come back from Scutari, all that could be hired were old women who felt an irresistible need for refreshment as their hours of duty came to an end, so poor Johnnie often waked out of sleep to find the air loaded with the fumes of a number of wee drappies, and the polluted air would become a demon and take him by the throat and shake him. He was distraught and emaciated: the latter probably for the reason that old Tyrian Purple kept him on a diet consisting of little but that unfounded rumour of nourishment called 'Broth'. Neither my grandmother nor anybody else in the house was greatly surprised when Johnnie took to coughing blood and old Tyrian Purple quavered, 'I'm sorry to have to tell you, Mrs Mackenzie, that I think our Johnnie has just a wee touch of consumption.' She looked at him in astonishment but not in surprise.

When she heard him utter the words she had expected, she was amazed because they differed slightly from her expectation; he had not alluded to the will of God. He must be upset, for the will of God was always mentioned when supremely disagreeable events had occurred. The phrase had been used again and again when her husband had died. It was surely proper that it should be used now, for it was inevitable that Johnnie should die too if he had consumption, and that quite soon. She was not being hysterical in her fear: in the middle of the nineteenth century the death rate from tuberculosis of the lungs was higher than can be believed by the present generation, and she must have seen not some but a number of friends and associates struck down by what was called by the people 'a rising of the lights'. She continued to wonder why God was not being named as responsible for this new abduction from her life; and she knew the pain of an instantaneous conversion to atheism.

She glared at old Tyrian Purple to tell him that if he had said those words, it were better he had not. Assuming, she said afterwards, the air of a patient sheep, he continued in a spirit of gentle rebuke, 'What I was endeavouring to tell you, Mrs Mackenzie, is that your Johnnie's not gone very far down that brae we all know of, and if you'll listen quietly, you'll hear why I think he's going to turn around and come up to the high ground again, and live to be an old, old man, if you'll but steel your mother's heart and send him straight out to Australia.'

My grandmother gaped at him. She knew nothing about Australia, except that Captain Cook had gone there voluntarily and a number of convicts had not, that it contained many kangaroos and some gold mines, and that it was at the bottom of the map. She did not even know how long it took to get there. She stammered, 'What for must I send Johnnie to Australia?'

Tyrian Purple then delivered an address, which was remarkable considering Pasteur was already a middle-aged man, but would have been listened to with the ear of faith by many medical practitioners of the time. He alleged it to be a well-known fact that no white person

born in Australia had ever suffered from consumption, and that some
members of the French Academy of Medical Sciences had reflected on
this and had for some years made a practice of sending all their
wealthier patients out to live in Australia; and they had found that
though the advanced cases made no improvement, the early cases
recovered and had no relapses.

This was, he explained, natural enough. It had long been evident,
in spite of all the daft theories which were blowing round the town
recently, that the disease was carried about the world and dispersed to
human beings by miasmas. Well, it now seemed that there were
miasmas which dispersed not disease but health; and they could not
abide consumption.

'So we must have our Johnnie out of bed in a month,' said old
Tyrian Purple. 'Fill him up with plenty of that bonny broth I see in
these big cups upstairs, and maybe you've friends who would make
some canny enquiries about a comfortable ship that'll be sailing to
Australia.'

My grandmother broke in with white fury, 'Australia! Australia!'

Aunt Isa, my mother and Jessie heard her and crept into the room,
and gathered round her, and tried to caress her back to calm. She
struck their hands away. 'Australia!' she cried again. 'How is that sick
boy upstairs to get up and go to Australia in a month's time? Who is to
take care of him out in Australia? There is not so much money in this
house as you think. We have to work. I cannot leave the shop. I could
not send one of the girls alone. What will my husband think of me,
letting one of my bairns go so far from me and all his brothers and
sisters? Australia! Australia! Australia!'

'Mrs Mackenzie,' said old Tyrian Purple, speaking over-politely out
of pursed lips, 'you're no taking this as well as I hoped you might. I
think when you're more yourself you'll see you've been singularly
blessed in being given a sudden revelation of the design traced by a
Hand Greater than Ours. I myself, if I may mention it, intend to go on
my knees together and thank the Lord for releasing one of His secrets
at a time when He may lighten the lot of a brave wee lady.'

Because my grandmother's face was streaked with tears and she was
still shaking with sobs, nobody rang for one of the servant-maids to
show old Tyrian Purple out of the door, so Jessie did that. She came
back bravely giggling. The old silly had told her on the mat how all his

life he had admired my grandmother and had mentioned that when she had come to Edinburgh as a bride people called her the Fairy Bride.

Everybody laughed except Aunt Isa, who gloomed and said, 'If anybody called her that, he must have known he was taking a liberty.'

'But nobody did,' said my grandmother, 'Yon old humbug made that up between this room and the front door.' There was a long pause and she went on, 'It seems our poor Johnnie's got consumption.'

The three groaned that they all knew that, the blood could mean nothing else, and waited.

She told them how some French scientist had discovered that mild cases of consumption were healed in Australia, merely by being there, and how difficult it seemed for her to arrange the ways and means of getting Johnnie out there, and, 'Oh, how I wish I could talk this over with Alick,' and lost her daughters for ever. That remark was about twenty years out of date. They were never to give her unqualified obedience and respect again; they were always to suspect she undervalued them and what they did for her.

Their resentment might then and there have escaped from their control, and what remained of the family disrupted, had not their brother Joey been on their side, and he fought all his wars according to the code of the angels. He would raise no devils. His comment on my grandmother's desire to consult Alick he dismissed as 'Daft, daft, but mark you, she's no trying to defend him, she's just pretending that nothing happened and he didn't do what he did. Oh, leave her be.' That was a favourite expression of his, but that seemed the last time he used it for some time. He perpetually ran errands in the interest of his Johnnie which often threw a light on the peculiar gaiety and resources of him and his brother. He and Johnnie had been great runners-about in the city, turning up roads simply because they had never noticed them before, indeed pursuing any form of the strange.

One Saturday afternoon, it seemed, they had passed a chapel hall on the fringes of the city, with a very small man, a wee man dressed in skins over a neat suit, standing at the door beside a board announcing that there was being held within the annual meeting of the Society of Picts (who were, if anybody does not know it, the dwarfish, primitive people which inhabited Scotland until the advent of the Celts, and were finally exterminated by the Romans) and that all Picts were welcome. My young uncles had found it an irresistible attraction, and were upset when the small man at the door had sniffed and said, 'You're gey large for Picts, we're no eident to welcome the usurpers.'* But there then appeared a bearded man, like themselves of normal height, who falsely said, 'These are my cousins, and we're all Picts, but we don't look it for we're a terrible family for marrying out of our ain folk and into Celt families,' and Johnnie and Joey sighed, 'Och, ay, we just canna help inter-marrying.' The three of them had a happy afternoon, though rather a long one, for Pictish laments on defeat in warfare proved not to be short, and they finished by having some drinks in a pub, and learning that their new friend was a lecturer in medicine at Edinburgh, and his special interest was in diseases of the lungs.

Joey took my mother to see this man, in some hospital, she could never remember which it had been; it was in a squalid quarter of the town which she had never visited. They sat facing the doctor at a small wooden table, so old that its surface was flaking off in slivers; high dirty windows admitted depreciated light, and now and then boots rang on an iron staircase just outside the door. The doctor had a kind face; though he would have shocked his patients today, for according to the custom of the time, he wore no overall and his black suit was stained. The doctor said, 'Joey, you look tired,' and Joey said, 'Oh, Angus, I'm not tired, we Mackenzies don't tire easily, but it's the strain. Isabella here's feeling it too. It's brother Johnnie.' He explained that Johnnie had been stricken down with consumption, and that the family doctor had this idea that if he went out and settled in Australia he might benefit from the mere act of living within that continent, owing to the local abundance of beneficial miasmas.

The doctor said he was not conversant with the idea of beneficent miasmas, but no doubt it was looking for them that made kangaroos jump such long distances. The three made the most of the little joke, and then Angus told them he knew a lot about old Tyrian Purple and considered him old-fashioned but no fool. It would be dangerous to reject his advice out of hand; and yes, the journey to Australia might be a good idea. Early cases of consumption often benefitted from long sea voyages. But he could not express any opinion about a long stay. Accommodation for an invalid – and even ordinary accommodation for the healthy – might be very rough even in such places as

Melbourne and Sydney. But he would enquire. He would enquire, he went on brooding. He would enquire. Of course a lot would depend on Johnnie's state. 'How are his spirits?' he asked.

'Oh, down, down,' groaned Joey. 'He disna want to die, Angus. Man, you cannot think how Johnnie disna want to die. He is a shadow of himself, and he kens well he may go. When old Tyrian Purple tells me how fine my chest is after the trouble I had at the same time as Johnnie and harps on the long life I have before me, I feel ashamed. God knows I'd split the length of life I have before me right down the middle and give half to Johnnie.' My mother thought that she herself could give half her life to save Johnnie; but Joey could have her whole life from the minute she knew he wanted it.

That visit turned out to be a good gamble; Angus was the kind of man whose labours for his friends are fruitful. From one of his seniors he heard of a young consumptive named Alistair, son of a General, who was going out to Melbourne to test the beneficence of the miasmas, under the care of an old soldier who had been a hospital orderly. The General, a needy landowner, was glad to find that there was someone who was willing to be responsible for half the orderly's pay, as well as be companion to the boy. He also handed on the name of a boarding-house well recommended in Melbourne where he intended to send the boy. That settled, Joey begged his mother to let him go and talk over her affairs with her banker. When he came back he seemed not too pleased with what he had learned; but he had gained some information that lifted a load off all our minds.

As my grandmother drew into middle life, and her elopement with a musician changed from a scandal to a romantic legend, her relatives gave her the benefit of the Scottish belief that it is unnatural, truly *nefas*, to omit one's relatives from one's last will and testament in favour of friends or charities. The resultant legacies were never sensationally large; but she drew a quite surprising rental from a stretch of land adjoining a racecourse near an English town which she was never to visit. Joey proposed that she should sell this and now set the proceeds aside, consider them as Johnnie's own, and send the income regularly to him in Australia. She hesitated to consent, and he told her, smiling, 'None of us will grudge Johnnie that.' But for another minute she refrained from taking the pen he offered and signing the letter of instructions to her banker. A vein standing out on his forehead, he told his two sisters afterwards, 'She came near to saying to me that she'd like to consult Alick first. Oh, our mother!'

By this time their first anger against their eldest brother had changed into cold indignation, such as they might have felt against an intrusive stranger, and indeed that was how he appeared when, rumours of Johnnie's misfortune having at last pierced his preoccupations, he paid an impeccable visit on the invalid. He came when Johnnie was just waking from a deep sleep, and the boy looked up with a smile which showed that, as sundials boast, he marked only the sunny hours, and his visitor was seen at a grave disadvantage. This braced the household. Thereafter the business of getting Johnnie strong enough to travel, organizing his journey and finding him a foothold in Australia, was conducted with the briskness of a military operation.

One of the means adopted by Joey to get his brother out of bed and on to his feet strikes me as a remarkable display of character and common sense. I have said that Johnnie's prescribed meals consisted chiefly of cups of broth, and I am sure I am speaking the truth, for his diet was engraved on my mother's mind till the day of her death. He was given pints, and if he would take it, quarts, of beef tea and chicken stock, gruel made of fine outmeal and served not with milk but with whey, and very occasionally morsels of honeycomb tripe and lambs' testicles. He was given no milk, meat, fish, eggs, vegetables or fruit. This was not the diet prescribed for known consumptives, which went to other extremes of 'goodness'; this was aimed at the elimination of chest infections such as bronchitis, trachyitis, pneumonia, which it was decided to eliminate first. But Joey, giving Johnnie his blanket bath one day, exclaimed, 'Good God, Johnnie, your ribs look more like a bird cage! Are all these damned slops enough for you? Do you not crave something solid?' Poor Johnnie said, 'I'd give my soul for a bit of fresh fish.' 'We'll try you on it,' said Joey, 'and if you die we'll bury you and say no more about it.'

In those days, and for long after, though not now, Edinburgh was a gourmet's dream of fish of all sorts, coming up only hours old from the Firth of Forth. There was some argument with Aunt Isa and the servant-girls, all by temperament given to doing what the witch-doctors told them; but Joey gave his orders, and got peace by coaxing his mother to confirm these orders. When the younger people in the house saw her defying the old witch-doctor and treating Joey as a new and superior witch-doctor, it was treated as a famous victory. Johnnie wolfed the proteins and the fats and grew more vigorous every day. This is enough to make me respect Joey. He was campaigning against a real death. When it was my turn to live with my grandmother in Edinburgh in the early twentieth century, typhoid cases showed a very high death rate, and it is to be supposed that many of these patients died of starvation. The accepted treatment was to give them virtually no food at all, except milk and water, for a period of up to twelve weeks.

Johnnie was up and about and ready to go on his journey in good time, so much better that sometimes he longed to get out of the house and go out with some of his friends and have a game of cards; and having been in bed so long that he had forgotten the conventions of the dining room and the drawing room or wherever his mother and Aunt Isa might be, he once said so at supper.

'What's that?' asked my grandmother sharply. 'Playing cards? I've heard nowt of this. Do you play cards? Where do you play cards? Not in this house that I've noticed. You've never been one to take a hand at whist or bezique in this house. Then where do you play cards? And I'll ask more, do you play cards for money?'

'Oh, mother,' said Johnnie, 'I go here and there with young men of my own age, and you know well the fathers of some of them, and there's others with fathers that are too grand for us, and we do play cards for money, and ye canna complain – it's a matter of bawbees,* for I have no more than bawbees in my pouch!'

'Ye'll have less if you play cards for money,' said my grandmother. 'That's for grown men, not for young boys.'

'Oh, mother, we're no weans,'* said Johnnie with a straight face, 'and anyway the bairns are catching up with us – you'll see weans of four and five running barefoot up the steps of all the clubs in the New Town and sitting down at the green tables with Dukes and Marquesses and taking their gold snuff-boxes off them.'

'Dinna give me these havers,'* said my grandmother, standing up. 'Gambling is a terrible thing, and though the high and mighty do it, it's my opinion, and it was your father's, that there's that about it which is gey and low.'*

'Oh, mother,' said Johnnie, 'ye canna take a joke. It was to see my friends I wanted out. I've told you about them, and some of them have been here, and they're good lads and you liked them, and if we sometimes play cards, it's truly nothing to carry in your heart – it's nothing; and I wanted to see the lads not for that, but because I am going away and I may never see them again.'

From behind him, Joey nodded his head at my grandmother as if to say, 'Ay, there's that.' My grandmother nodded back and said, 'Never say that again,' and went back to her chair, but could not keep her peace. 'But wherever you are, Australia or anywhere, you may be led to gamble. There's other things to do.' 'Ay,' said Johnnie, 'I know what ye mean, there's chasing lassies – and I'm grateful for such a thoughtful mother who suggests I put first things first.'

'Oh, will I never learn when my sons are making a fool of me,' said my grandmother, and later she said with a smile to my mother and Jessie, as they sat in her bedroom and brushed their hair before they went to bed, 'Johnnie's a cruel one to me, he had me thinking for a moment that he'd played cards for money. I couldna bear that. Oh, the harm I've seen from that.'

Johnnie and the General's son went the first part of the journey by rail, in the company of Joey and Willie. It had been assumed from the first that the women of the household would not be of the party, and this was unfortunate; their minds turned to the Scottish convention that women do not attend funerals. But the two brothers returned bright with the pleasure of what had later, against all expectation, taken on the quality of an outing. They had spent the greater part of a day in London, and were pleased to pronounce that it was not a patch on Edinburgh. 'It has no got the variety, it has no the majesty – it's too spread out – the brothers Adams' hand is spread too meanly on the place. Mind you, St Paul's is grand. We could do with St Paul's in Edinburgh and there'd be nothing against the move. It would look far better there.' But then again the Thames was nothing. 'Earth hath not anything so fair – the thing's ridiculous. But of course you have to remember that Wordsworth was an Englishman doing his best with what he'd got.'

Pressed for news of how Johnnie had stood the day's fatigue, answers were given that he had enjoyed himself and they had been careful not to let him get tired. 'We made him sit down on a bench, and we stayed there quite a time, for it was quite a convenient spot. We three Scots were able to sit and look at the English Houses of Parliament and what a miserable lot of gingerbread that is. Och, we had a fine time.'

'But go on about Johnnie.'

'He was fine, I tell you, he was fine.'

'Did he eat? You saw that he didna miss his proper meals?'

'Oh, mother, no. We all ate like horses, with the excitement. At an inn, I forget the name. We had beefsteak pudding and greens and baked potatoes, and treacle tart. And Johnnie was delighted with the ship. It looked a weird thing, it's so long, so long it might be a floating log that's been hollowed out, and the mast looked like trees stripped by the wind, but when one gets aboard it's such a wide thing, such a solid thing, but it's so neat, the carpentry's so gimp, and Johnnie was so pleased with his cabin and his bunk, and the General and his son were there, saying goodbye, and they're civil people, very civil, and the old soldier's a good old man, and he speaks the Gaelic. They all took great notice of Johnnie's violin and viola, it seems there's flute-playing in the family. Oh, it'll all go well, mother, be sure it will go well.'

And it seemed to be so. The voyage gave them long days of delight. The passengers experienced the delight, now long denied us because the plane has ousted the ship, of breathing day by day air utterly undefiled by soil and gases. They learned that it is difficult to worry about what has happened or is going to happen to one on land, if one can watch a shoal of dolphins in a clear sea. Also the boys became attached to some of the passengers, some of the crew, and to the old soldier who was their nurse and guardian; and both Johnnie and Alistair, who were gregarious by nature, and had detested their isolation by illness, took great pleasure in these quickly won and easily maintained friendships. Alistair had been warned by his father that these bonds might disappear when the ship reached land, and he passed on the warning to Johnnie, who was so shocked that he wrote of this cynicism with horror in a letter to his family. Was it not mean and grudging to deny people credit for a special gift of seeing into the hearts of strangers and using the knowledge so gained to give them what they wanted to think over and laugh over?

'Why,' he wrote, 'there is an Oxford professor on board, a serious-minded man, who reads books on philosophy and Greek texts on deck, and is not fond of just talking either. He is sharing a cabin with an old clergyman, a poor doddering old man who is going out to Australia to live with his married daughter, because he has lost his wife and likes no part of what was left to him – he doesn't enjoy the boat, he sometimes weeps at table. Well, this Oxford professor has found out that of all things the poor silly old man loves puns and riddles, as if he had gone back to his childhood, and the professor, will you believe it, who keeps to himself most times, came to Alistair and me the other day and asked us if we could remember any stuff like that.'

The boys enjoyed the odd little chore and worked on it, scoring their greatest success with Charles Lamb's story of the Oxford scholar who met in the street a porter carrying a hare and asked him if it was his own hare or a wig. The old clergyman relished that story so much that every now and then he asked the professor to tell it to him over again. When the boys heard that, they asked the professor how it happened that an educated man had not heard that story which everybody knew, which they had known since their childhood, and the professor said, 'Ah, you are pitying and perhaps despising the old man for having forgotten something he must have read in his child-hood. But how could he have read Lamb's essays in his childhood, since there was not twenty years between his birth and Lamb's, and Lamb was over thirty when he made his first success? It is me you should pity, for I certainly am deteriorating, since I remember now that I have known that story for a long time, and it had gone clean out of my mind. The old man is simply me a few years ahead. So you, my boys, be careful, my boys! Oh, be careful!' At that point in his letter Johnnie was diverted by his enthusiasm for flying fish, but after some infatuated sentences he returned to argument. 'How can anybody say that a man like the professor will forget Alistair and me if we met again? Anyway, Alistair and I will never forget him. He was so patient with that daft old man.'

When Joey handed back that letter to my mother, he said, 'Poor

Johnnie, how he loves the human race.' They were sitting in the drawing room at Heriot Row, and it was a good thing he had finished with the letter for this was a winter afternoon, and the light was failing round them. There were small lamps on the tables, but it did not occur to them that they should light them. I must have made it clear that my mother's family could only be defined as artistically gifted mongrels, crossbred between aristocratic and peasant stocks, living in a bourgeois environment; but neither my mother nor my uncle Joey would ever have thought of lighting those table lamps. That was the duty of one or other of the three servant-maids. This was not entirely a matter of superiors being waited on by inferiors; it was in part due to a technological fantasy of Aunt Isa's. She believed that her nephews and nieces – and even her own sister – were so lacking in manual dexterity that they could not possibly attempt to light a lamp without causing an explosion of a force not to be achieved till the atom bomb was invented eighty years later.

'If ye put your great hands to it, there'll be not a wall standing between here and the Castle Rock,' she would tell my uncles and my aunts and my mother and my grandmother, though all were of proven dexterity as musicians or embroideresses. 'For peace sake, leave it to the lassies.' On this occasion, as the lassies were unaware that my uncle and my mother had gone there to be alone – not with each other, but with Johnnie's letter – they did not come to dispel the steely dusk. 'That was why he loved parties,' said Joey. 'All that company, in their Sunday best, with the famous chandelier of Number 41 shining down on them. Johnnie just gloried in all those human beings.'

I must explain, for the benefit of those unacquainted with the seignorial character of the New Town of Edinburgh, that my mother and Joey were recalling festivities of a sort unlikely to have taken place in the home of an English family of so small a fortune. Houses in London were built in a more humble spirit: noble residences were there reserved for the noble; but in Scotland, dwellings of the professional and mercantile classes held back from magnificence only just enough to give Dukes occasion to justify their pride. My grandmother's neighbour, Sir James Simpson, the inventor of chloroform, had a whole house to himself, which today houses without strain the organization of the Church of Scotland.* My grandmother had but half a house, but her dining room and drawing room were spacious and elegant; and the setting determined the style of the performance. We did not entertain Dukes and Duchesses: junior members of such families sometimes, if they were musical, looked in on us, but we knew they were gipsying. We regularly entertained fry that were nevertheless good fish: musicians, painters, lawyers, doctors, university staff and their pretty daughters.

I have not mentioned the most important fact about these parties. It was stated by Joey, as the darkness fell. 'There's been no sae many parties since Alick left.' These parties had a significance which they should not have had: they determined the destiny of the individual members of the Mackenzie family to a degree which made it impossible for them to be judged on their merits. When 41 Heriot Row had been the home of Alexander Mackenzie, Musical Director of the Theatre Royal, Edinburgh, songwriter and composer, and his pretty wife, and the children that came to them annually, they formed the classic family group that increases and multiplies as does the grain in its barns, the cattle in its pastures. If Alexander had not died of an undiagnosed disease in his thirties, that classic family group would have been nourished by the approval of the community, and their roots would have struck deep as they took over an area and made it their own, entwining their roots with those of like growth. Every stalk and leaf and flower would have been accepted by the environment. They would have seeded and spread themselves as far as the wind would take them. Had my grandfather not died, his hospitality would have lit up his rooms with parties, at which my mother and Jessie would have appeared in bright and flowing dresses, and would have entered into marriages that might have been long and public examples of happiness; and my uncles would have met strange girls as pretty as their sisters, and been civil to their fathers and mothers and, proved stable enough to extend the group, would have been helped to whatever eminence their gifts entitled them.

Because my grandmother had been still young and very pretty when she was left a widow, and because so many householders in the Old and New Town felt tenderness towards her husband's ghost, the Mackenzies had been granted the right to enjoy something, if not all, of the prestige of a classical family group. Then Alick came back, and the family really had a right to enjoy that prestige; for what was the title to it? That there should be a man at the head of it. Alick was now that man; he could work the magic, the botanical magic, whereby a set of males and females turned into a unified growth. There were then more parties, frequent parties, if not so frequent as they had been in the days when Alexander Mackenzie was alive. But my mother and her sister had the double handicap of being dowerless and, at the time of Alick's return, too young to be ingenious in claiming a husband, the more so because my mother was absorbed in her musical studies and Jessie was cloistered by her shyness: and the boys were in poor health.

Then Alick went away, to a home just round the corner, but effectively as far off as Turkestan; and the twice patched-up classical family group at 41 Heriot Row fell to pieces. I repeat that this was simply because there was no man at the head of the house. My grandmother, now middle-aged and not so pretty as she had been, was no longer visited as a special case and treated as an honorary father. She and her family had committed no faults, they had not failed to fulfil any function demanded of them by law or custom, but they were, from the oldest to the youngest, punished not by fine or imprisonment, but by a far worse penalty. They could have paid named fines and served allotted sentences, but it was for an indeterminate period, possibly for ever, that the Victorian community refused to contemplate with any glow of warmth a family not headed by a man. It would be said today that such people were boring, whether they were or not: and they would receive fewer invitations, and their own would be less often accepted. The sons and daughters would find it an effort to persuade fathers and mothers of families not under such bans to become fathers-in-law and mothers-in-law of this headless, uninfluential family. That was the inconvenience which, in that particular evening under the unlit chandelier in my grandmother's drawing room, was pressing hard on my mother and her brother Joey.

JOEY

On my mother the blade had already struck its first blow. She was in her middle twenties, within call, or rather wail, of the thirties. There was no reason why she should not have married. Her conversation was quick, amiable, witty, and always it was the amiability which was the determining force. It is hardly necessary for me to describe her appearance because there is a picture in the Hermitage at Moscow, painted by Manet and called 'In the Conservatory',* representing a woman sitting on a bench among palms and semi-tropical flowers, and a man leaning on the back of the bench. The woman's dark curling hair, her regular features, and her long hands, give the essence of my mother's appearance; and the little hat, turned up at the back with a neat confusion of feathers, a plain grey silk suit, with a long belted jacket, and a flounced shirt, and a black cat-bow tying in a white *jabot* at the throat, and narrow white frills at the wrists – these are such clothes as my mother wore in her old photographs.

The only difference lies in the eyes. The lady in the conservatory has the fixed but compliant eyes of a china doll; my mother saw with black fire – not fire to burn, fire to illuminate, like summer lightning, only black. But there is one curious, and prophetic, similarity. Manet's lady has very large ears, and my mother was to end her life under the same disadvantage, though those early photographs show only the two conventional Victorian sea-shells. Her family suffered from a bizarre genetic flaw: some of our bones and cartilages continue to develop throughout our lives. My mother was to end with nothing like Manet's lady's neat profile; she was to have a Roman nose, large ears, large hands, large feet, by the time she died, and I was to know just the same disfigurement. I took small-size gloves and size 4 shoes when I was young, and now my gloves are as big as I can buy and my shoes are man-sized. Mr James Lees-Milne, the apostle of good taste, has been very funny in print over these ridiculous defects of mine,* but it was unnecessary. I have long been as embarrassed as even his nature could hope over my defects.

But I talk of the defects that come of ageing. In my youth my mother would have seemed to most men an attractive woman; I would even say, a woman whom it would be pleasant to marry. This was not simply because of her looks, which really were delightful: both she and the Manet lady have the look of songbirds, trim little packages of celebration wrapped up in delicately coloured layers of silk, muslin, and the primal garment of skin. But it was also due to something spiritual, which was not exactly hope, but a related virtue. Arriving after a journey by train at a place where nothing but hardship awaited her, she would have walked out of the railway station looking from side to side, as if to be sure of seeing the thirteenth-century cathedral in perfect condition, unaccountably omitted from the guidebooks but, she thought, possibly still there – and indeed she got what she wanted: she was sure of seeing anything that was there and had its place in the catalogue of attempted perfections.

But she was not surprised when she found nothing remarkable. She understood the thesis of tragedy: that the good is self-consuming, not through its own fault but through the nature of things. Men and women live and breed through the generations, so that their achievements are beaten down by the army of their descendants, too densely crowded to have room for achievement. A man loves a woman, and their children form an unnegotiable family. People develop their musical gifts, and when enough have done that, the musical world becomes so complicated that for a gifted musician to fight his or her way to share his gift with his audience is like a journey through the jungle. And so on, and so on. But my mother had already learned to live, although aware that life is hardly worth living, and this is surely the most useful quality a wife or husband can possess. Yet at that moment a hundred years ago or so my poor mother was sitting there in the dusk reflecting that she met fewer and fewer unmarried men, and that the only man not a relation of hers who was constantly at her side was the artist who seemed never to have heard of a proposal of marriage. She also had in mind the similar plight of her sister Jessie;

who was so very pretty that wherever she went smiling old gentlemen presented her with posies, but who had never yet received a love letter.

My poor mother had a double cause for dissatisfaction. Obviously she was at a disadvantage in taking up a musical career, compared with any young man of like endowment. She could not play in a theatre orchestra, or in any other orchestra; she could not mix with foreign musicians in comradeship and be passed on to this teacher in Germany and that one in France and that other in Rome; she now could not, since Alick had left home, meet such musicians as Hans von Bülow and Anton Rubinstein and Joachim and Clara Schumann,* and could not even make her way into less exalted circles; indeed, the more rough and ready the artistic *milieu* was, the more reluctant it would have been to welcome any women but singers on to their platforms or into their homes.

But she was not alone in her professional uncertainties. Joey began to talk of his anxieties about his future. In the panic excitement over Johnnie's 'wee bit' of consumption and his dispatch to the beneficent miasmas of Australia, it had escaped general notice that Joey's future, which had seem to stand firm as a rock, had vanished as if it had been a nonsensical dream, whereas nothing could have been more practical and feasible. It had been reckoned that his beautiful, clear, flexible tenor voice might take him into opera, and that anywhere in Europe he chose to go. He was also a flautist who might even have reconciled Mozart to his instrument. (Mozart said flutes were never in tune.) But he had, like Johnnie, suffered from chest infections; he had not developed consumption, but his winters were rough with bronchitis and asthma, neither of which help singers or flautists. To this predicament he had given much thought; he had taken up the violin, for which he had always had some talent, and he had planned to enter the orchestra of the Theatre Royal, and in the meantime was studying opera, so that he could join the staff of some great opera house. But, he warned his sister, nothing must be said about this, for none of it might happen.

'Oh, but it must happen,' said my mother. 'It will happen. You've always been the lucky one, things will always turn out lucky for you.'

'No,' said Joey, 'it may none of it happen. I could never leave you women here without a man. The four of you could never get on with you on your lones.'

The truth of this statement, and the loyalty and willingness for self-sacrifice manifest in the way it was made, so moved my mother that she rose and pulled the bell so that she could tell the servant-maid to bring in the tapers and light the lamps as if to see, literally see, what was best. 'Oh Joey,' she said, 'you must not throw away your life just for us. We'll look after ourselves. And you forget, you're not the only man in the house, there's Willie.'

At that Joey rose from his seat and walked across the still unlighted room to stare at the passers-by, who were hurrying along under the slanting rain, so wrapped up they might have been footpads disguised to carry on their trade, though, as he pointed out, they were more likely to be the victims than the perpetrators of such violence, who would more likely be waiting within some warm doorway in a milder discomfort. 'Life was like that,' they said, smiling, but not much.

Fiona or Mary or whichever maid of ours came in and lit the lamp, and they were silent until she had gone. 'Has it never struck you,' Joey went on, without turning round, 'that considering Willie's so young, he drinks an awful lot? He goes from one dram to another all day long. Slowly, I grant you. But he disna turn back. And he gaes so *darkly* from dram to dram.'

My mother was too astonished to do more than exclaim, 'What, Willie?' She saw her youngest brother as an unusually silent young man, whose taciturnity was probably to be explained by a mystical inner life; his landscapes were strictly naturalistic yet part of a wider survey. He was little at home, was the last to rise in the morning but stayed out till all hours of the night, but he had the excuse of working late and long on an engraving enterprise with a partner who had other employment during the day; and he gave the womenfolk in the family and the maid-servants pretty and thoughtfully chosen presents at the New Year and on their birthdays.

'Willie!' my mother exclaimed again. 'Willie!' she breathed in deep pain. Johnnie had gone far away and might never return; Joey was talking of throwing his life away; and Willie, it appeared, was a drunkard. Joey, who had gone to stand in front of the mantelpiece, swung round and faced her, and she was struck dumb, pierced by his beauty. When she described how he looked, thirty-five years later, I could understand why his appearance, and nothing else about him, had seemed to her an assurance that no pain could come to him, or her, or any of their family.

His hair was golden-brown, cut Victorian-short at the sides, but with a wide, thick strand falling back from his brow, and fanning out; this was called a 'flash', and was first worn, I believe, when men gave up the periwig. It made them look as if their days were spent in the open air; it gave them a part in a play. He had 'the laughing mouth' of my grandfather, but serious eyes, dark blue and, in a good sense, calculating. He had, for a male, an unusually long and slim waist, and a well-set head, and my mother felt a pang of indignation because he was never to stand on the stage of a famous opera house, a pure note maintaining his lips in a perfect circle, under the double beam of limelight and the audience's rapture, the delicate outline of his body drawn in exaggerated form against the backcloth by some splendid or piteous stage costume, and the orchestra beneath in the pit holding up everything: his voice, the composer's intention, the whole event, just as the foundations in the ground beneath the orchestra and the stage and the auditorium held them up and the galleries and the dome and its great chandelier; and held up too, it always seemed, if one were involved, the night sky above. My mother flamed with revolt at the threat to Joey's manifest destiny. It strikes me as extraordinary that my mother described what she thought and saw at that moment but never told me in what operas she wished her brother to appear. She had seen many operas: by Mozart, Rossini, Bellini, Gluck, Handel, Donizetti, Cherubini, Weber, and the early Wagner, and more.* She had never heard of the Ring, nor of the most luscious of Verdi, or of Puccini, or of Tchaikovsky, or of Ravel, or of Debussy, or of Bartok, because they all belonged to the future. Yet she was to hear of them and understand them before she died; and they are so much a part of my life that I cannot imagine what the world was like without them.

It still astonishes me, the construction of life as that moment reveals it. Human beings are constantly having to face crises and resolve them with no hope beyond substituting a new and less painful situation for the existing one; the most we can effect is a slight reduction in the amount of pain in the universe. Its abolition is plainly an impossible dream.

My mother, smiling across the room at her brother, found herself
wondering whether, had Joey realized his ambition, he would have
been a *tenore leggiero* or a *tenore robusto*, and she could not decide, for
though he was as delicate as fine bones could make him, he was also
strong, and her heart seemed to swell in her breast as absolute assurance came to her that he was so well fitted to be an opera singer that
no matter what happened, that is what he would be. It must happen.
But he was shaking his forefinger at her and bidding her give him her
strict attention, in a schoolmasterly way comically incongruous with
his brilliantly coloured youth; and, thinking that he wanted her to
join him in some last hope which had suddenly occurred to him, she
reluctantly brought her imagination back from the gilt and heat and
ecstasy of a Continental opera house, and that pure and long sustained
high note. What he said astonished her by its combination of sober
realism and winged goodness. Joey had, it seemed, succeeded rather
better in his studies than his family knew; he was, indeed, within sight
of employment at the Theatre Royal under the management of the
famous Mr Wyndham,* partly owing to these recent successes, and
partly through the influence of some well-disposed old men he had
chanced to meet, judges and that, and partly because his father's name
was so well remembered. He hoped to make good money and good
friends before long; and he would perhaps be able to repair my
mother's career, and in any case, he thought, their home would
become a gayer place. 'I am the head of the family now,' he said, and
paused, as if it sounded strange to him. And it sounded strange to my
mother also. He went on, 'It is my duty to protect you all. And if you
and Jessie do not marry, I swear to God I will not marry either.'

My mother could hardly speak. She was astonished by Joey's goodness: his *pietas*, as the Romans would have more precisely defined it.
She was, indeed, appalled by it. Since she herself desired to marry the
artist who did not want to marry her, she recognized the terrible
nature of his vow. She breathed, 'Oh, no! Not that. Jessie and I want
you to be happy,' and then was overcome by a purely physical distress.
There was a painful singing in her ears, and she felt faint and jarred
and shocked, as she might have had she been travelling in a train
which had crashed into another. Her mind was for a second wholly

occupied by fear. But when the darkness cleared and she heard her
brother telling her that she and Jessie must submit to his intention, it
was his duty and he could not feel at peace with himself if he did not
fulfil it, then her apprehension changed to exalted confidence. The
shock that she had received had seemed at first the same as she might
have received from a gross mechanical cause, but Joey's innocent
handsomeness, the free but not disorderly spring of golden-brown hair
from his high forehead, his slight touch of formality, his cherishing
way of speaking about Jessie and herself, made her feel that that shock
was due to a sudden rearrangement of the place, or places, where
human beings live. The physical world had suddenly coalesced with
the spiritual world: real life and the something which was the reason
for going to church had become one. She assumed that events of a
novel and benevolent kind would follow.

It is impossible that, looked at from any angle, her premonition
could be regarded as fulfilled. The routine at Number 41 Heriot Row
continued as before, until one morning, when my mother came down
to breakfast and found herself in the dining room alone with Joey, who
was up half an hour earlier than usual. She did not at first note how he
looked, for he kept to the Scottish custom of eating his porridge while
he walked about the room bowl in hand, and often, as on that
morning, came to a halt at the bow window, where he would stand
and watch the passers-by. He hardly greeted her, though his mutter
was good-natured enough, and she did not see his face, since he was
sitting at the table, till he turned to put down his bowl on the
sideboard and leave the room. Then she exclaimed, 'Joey, are you
sickening for something again? You're so white, and you've got a
blackberry stain round your eyes.'

'Och, I'm fine,' he told her, but the ghost of his voice was standing
in his throat and crowing.

'Oh, Joey, Joey,' cried my mother, 'I hear your asthma's come back,
will you not go back to your bed?'

'I'm fine, I'm fine,' said the ghost of his voice, and in no time she
heard the front door bang behind him. She went out herself to do her
day's work, half-teaching, half-learning, and hurried home, to find he
had come back in the late afternoon, and gone to bed, after getting
the servant-maid to bring up his asthma kettle. She ran up the little
staircase which led to the boys' room, and laid her cheek against the

door, and listened, but heard none of that ugly howling on the breath. She knocked, but there was no answer, and she slowly and softly opened the door, and he looked across the room at her, from a deep cleft in the pillows.

'Hush,' she said, and listened. Yes, he had an asthmatic attack, but it was either nearing its end or was not severe. 'Oh, Joey, what can I bring you?' she asked, and he answered, 'Not a thing, my love, but later you'd oblige me by seeing that Aunt Isa doesna send me up a gallon of broth – you know how she overdoes her errands of mercy.'

'I'll bring you just a cup,' she promised, and as he had smiled, turned his head away, and closed his eyes, she left.

As I have said, in my grandmother's household – and I think in all Edinburgh households at that time – it was felt that there was one useful thing they could do for any victims of catastrophe, and that was to give them cups of beef broth. Huge joints of superb meat and much fuel and hours of scrupulous care were wasted on preparing this useless brew, and my mother felt an acute revulsion against the practice at this odd moment. After she had sent one of the maids up with this ritual food, she then went to the bedroom she shared with her sister Jessie, whom she found sewing the brush-braid on the hem of one of my grandmother's dresses, a job which had to be done very frequently when long skirts were worn, since they were so very long that they hoovered the pavements.

They spoke for a moment of Joey, and then my mother, who had had a hard day, took off her dress and lay down on her bed and fell into a doze. She heard her sister say, 'I'll give your cuff a wee mend, it's gone by the buttonhole,' and she murmured, 'Don't trouble, you have so much to do,' without opening her eyes; and she was sad, but only sad as one is in a dream, because Jessie went on to say she did not mind mending the cuff at all: she had nothing to do when she finished their mother's skirt. She had often nothing to do these days, which was bound to happen if one thought of it; there had been nine in the house, eleven before the two Campbells had gone. Much less mending, and she had nothing else to do. Her voice was desolate, but my mother was too sleepy to set about comforting her and felt that anyway it would be difficult to cheer her up, for she really had no basis for her conviction that all was to be well with them, except her conversation with Joey in the darkened drawing room some

nights before, and that was incommunicable, particularly as Jessie had
a literal mind.

When my mother came down to breakfast the next morning she
asked the servant-maid who brought in the tea whether she had seen
Joey yet and if he seemed better, and was told to her surprise, for Joey
was no early riser, that he had left the house an hour or two before.

'But I doubt he was well enough to go to his lessons!' she exclaimed.
'Was his asthma gone?'

'Ay, he might never have had it in all his life. I didna hear a wheeze
out of him,' was the answer, 'but he seemed troubled. I'd say he'd
something on his mind.'

My mother thought how deceptive human bodies were: just because
Joey's bronchial tubes were blocked, this girl had thought him
troubled when, in fact, he was settled in his mind as he had never
been since he was a small child; he had truly become what one would
like a man to be in making that offer of self-sacrifice – which,
however, she did not mean to accept. Though her mind rarely ran on
her own affairs when she was teaching or having a lesson, it happened
several times during that day (and had each day since she and Joey had
had their conversation) that some sight or sound had pleased her, and
she had found herself passing on naturally from pleasure to pleasure to
the contemplation of Joey's promise, made with such masculine
strength it could be believed, as would not have been possible before,
that he worked to care for her and all the women of his family.

Such a moment recurred when, at the end of her working day, she
returned to her home in Heriot Row, to be instantly forgotten because
she noticed at once that the front door was not locked. This was
extraordinary. By a curious convention – I do not know if this was
peculiar to my grandmother or was a local custom – the door was left
shut but not locked during the hours of daylight, so that any passer-by
had only to turn the handle and walk in, but was locked, and carefully
locked, as soon as the dusk fell. This evening, however, although
it was so late in the year that when my mother came home it had
been dark for a couple of hours, she was able to walk straight into
the hall.

She found it presented an odd appearance. It did that at all times to eyes not accustomed to the ambition of early nineteenth-century neo-classical architecture, particularly as felt by Scottish architects and householders: the hall would have graced the town house or country seat of a noble friend of Horace Walpole, but was compressed (and that not so much as might be expected by an English visitor) for the use of the middle classes: materially compressed, not imaginatively so – there was no tampering with the liberating dimensions of the vision. Three ornate doors opened off the hall: the one to the right gave entry to the drawing room and the one to the left to the dining room, and the third, in the back wall, to the music room and the kitchen premises in the basement. There was also a staircase, stately though not long, which achieved an illusion of a gallery as it mounted and joined the passage where the family bedrooms were.

When my mother entered she saw that all the lamps in the hall were lit, as if guests were expected, but that the door to the kitchen premises was open and that all three servant-maids were standing there, the cook in her working clothes, her skirt pinned up over her petticoats. They took little notice of my mother, only making vague movements which showed awareness that they should be taking notice of her, and then continuing to do what they had been doing when she came in, which was to stare at the closed dining-room door. On the staircase was another sight which would have been described by the inhabitants of the New Town as 'extraordinary' in their public conversation, but within their houses as 'by-ordinar', which is a richer word, with overtones which run from the unusual to the fearful, according to the pronunciation. My aunt Jessie was sitting on one of the lower steps with her head buried in her hands.

My mother went to her, knelt, and put her arms round her, and said, 'Dinna greet, my darling!', which meant 'Don't cry.' She was sure that whatever had gone wrong it would be righted as soon as Joey came home, and that should be in a few minutes. Jessie lowered her hands and said pettishly, 'I am *not* crying. But I don't know what's happening. They're in there. He's in trouble.' My mother remembered what Joey had said to her. 'What, Willie's in trouble?'

'No! ' screamed Jessie. 'Joey's in trouble. Joey.'

'Who turned you out?' asked my mother, but did not wait for an answer: she always felt protective towards Jessie because she herself was not tall, and her sister was smaller still. She threw down her gloves and her reticule on the stairs and walked across the hall and opened the dining-room door, and stopped dead on the threshold, because she was uncertain lest she was not going to burst into laughter, and uncertain too that laughter was not the proper response to what she saw.

My grandmother was sitting at the head of the dinner table, which would normally have been set for supper at that hour but was shining in its naked polish, in a chair with arms, such as was reserved for the head of the house; and Aunt Isa was sitting beside her, in a chair without arms, which was set close to her sister's chair but slightly behind it. On the other side of the table were three chairs pulled right away from the table, so that there could be no question that whoever sat on them did so as friends of the family summoned to a social gathering: and these were occupied by three members of the Edinburgh police force. This was why my mother had so strong an inclination to laugh.

The police force was a body doomed to excite at one and the same time respect and mirth. Edinburgh citizens loved their policemen, particularly those whose memories went back thirty or forty years and recalled the watchmen who had then taken care of life and property; mostly old soldiers, so hardened by years of savage warfare till they were sometimes uncertain in their old age as to which side they were on in the war between law and the less serious forces of crime. The Mackenzie children had all been taught to be respectful to the policemen as people who did the city a service. But unfortunately the guardians of the peace looked funny in their uniforms, very funny. That was why they found their way so quickly into the harlequinades of pantomimes. The length of their swallow-tail coats, the cut of their trousers, and their top hats, were somehow wrong, and made them look as if they were amiable animals dressed up as men; it was as if the hand of Walt Disney had stretched out from the future and added mischievous strokes to designs drawn in all sobriety for the use of the Home Office. There was no stopping the course of this supernatural event: when the public saw the police clad in this grotesque attire it laughed as its descendants were to laugh at Donald Duck and Tom and Jerry. And as is the sad fact when people in authority find themselves the object of affection and respect and derision, the police did not find the psychological situation easy. It would have been much simpler for them if ridicule had been the only reaction they sparked off, and then they could have met that with hatred. But all they felt justified in doing, since they were just men, was to bear themselves with greater dignity, and we all know what happens when we do that. The laughter grows stronger.

But my mother could control her disposition to laugh because one of them, who was of high rank, she had known all her life, and had answered his enquiries about his children's education. He, being ambitious about such a matter, as Scots are, had wanted to send them to school in Germany, if it could be managed, and sought her out after she came back from Düsseldorf. But when she smiled at him and bowed, she was frozen by what she saw on his face, which was sheer horror. She looked at the other two men, and they too were looking at her as if it were an indecency that she should have entered what was, after all, only the family dining room.

She turned away from them and looked at her mother and her aunt; and they too were staring untenderly at her as if her presence there was a graceless intrusion. Her mother said, 'Isabella, I've business with these gentlemen. I'll not be free this hour or two. If you want your supper, get the lassies to give you a tray in the music room.' She stopped and her teeth began to chatter.

My mother said nothing for a minute, and came to the conclusion that nothing in life could possibly justify this extraordinary fuss. It was just a carry-on, like the Greek myths. She said firmly, 'Jessie's upset. She's sitting on the stairs. Will you or Aunt Isa not come out and talk to her for a minute and explain this stramash?* Then I'll get her to bed, and see she gets supper.'

The horror did not leave the faces of her mother and her aunt, nor of the policemen, one of whom sighed deeply, as in pity. Her mother said, 'Isabella, will you please do as I bid. And when our business here is finished, I'll come out and deal with what needs to be dealt with.'

At this point my mother was taken over and controlled by her certainty that no event, none at all, could possibly excuse the way that Jessica and she were not being allowed to know what was going on in their own home, although they were both grown women. This was intolerable not only because she could not bear Joey to be attacked, but also because of her mother's cavalier treatment of

Jessica's distress; and she had a notion that there was a certain good sense in the three servant-maids which would have prevented them being so agitated about what was going on in the dining room unless there was cause. She was preparing to stand firm, to insist that her mother go out and soothe Jessie, when there were sounds of an arrival at the house, first carriage wheels, then the jangle of the bell and the hammer of the knocker, and the patter of a servant-maid's rush to the front door.

In a minute there was a knock on the door of the dining room, and there came in the old Irishman who was the 'Highland Porter' whose services were used by the Mackenzie family and their neighbours to run errands. He gaped about him, astonished at seeing the policemen bearing company with my grandmother and Aunt Isa. He had only time to say he had found the gentlemen at home and had brought them with him, when he was plucked backwards and his place was taken by old Tyrian Purple and a man whose name I cannot remember – it was one of those Scottish names found in such abundance that it fuses with other names of like frequency, and the identity of the individual is impossible to keep in mind, however distinguished, as one moss plant on a mountain side covered with mosses of one sort and another becomes hard to keep in mind. This man, Mr Menzies or Wallace or Thompson or whatever, had not only a name borne by many other Scotsmen, he looked like many other Scotsmen. He was my grandmother's lawyer and had dealt most kindly with her affairs and, himself musical, had followed with pleasure her children's achievements; and all the handsomeness he had shown in this way had given him very pleasing features. I have seen a bust of him which it was agreeable to contemplate; it showed what humans can look like if they reject meanness and callousness. But on that amiable face there was at that moment written nothing but sheer horror at my mother's presence in that room; and nothing else was written on old Tyrian Purple's face either.

Indeed the expressions now visible on old Tyrian Purple's inflamed features, on the lawyer's marmoreal face, chiselled by concentration on things of good repute, struck her as having suddenly become nasty. Old Tyrian Purple's face was coarsened by some dirty excitement to which she could not give a name; the fine features of the lawyer seemed not noble but blank coverage to ugly processes, like a lavatory door. They were thinking esuriently of what they had no right to enjoy, for they were at the same time suggesting a total rejection of it. She could see trouser buttons, shirt tails, all the uninviting side of masculinity, all its sluttishness, and wanted to flee, but they had been insincere: old Tyrian Purple had said to her, 'This is no place for young leddies, Miss Isabella, so do as your mother bids and go to the fine wee leddy your sister,' and Mr Wallace or Mr Thompson had bade her bide her time; she would have to meet so much sorrow before she was done that she should be grateful to her elders for sparing her what they could, but they did not move from their place between her and the door.

Oh, how hugely they were enjoying it! and their enjoyment was arrived at by a circuitous route to a point where it involved her own humiliation. She pushed them out of the way and went out of the door and started to cross the hall, so that she might reach Jessie, who, she saw, was still sitting on the stairs with her head in her hands. But she felt so sick and faint that she had to sit down and rest until her heart slowed down, during which time it occurred to her that really the fuss that was being made by the people in the dining room could not be as pointless as she supposed. There must have been some allegation, made by someone about someone, which almost certainly, considering they were all looking so fatuous, so masculine, must be nonsensical. She set her mind to solve this riddle very carefully. She was anxious to get an answer before Joey came home, because he was so near revert-ing to illness that it seemed possible he was threatened with something as dislocating to his life as Johnnie's disorder had been to his. It seemed to her that all their brothers were to be snatched away: they had lost Alick through something as mindless as illness, Johnnie was ill, and Willie, she supposed, would be an alien in their house before long; in other Edinburgh households she had seen such thick and lumpy versions of phantoms that had drunk themselves out of life. She began to pant as if she too were asthmatic, and one of the servants brought her a glass of water, but it blew back in bubbles from her mouth, and Jessie too came to her. Then there was the turning of a key in the lock; and Joey was with them.

They caught at him, and then let him go, taking their hands away, not to throw the least fraction of weight on him, for they could hear the dragging of his breath. They besought him to tell them what trouble he was in, so that they could band together, get the police out of the house, send old Tyrian Purple and the lawyer packing, and get their mother and their aunt to stop conspiring with these people to whom they had given too much liberty to go about their home. Joey sank down into a chair and laughed up at them through his gasps. 'I'm in no trouble, my bonny sisters,' he said, 'but dear knows, some people seem to wish I was.'

It seemed that a month or two earlier he had been playing the accompaniments for a young tenor at a musical party given by the bearer of one of the great and glittering titles of Scotland, at his splendid house in Charlotte Square. Alick and his wife had of course been there, and Joey had for that reason retreated to one of the smaller drawing rooms, where two or three people were looking at a portfolio of drawings and etchings left lying out for the guests' amusement. Joey pained to describe them for a second. Among them were what (I think) must have been detached engravings from the portfolio made by Robert Adam with the aid of his French assistant, Clerisseau,* when he had visited the Illyrian coast and pilfered a new style of architecture from the ruins of Diocletian's theatre by those innocent thefts the eye can commit. Joey soon got into conversation with two men, who were delighted by the plates as much as he was: a stout, pale young man, not well favoured, and an elderly man, far better looking and more elegantly dressed, but not, it could be guessed, of nearly as much consequence as his companion – though that hardly needed remarking, for probably few people were. The roly-poly made a remark that owned to a peculiar form of poverty often imposed by great wealth. Peevishly he told the older man that he believed that they had a set of these same engravings in his own library, but he was very doubtful whether he could ever find them; with all the heap of things that were there, he had never had time since his father's death to put the place in order. Joey was amused but not greatly interested. The couple then apologized to him for not having gone to the saloon where he and his tenor had performed, and as Joey stood up to leave them and go home, they announced their identities. The young man was a Scottish peer and the other a Colonel with a familiar name, and as they seemed to be uninterested in music he expected to see no more of them.

But they had taken down his address, and wrote to him not long afterwards, telling him that they had met a friend who had heard him and the tenor at the party in Charlotte Square, and wished to meet him, so that he might arrange for a like performance at his own home. Eager as Joey was to get on with his interrupted career, he had not greatly fancied the engagement, or the proposed meeting to discuss it. Jessie asked, 'Why not?' and Joey answered, 'Och, I just didn't fancy either of them.'

After a pause he added that he had another reason for reluctance to follow up the invitation. They had proposed that they should all four of them meet at a sort of club, where it was possible to eat good saddle of mutton and drink good claret in surroundings just a little out of the ordinary. They recommended it highly, saying that it was quite refreshing to find such a place in Edinburgh, it was more like what one might find in Paris or Brussels. In the end they repeated the invitation three or four times, and Joey had accepted it out of sheer weariness. He had disliked these importunities, he explained, largely because of the place where they were to meet. They had given him the address and he had recognized it as a place which had already attracted the curiosity of himself and his brothers and sisters by something a little odder than mere oddity. I cannot remember whether my mother said it was in India Street or India Place, but it was within a short distance of Heriot Row, and it was at the corner of a street and a mews. The curtains were always drawn, and the iron gate opening to the area steps was fastened by a noticeably large padlock, with a round inset on which there was the raised figure of a boy naked to the waist wearing floppy trousers; and in the area below there slept or barked a chained collie dog, noisy like a farm dog. The total effect suggested that the occupier was up to no good, but that it did not amount to much: it might have been that a person not in good standing used it to store booty not actually stolen but irregularly acquired. Joey had, he said, succumbed in the end to his two unwanted friends' invitations, because he wanted to see the inside that had for so long puzzled and amused him by its outside. It seemed to him an odd thing that a house in the middle of the New Town should have a fierce watch-dog. He meant to leave as soon as he could.

But after he had been admitted into the house, he wished he had never set foot inside the door. The place, he told his sisters hesitantly, was not right. An impudent-looking chiel had let him in and had taken him through a hall, past an open door that showed some rough-looking lads drinking at a long table in a shabby room, and into a little office, where he was left to sit on a hard chair and read a day-old copy of *The Scotsman*.

At this point, mysteriously, Joey seemed to lose interest in his own story. He had been speaking more and more slowly, and now he sat back, fell silent, frowning and wiping his forehead with his handkerchief. His sisters watched him in perplexity. 'Go on,' they said, 'go on.' He sighed, made a weak gesture of despair, told them regretfully that he was so puzzled by his reception that he would have got up and found his way out, had it not been that a door opened in the shadows and a wee man, not like an innkeeper or a waiter, but more like a lawyer's clerk, had come in and asked him in a low voice who he was and who had invited him, inclining his ear to him as if to hint that the answer should be as soft as the question. At Joey's reply, he grinned as if in congratulation, and led him to a large room, quite well furnished, in which there were several round tables set out with silver and glass for supper, but the only diners were the peer and the Colonel, who were sitting at a table set for four, drinking claret and busy with some marrow-bones. At this point Joey lost his speech again; he laid his hand across his mouth and shuddered, while my mother and Jessie begged him to go on, to tell them everything. 'For goodness sake, Joey,' wailed Jessie, 'tell us what they did to you?'

'Och, they didna do anything to me,' breathed Joey.

It must be obvious that I am labouring under great difficulties in telling this story with any approximation to accuracy. All this happened in the last century and it is nearly sixty years since my mother gave me her account of it, not long before her death.* But she repeated it to me twice, and I kept notes, and the two versions differed not at all. When she reproduced the conversations that had passed, she rendered the family's conversations within their house as couched in a quite broad Scots accent, which was immediately abandoned if there was talk with a stranger; and her hands bore out what she told me, curving tenderly round the palm when she spoke of her brother. The story is so true that I would not tell it if I were not impelled to do so by anger on behalf of women in general, and of my mother in particular.

When they had shaken Joey back to speech, he described how his new and determined friends had greeted him cordially and seemed in very good spirits, much more at ease than they had been at the party in Charlotte Square. They were indeed so flattering in their welcome that he suspended his judgement on the house they were in, and indeed his hosts were very attentive, almost as if they knew of his physical delicacy. They made the boy who was waiting on them bring him a more comfortable chair, poured him out a glass of finer claret than he had thought this place would provide, and drank to his health before they all sat down. They were praising their friend who was yet to appear when there was a sound of a loud shout coming from a room on the floor above them, which was followed by a long shriek. Joey and the others rose to their feet. The dog out in the area began to bark. There was a bump, as if some heavy object had fallen, again somewhere on an upper storey. They all turned about. A door in the wall behind them, which they had not noticed, slowly opened and remained ajar, till there slowly fell through the opening the blood-stained body of a young man, to lie face downward on the floor.

The world was swinging in circles round Joey. There was a senseless body at his feet; there was somewhere nearby in the house a violent man armed with a weapon. He said to his new friends, 'How do we get hold of the landlord?' It seemed to him, as he remembered the lads he had seen drinking in the pothouse sort of room as he came into the house, that there would be little difficulty, if the Colonel and the landlord would take charge, in fetching a doctor and the police and before they came, overcoming the maniac and getting him under lock and key. But his courage was of course overlapped by another and unnatural fear, caused by the fear, which was also unnatural, manifested on the faces of the young peer and the Colonel. Both were as green as if they were seasick; one of the Colonel's hands, stiff and strong as some large bird's talon, had closed on one of Joey's wrists, and the young peer was applying his soft weight to put Joey off balance so that he had to run with the two men in the direction they were going, which was along the hall and out of the front door, now open and thronged with a number of people getting out into the street as fast as they could, more people than Joey would have supposed the house could hold. Some were well dressed, and of these some obviously of the same quality as the young peer and the Colonel, and others were the rough lads who had been drinking in the pothouse room, whom Joey had envisaged as fetching the doctor and the police, but who seemed on no such errand. They were going down the steps into the street and round the corner into the darkness of the mews as quietly as might be, not talking amongst themselves.

It was the more respectable fugitives from the house, who might have been expected to have the advantage over these keelie boys in all circumstances, that seemed least able to cope with the catastrophe, whatever it was. They stood about on the pavement, unable to decide which way to go, while the chained dog told the whole street that something was up; and then some of them ran for it, scattering here and there in obvious panic. The Colonel and the young peer, without leaving hold of Joey, started off in one direction, turned back and tried another rat-hole to safety, and were heading down to some alley branching off an alley, going off a street into the darkness, when Joey pointed out that he was quite near his own home and would be obliged if they would let him go to it. The Colonel had not seemed to grasp that Joey's request was a polite disguise for an intimation that he wanted to see no more of him and his companion, neither on that night nor at any future time. He had rather bade Joey farewell as to a comrade-in-arms. Joey had let himself in at Heriot Row and thrown himself into bed and slept, and had woken up, wondering if ill would come of his misadventure, and thinking that it probably would not. Who was to know he had been in that peculiar place? – the like of which, he vowed, he would never enter again as long as he lived. It was towards evening that he had heard that the police knew well why the dog had been barking, and he had not slept more than an hour or two that night. 'That's why,' he told my mother, 'I looked so bad this morning that you thought I had my asthma back again.'

It was at that point that the startled household had yet another caller. A Highland Porter had come to announce that he had, as ordered, left a letter on Mr McKay Jameson, who was my grandmother's banker, and a true friend to her all the years of her widowhood, the person she would naturally have consulted in any such crisis as seemed to be threatening the household at Heriot Row. It appeared that he, unfortunately, was unable to obey her present summons. His wife had come to the door to tell the Highland Porter that her husband had gone down to spend the night with an important client of his at Linlithgow and would not be back till the morn. Joey received the news with anger. He and his sisters knew that Mr McKay Jameson had a grown son, holding a high position in his father's bank, who lived at home, and could have come in his father's stead, if not at this time, later. This refusal was more than a refusal, coming from these professed friends. It smelt of desertion. Joey got up and straightened himself and went in to tell his mother and aunt and the police and old Tyrian Purple and Mr Menzies or Mr Wallace or Mr Thompson or whatever, and came out as pale as death.

His sisters cried out to him that all this was nonsense. How could he have killed a man? He had no weapon!

Joey looked back at them in amazement. 'There's naebody been killed.'

'Naebody's been killed! But what about the man on the floor?'

'He's no deid. He's in the Royal Infirmary and doing fine.'

'Then what are you afraid of? What is all this nonsense?'

Joey stared at them and held his head between his hands. 'I should-na have been there. In that house. But I didna ken the kind of house it was.'

'Why? Were there, were there any bad girls there?'

'Och, no. Och, no, no, indeed! There wasna the wee toe of a bad girl to be found in yon establishment between the roof and the cellar.'

'Well then, what was wrong with the place?'

'Och, Jessie, Isabella, leave me be. I canna tell ye. I canna possibly tell ye. Don't plague me. It's something that a decent man would never speak of to either of you, or to any woman in this house.'

Unfortunately Joey was telling the truth. I have many grievances against men. When life is obviously too difficult to be lived by the human species, with its limited intellectual equipment, males have a special tendency to make life still more agonizing by adding un-necessary difficulties solely for their sporting interest. They make rules for society, to be followed by everybody, gentle or simple, idiot or competent, as if they were laying out a new course for the Grand National to satisfy the jaded tastes of the sporting public. In all ages male homosexuality has been prevalent, and there are arguments for and against tolerating it. It might be judged a good thing because it fulfils a useful purpose in this age of keeping down the population, and for the further reason that many good and wise men have been of that disposition; and because it is undoubtedly a natural disposition in many persons, and it is a serious matter to deprive men and women of their right to sexual fulfilment, which is an inherent part of the human machine. But tolerance of homosexuality may be judged a bad thing because it loads the community with people who, having no children, will not work for its future; because many bad and foolish men have been of that disposition; and because it is wrong to encourage men to seek sexual fulfilment of a sort widely considered abnormal and therefore likely to isolate them and put them under special stress. It has been impossible, because of the masculine tenderness for their painful and unreasonable situation, to debate this matter coolly; and therefore, as I write, homosexuals have been put into a position of peril. Homosexual practices have been made legal; but a very large part of the population still abhors them and will turn on any homosexual who avails himself of the legal rights accorded his kind, should his activities become public, and will rend him to pieces without mercy.*

But the situation was worse a hundred years ago, when the ordinary man either loathed or pretended to loathe homosexuality so that he did not dare or care to mention it, and the knowledge of it reached no respectable women; although at the same time it was in fact so little loathed that it was widely practised. It was this ridiculous humbug which destroyed my grandmother's household in Heriot Row, which was to inflict the painful and incurable disease of deep sorrow in my mother, and indeed all members of that family. The mysterious house to which Joey had been taken was, of course, a homosexual brothel, and the young peer and his friend (who was one of a distinguished military family from just south of the Border) were homosexuals who had been attracted by Joey's remarkable good looks, and by an element in his behaviour which they might easily have misunderstood.

All the young Mackenzies worked at their professions so hard that there was little time left for their emotional lives. I can imagine that the baleful Mary Ironside owed her power to abstract Alick from their midst to her remarkable beauty, which reminded him of all that he had missed in his abnormal life of running from country to country and laying his hand on one musical instrument and then another all through his childhood and youth and early manhood. Joey was now deeply preoccupied with his muscial career, though it was limited to Edinburgh and the Lowlands and a visit or two to Dublin; he was always meeting people to have lessons from them or arrange performances and smiling at them because they were musicians too, and were helping him. But the young peer and the Colonel had been deluded by missionary zeal into misinterpreting his amiability.

Their error had become important, for the reason that either the young man whose bleeding body had fallen into the supper room, or the man who had stabbed him, was a person of consequence.* I would assume it was the assailant, and that the authorities suspected that the other, the assaulted person, who was probably a person of no consequence, had the intention of forcing them to take the proper steps and initiate a prosecution for the infliction of grievous bodily harm, under the pretence that he, as innocently as Joey, had thought the evening's business was a supper party. And that to prevent that, all persons concerned had to be put into a state of fear.

This does deep discredit to the respectable persons who were my grandmother's trusted advisers. It has to be realized, in the first place, that my grandmother and none of the female members of the household in Heriot Row had the slightest idea of what had been going on in the enigmatic eating-house. My mother was quite certain that her mother went to her grave unaware that men ever had sexual relations with each other; she herself was unaware of such a practice until, more than ten years after her marriage, Oscar Wilde was prosecuted, and my father gave her not very explicit but relevant information. All that my grandmother and the other females had to go on was that Joey had been drinking claret and sucking marrow-bones in an eating-house when someone who had been stabbed appeared in the room, and for that reason Joey must for ever after be shadowed by some monstrous crime – but not, as would have seemed more likely than anything else to all women of that time, of murder.

Old Tyrian Purple and the family lawyer – her banker never turned up at all: a huge, amorphous cloud of business had suddenly enveloped him – blinked and looked down their noses and told her that the eating-house was a place where nameless abominations were committed, odious practices condemned in the Bible, but it was no use her asking them to indicate the texts; no decent women would have understood them. Had she done so, she would herself have become distraught, and she would have been for ever after repellent to all respectable citizens were it known that she had grasped this horrible information. There was the further danger in the family situation that were it suspected that the information had somehow seeped through to the young women of the family, it would be better for them if they had never been born. Not for anything in the world would any man think of marrying a young woman whose mind had suffered this pollution.

The same message showed in the shamed and sympathetic evasion of the police. It was no wonder that a retired general, in some way connected with the force, husband to an old friend of my grandmother's, actually showed signs of fainting during a conversation on the subject which his duty required of him. Fortified with brandy, he recovered sufficiently to visit her the day after the council my mother had interrupted, to suggest to my grandmother that she would be serving everybody's interests best, including her own, if she sent Joey out of the country as soon as possible. When she cried out, he remarked that she would surely not find that so difficult, as she had only a short time before sent another of her sons all the way to Australia. She asked him if he remembered the story of the cook who, rebuked for cruelty in skinning eels when they were still alive, replied that the creatures got used to it. As he looked puzzled, she explained that sending one's children away from their homes to go to the other side of the world was an action which, she suspected, became more and not less painful when it was repeated.

Her position was worse than it appears. Here was this strange story that something went on in an eating-house in the New Town of Edinburgh, which was so frightful that merely to sit down within the tainted walls with the intention of drinking claret and sucking marrow-bones would stain one for ever, so that one must leave one's hearth and become a solitary wanderer in another continent lest all one's kin should be disgraced: obvious nonsense. The world simply could not be as daft as that. But here were men who passed for the sanest in the community assuring my grandmother that this was the very truth; and what was more disconcerting still, so did the victim of this Hallowe'en nonsense. Joey himself was adamant in maintaining that old Tyrian Purple and the lawyer and the General were perfectly right: he could not possibly name to his female relatives the crime of which he was falsely accused. If it were known that they were aware of its existence, they would lose the respect of their kind, and it was right that they should. And, as Joey had been connected with this crime by his presence at the unlucky supper party, he himself thought it was just as well if he went as soon as possible across the seas. In all seriousness he held it to be natural and right that he should become an outcast, if this case came into court, or near enough to that to be widely known. He was willing to sail anywhere, as soon as a berth could be found for him.

The agony of his family was more than might at first be imagined, because my grandmother had had proof of his innocence. He always handed her such of his letters at breakfast time as might interest her because they referred to his profession; and he had handed her all the invitations he had from the odd pair, and she had been struck by the distaste he had felt for these approaches. Also she remembered the innocent interest all her children had felt regarding the curious house in India Street or India Place, and he had even mentioned that if he went there he would be able to amuse his brothers and sisters with an account of what it was like inside.

I do not know if my grandmother believed these rumours of infections and omnipotent evil, but I used to think she did not. I knew her only in her disappointed old age, but there were overtones to her disappointment: it had a cutting edge to it which makes me suspect that she believed rather that the world did not believe this absurd fiction, but for some maniacal reason found relief in pretending that they did. This was the state of mind common to her, her sister, and her two daughters when they yielded to the pressure put upon them, and sent Joey off to Canada to work on a ranch belonging to a relative of the General connected with the police, I think in New Brunswick. My grandmother had been anxious that he should go to North America rather than join his brother Johnnie in Australia, for the reason that the sea voyage was shorter; she wanted to go out and visit him, as she could hope to do often if the situation was as maniacal as it was said to be, and he could not return. The whole family would visit him, it was hoped.

But some time after he sailed – I cannot say how long, long enough for him to write some letters saying how much he liked his employer and how beautiful the landscape was, and how he was doing work which would not spoil his hands for playing: the length of the interval was to be driven out of everybody's memory – a telegram arrived at Heriot Row, addressed to my grandmother, but opened by my mother, who was the only member of the family at home. It stated that Joey had died as a result of an accident in which a runaway waggon-horse was involved. An axe had come loose and had cut his hand, and he had contracted lockjaw. It unfortunately happened that there was a medical dictionary in the house which gave a full account of the symptoms of lockjaw.

PART TWO

ISABELLA

CAPRI

From then on events followed a course which meant that I was never to see for myself the glories of Heriot Row. The death of Joey divided the household as it had never been cut apart before. The old and the young were now enemies. To my grandmother and to Aunt Isa and to my mother's brother Willie it seemed that the exile of Joey was the only sensible step to take. To all the rest of the household his deportation seemed disgusting, a coarse offence like the idiocy of the gods in *Oedipus Rex*.

Years later, when I was a little girl and was part of a family salad of children on an August-sunned east coast, I picked up from the bubbling surf a rounded pebble with a look of a dollar's head, and ran across the warm sands to show it to my mother and Aunt Jessie, who were sitting in the lee of a breakwater. As I neared them I came to a halt. They looked like any other beach mamas in the uniform of the time: a white blouse, a long black narrow skirt, a white straw boater. But they were staring out to sea with the tears running down past the drooping corners of their mouths, and they had their handkerchiefs out. Aunt Jessie complained, her little voice making a piping trial at fierceness, 'We should never have let them send him away,' and my mother, to whom rage came more naturally, condemned a surrender made when it all could have been brazened out; and I crept away, no notice taken of me.

Alick did not come to his family's assistance. He was in Tuscany, looking for a house in which he could produce the half-dozen oratorios and as many symphonies as a composer needed to establish his status: he was to make the score. But Willie was kinder; he really could have done no more than he did. He had, however, abandoned all power to do anything effective. But my grandmother relapsed into an over-grateful gloom, and tried to make the best of the one son left at home; and then for a moment there was a flash of brightness, a return to the household life as it had been. Jessie married and married well, it was considered: a schoolmaster from the West of England, tall and hand-some, clever and capable, a headmaster of one of the new secondary schools at a quite early age.* My mother told me, as evidence of the sweetness of Jessie's character, that when she had told her of Jack's proposal, she had put her arms round her and said, 'Isabella, it is ridiculous, fair ridiculous, that I should marry before you.'

That was indeed a most generous remark for one girl to make to another at that period. But later, when Jessie left Heriot Row to go to her wedding, there was a moment when they found themselves alone, all the fuss of the occasion having diverted itself to other rooms, and they stood facing one another in what had always been their bedroom, and Jessie said out of the shelter of her veil, her perfect little forefinger pressed on her perfect little chin, her eyes round, 'I have no idea what is going to happen to me.' This was a realistic remark for a bride to make, particularly when she had no dowry; and that Jessie certainly had to do without. There was a Scots idea that a dowry offered encouragement to the mercenary male in search of an heiress. This was a logical but not sensible or loving idea, and I suspect it of being invented by Scottish fathers who liked to keep what they had till the last will and testament came into effect.

After Jessie's marriage, my grandmother's health grew worse and old Tyrian Purple decided that she ought to winter abroad; and my mother was told she had to give up her teaching and her own lessons and take her mother to Capri. This gravely threatened her hope to become a professional pianist; she must resign herself to living for the rest of her life on a small income, unless her mother had accumulated some capital from her savings and her family legacies. Neither my mother's relatives nor any of the family lawyers took any steps to inform her on this matter, which was plainly regarded as none of her business. She felt quite insecure about her old age, but could not worry much about that. She was anxious to leave Heriot Row because she missed Joey and Johnnie: she had not realized how much they had sung about the house, and the silence of the flat grew more and more a statement of statistical tragedy. The place had not so long before housed thirteen people, most of whom were young. There was now left just her mother, her aunt, the ruined and silent Willie, and the servant-maids. Sometimes Jessie Watson Campbell came over from France, but her adoption by the Orléanaise family to whom she had originally gone as a governess was now complete. She was tied to them as if she were their true daughter.

My mother was quite pleased to go abroad. She once passed in the street a woman who was saying to a companion, 'Anything can happen abroad,' and it seemed an omen. In fact, nothing happened to her on Capri, or rather nothing of the sort she had hoped for, though of course she was happy as the British always are when they are away from their natal rains. It was the first time she had enjoyed the pleasure of idle travel, for when she had been in Germany she had been learning and teaching. Now she had nothing to do but sit in the morning sun, near scented plants, to eat some unfamiliar food and go upstairs afterwards and lie down on her bed under the mosquito net (which always reminded her of Jessie's wedding veil) and listen to the creak of the cicadas till she slept and forgot that Joey was dead. Waking, she walked through the vineyards, Joey going before her, Joey walking behind her, Joey on each side of her, up to the pie-crust edge of the cliff, where they all knelt and looked down on the hyacinth-blue breaking on the rocks so far below that the white foam seemed static, like carved white wood. Nothing was to be seen that was not beautiful like the Bass Rock, but usually the weather was gentle: unless the Tramontan wind* was blowing from the north or the Sirocco from Africa, it was a caress on the skin.

My mother played the piano to the wonder of all, on a number of pianos that were exiled on Capri like classical princesses captured at sea. She even played reels and strathspeys* at a café one night, to let a Scots party show the islanders what Scottish dancing was like. And then a clergyman and his wife and son and daughter took pity on her, and took her to the mainland for two days because, they said, she was seeing nothing. 'But what was there to see?' she asked herself, as she pretended delight.

It was a foolish question, as she told me many years later. Even if a young person was born into an ancient town, his or her first glimpse of another ancient town is a revelation, of themselves, of the potentialities of human society, of the junction of time. My mother had been

born and brought up in Edinburgh, and therefore knew, from the
Castle and the Old Town, of humanity's first refuge from its own
ferocity and the perils of the wild. On the mould of Edinburgh's early
conflicts there was, by the time my mother was born, superimposed
the image of peace, as devised by the eighteenth and nineteenth
centuries, a growing certainty that man could have safety by abandoning the butchery of his own kind. But other cities argue towards quite
different conclusions. My mother found that Naples held out no
promise whatsoever regarding the improvement of the human lot
through the ages. It just accepted that the destiny of individual human
beings was likely to follow a certain limited number of patterns,
ranging from the agreeable to the disagreeable, and concentrating
with most passion on the disagreeable.

Those tenements built as palaces and still palatial in mass and arch
and vista, and festooned with drying clothes hanging from every
window (what shocks the change from splendour to the sordid must
have given the population); the beggars that edged like lice through
the crowd, thrusting out through rents in their filthy clothes what the
vicar's wife, having been a nurse, recognized as counterfeit stumps of
arms and legs; the churches smeared with ornamentation like children
with mouths smeared with jam and honey; the lovely little bronzed
boys and girls; the young men hurrying supple through the sunshine,
like jets from a fountain of masculinity, the young girls with eyes
and lips lucent as crystallized fruits. And the repulsive crowd that
pressed in on them, made up of themselves as they would be when
time had had its way with them, men with their obesity thickening
and softening and purpling so that its proper place was at the butcher's
along with the tripe and the offal, the women at once swollen and
shrunken, their busts falling parallel to their waists but lax as empty
toy balloons. All was gilded by the light cast by its stance in the
bleached sky, and also by the reflection from the sea that washed the
harbour side of the splendid highway where the churches and palaces
formed a shining arc on the landward side, while in the harbour waters
masculinity had sent out ships so heavy in hulk and sail that they
boasted of miraculous seamanship, and others so small and fragile and
knitting-needle-masted that they boasted of wayward courage. But the
sea, set ablaze by the white sun above it, was its own barrier. Soon
nothing could be seen but the blindness it caused. The mood of the

Rebecca West's grandfather, Alexander Mackenzie (1819-57), Leader of Edinburgh's Theatre Royal Orchestra and editor of *The National Dance Music of Scotland*

Grandmother Janet Campbell Mackenzie. **Alison Selford**

Great-aunt Isabella Campbell. **Alison Selford**

Theatre Royal poster for 11 May 1848, during Alexander Mackenzie's musical directorship

Uncle Alick (Sir Alexander Mackenzie), Principal of the Royal Academy of Music from 1888, with a group of distinguished conductors in 1910. (Left to right) Sir Edward Elgar, Sir Dan Godfrey, Uncle Alick, Sir Charles Stanford; (standing) Sir Edward German and Sir Hubert Parry. **Alison Selford**

Rebecca's parents met on the ship S.S. *John Elder* and were married in Australia in 1883. **Norman Macleod**

Rebecca's parents: Isabella Mackenzie, c. 1890 (Alison Selford) and Charles Fairfield, a portrait by C.J. Lander, 1889. Norman Macleod

Drawings of his family by Charles Fairfield when
they were living in London in the 1890s. (Top)
his wife Isabella; (middle) his elder daughters
Lettie and Winnie, and (left) Rebecca (Cissie)
aged five. **Norman Macleod**

(Above) Winnie and Cissie photographed in the 1890s by John Bidgood, who married their aunt Jessie; (right) Cissie aged about eight. **Alison Selford**

Rebecca's parents outside their home at 21 Streatham Place. **Norman Macleod**

Pupils of Richmond High School at the turn of the century. Lettie is ninth from right, top row; Winnie second from left in the next row; Cissie fourth from right in the front. **Alison Selford**

Rebecca's aunt, Sophie Fairfield (née Blew-Jones). **Alison Selford**

Lettie graduating as one of the top candidates from the Faculty of Medicine, Edinburgh, 1907. **Alison Selford**

Rebecca's marriage to Henry Maxwell Andrews on 1 November 1930 at Abinger Parish Church, Abinger Hatch, Surrey. Alison Selford

Henry in Rangoon, where his parents lived for part of his childhood. University of Tulsa

Henry's mother, Mary Andrews (née Chavatsky). University of Tulsa

crowd changed: it grew angry, it turned about a dozen ways, and the streets were empty.

My mother found herself saying to the vicar's daughter, 'My brother would not have liked this place.' The vicar's daughter said nothing but 'Papa, Papa,' and it was as if she had said, 'Papa, you have never been able to help me, but can you not help this poor girl, who is, I think, not competent like me, and should be easier to console.' It seemed to my mother that she had heard the vicar's daughter say these words aloud, and she felt abashed that she had caused these nice people trouble. But the vicar drew in his breath, and dealt bravely with what he knew to be her preoccupation. He said, 'My dear, you need not be worried, your brother is in Heaven and nobody has ever said that Heaven will in any respect resemble Naples.' He squeezed her arm and led the party to a cool dark street.

On the second day they went to Pompeii, which had been excavated with serious intent for at least a century but must, I think, have retained some simplicity, lost today. After they had been sightseeing in the morning cool, they had lunch at a little farm amongst the vineyards that climbed towards the heights of Vesuvius. They sat in the shadow of a mulberry tree, turning their backs on the sea that was again a merciless screen against sight, and drank a wine called the Tear of Christ, although the vicar's wife clicked her tongue. But she yielded to its taste though she could not speak that name. Lunch was beautiful: there were little roast birds and a very delicate kind of pasta. It had appeared because the vicar and his wife had another son, who was working in New York. He had showed some kindness to the wife of a Neapolitan, who had been singing at the opera house, and the singer's wife had written to arrange the feast. The story had only a day before declared it was to have a sequel, for the vicar's son had written saying he was now engaged to the daughter of the singer.

To the story my mother could not listen attentively: she was thinking, 'All the time things happen to people, but nothing ever happens to me.' She scratched at the ground with the toe of her shoe and marvelled at the blackness of the earth, and nodded her head and raised her eyebrows as the vicar's wife pointed out that the soil was volcanic ash. She felt encouraged by the thought of this lovely stuff, soil-cooked under the hot sun on the hot volcanic slope till it had become pure nourishment, and seasoned with salt left by the sea in its long slow retreat. There was the savour of the Mediterranean everywhere. There were surely forces which moved, which engendered.

The truth was that my mother had a great and enduring passion for volcanoes, of which she was faintly ashamed. It seemed to establish a link between her and the lunatics who are feared as arsonists. All the same, the ascent of Vesuvius, which was the third stage of her tour with the vicar and his family, was one of the most cherished memories of her life and anyone who knew her would have known it would be so, that from the moment she had arrived on Capri and saw Vesuvius by night, its fires, sunk deep within its crater, reflected in the dark clouds above it, she had desired to be nearer this thing, that was no more like an animal than is a star, but had something to do with the life that gives an animal its importance, its fate. But the ascent at first disappointed her; she had for a time to ride a mule (meeting for the first time that almost abstract principle of non-cooperation), for there had not then been built the electric railway that ran up to the core of the volcano, or the wire rope railway that ran above it to the terrace, giving an oblique view down to the sculpturing, roaring fires.

Then the party dismounted and trudged up through a charred world, hard on the eyes when the wind blew, always hard on the feet, though my mother was well prepared: she was wearing the boots she wore for hill-walking in Scotland. (She had hidden them in her luggage, and when her mother said, 'Now, you're not to think of climbing that volcano, what is it,' she had answered, 'Oh, no, mother, and I doubt there'll be the opportunity.') Some soldiers escorted them along the path, swaggering like an opera chorus impersonating soldiers, and letting their voices loose in what was known in Heriot Row as *canto insensitivo* (a term invented by my grandfather when rehearsing an opera at the Edinburgh Theatre Royal). But the sunshine darkened about them; somewhere a huge cloud of smoke spread out over the sky as if some vast invisible hand were shaking itself free of thickening dust, and they pushed forward, this immense cloudy gesture developing before their upturned eyes and a tremor running through the earth under their feet.

They found themselves near a balustrade, and prepared to mount it and look down into the crater, but suddenly there leaped into the air before them a flame like a rearing dragon. It died and sank, and five other flames followed it, while sometimes the huge hand of cloud above them shook out more dust. This the tourists saw over their shoulders as the soldiers, no longer singing, turned them about and hurried them down the charred path, which was now rocking under their feet. My mother's account of it was like the distant recollection of a love affair: events had seemed ineffably precious, and still did, but it was not clear why. Who wants clouds contending with dust in the sky, and then conflict gritting one's eyes and teeth, who wants flame that leaps up and roars and is fire?

Another evening that was to make her happy every time it came back to memory was when she walked in the trenches of green shadow cast by orange trees, enclosed by the walls and roof of illumined leaves hung with curious refreshing fruits. So much brightness made her think of Joey. But there was one great disappointment about the journey. She and her mother had expected to spend the better part of a day in Rome on their return journey; how important this was to both of them can only be grasped by anyone who takes the trouble to read Nathaniel Hawthorne's *The Marble Faun* or Henry James's *Roderick Hudson*, not by reading anything written by any of my generation, who preferred Venice and the smaller cities, and Florence for the pictures. I would still go to Rome to see the Piazza Navona, which seems one of the great marvels of the world, a proof of what humanity can do when it makes its effort, and does not despise size, pure size; and I can remember a time when the town, largely because of the lovely second- and third-rate classical buildings and the Renaissance villas now destroyed, was much more beautiful than it is now. But my mother's and grandmother's generations expected from it a direct link between the Renaissance and the classical times, which would indeed have had to be tough metal to subsist after all those barbaric invasions and, more potent still, those earthquakes.

Whatever they expected they were not to gratify their expectation. My mother never set foot outside the ladies' waiting room in the railway station in Rome. My grandmother had no sooner left Naples than her neuralgia took command. She was unable to see, she was shaken by her heartbeats, and had to spend all day in the waiting room. Occasionally, with a timidity wholly out of character, she begged her daughter not to leave her. As the wasted day went by my mother grew more and more uneasy. She was not afraid that her mother was seriously ill; she had seen her have many such attacks. But she felt that possibly she had some quite sensible reason for allowing such an attack to break out on an important occasion.

THE HEINEMANNS

After they had been back in Heriot Row for a few days it became obvious that my mother's suspicion was correct. My grandmother's lawyer had died some weeks before she and my mother had left for Italy, and his son had taken his place. After their return he called frequently at the flat in Heriot Row and had long interviews with my grandmother and Aunt Isa. Needless to say, my mother was not informed of any matters discussed at the meetings.

It must be reiterated that she might, so far as any knowledge of the financial state of her family was concerned, have been a child of ten or twelve. Her life was the better because Willie had gone down to paint in the Border Country, but she was lonely all the same, and one evening said she must look round and see if she could start teaching again. At that my grandmother and Aunt Isa exchanged significant looks, and told her she had better not do that until she had seen the two lawyers, who indeed had expressed a hope they might have a talk with her the very next day. 'What was there to talk about?' asked my mother, happily. She had a vague idea that her mother might have decided to try keeping only two servant-maids instead of three, though why there should be lawyers called in about that she could not imagine.

The next day, the lawyers told her that on the death of the head of the firm certain irregularities in the handling of the Mackenzie estate had been discovered. They had reason to suppose that these would have been dealt with by Mr—, had not the Lord taken him. Och, aye. The situation, the two partners said, shaking their heads with an air of integrity, had to be dealt with now, for it could not go running on any longer. My mother would have liked to point out that their firm had been paid for years to do just that, stop things that ought not to go running on from doing so, but being a musician she knew that one cannot argue with the conductor.

With intolerable slowness it was imparted to her that it was proving impossible for my grandmother's business to show a profit if it were run by deputies, and in view of her health the shop had better be sold, but the capital sum it was likely to fetch was unlikely to meet the costs of the Heriot Row establishment; and it was unfortunate, too, that the various legacies my mother had inherited had not been too fortunately invested. They sat for a moment and shook their heads like some curious cross between mandarins and Presbyterian elders. There was a suggestion that while all this was going on they had been somewhere else, far away.

'In our great grief,' they went on to say, 'we have had to advise Mrs Mackenzie that she sell the flat in Heriot Row. But she's been very lucky, very lucky indeed, or should we speak of Providence, in finding an entirely suitable residence. More suitable, we would have thought, for a widow lady than the flat in Heriot Row.'

'Where is it?' my mother interrupted.

After a long silence the lawyer with the largest whiskers said with sugared tones, 'It's in Duncan Street.'

My mother was too choked to speak. At last she said, 'Duncan Street in Newington?'

'Ay,' said both the lawyers, facing her with innocent eyes.

To each town its own shame. My mother had lived in the New Town since her birth; in many of the streets she had only to stop still and think and she could tell who lived in which house; thinking that, her mind wandered, and it surprised her how the children of the district were growing up: the ones that only a little time ago were coming to school at two o'clock were doing the full school day (the schools savagely kept younger pupils, the babies one might almost say, from half-past eight till two, the others from half-past eight till four in the afternoon, with twenty minutes off for mid-day lunch). Also, the long, perfectly proportioned squares and crescents and broad streets and gardens made a classic whole as the parts of a noble city should cohere and be at once new and old; and oh, the Castle, especially when the ragged robin was purple in the crevices of the great rock, and the pillars on Calton Hill, and the faraway view on to the blue, blue Firth of Forth, and the far hills of Fife.

And there was the idea of the New Town, which was noble and historical, for here lived people who were naturally anti-English and therefore longed to follow the Stuarts, and were disillusioned about them, but had to keep silent about their disillusionment, and had to learn to live under the Hanovers (and on a step lower than the English), although Queen Victoria, with her passion for the Highlands, was a great help. The Old Town, the canyons of older buildings where the poor lived, on the slope between the Castle and Holyrood, knew of that struggle, getting that knowledge the hard way, through undertaking daring and suicidal feats of loyalty or by the murder of enemies. But Newington was a colony: full of suburban houses where people lived who had come from provincial Lowland towns up to Edinburgh to engage in commercial or professional enterprises. They had not been engaged by the Scottish idea to be in that particular place.

I do not say that my mother engaged in political analysis of this sort as she stood in the lawyer's office. But she did in fact feel her roots were being torn up, and she would not be able to guess what her basis of friendship with her new neighbours could be.

Almost immediately she received another shock. Whatever the house in Duncan Street had or had not to offer, she was not going to live in it. The lawyers went on to explain that in view of Alick's departure to the Continent and Johnnie's and Jessie's departures and Joey's death, my grandmother and Aunt Isa had thought my mother would be the better for a complete change of scene, and not just a change of house; one might go so far as calling it a different life.

The lawyers reminded her that you, Miss Isabella, with your gifted wee hands, had been engaged to play Schumann at a musical party given by the German consul in Edinburgh, and this had been attended by a German banker and his American wife resident in London, people named Heinemann. The couple had been, as people used to say then, 'struck' by my mother's performance. This was, I was to discover afterwards, partly due to their genuine love of music, and partly to their admiration for her looks, which I now realize were remarkable, though not useful to a woman who had no position in society. She always looked remarkable, as remarkable as Sarah

Bernhardt, or Yvette Guilbert, but this serves no rescue if one has not established the right to look remarkable by a successful career or been born with a large private income. But her appearance was enough to make people turn round and look at her when she came into a room; and that enabled her to help the Heinemanns in the problem that was facing them.

They were extremely rich, but more isolated than might have been expected. This was partly because Mr Heinemann's business obliged him to live in London. He was from Hanover and she was an American, a Miss Dabney from the South. Neither had ties in England, though Mr Heinemann was a British subject, for the reason that after 1714, when the Elector of Hanover became George I of England, the inhabitants of the Duchy of Hanover all enjoyed double nationality as Hanoverians and British; but this ceased in 1837 when Victoria came to the throne, for the Hanoverian constitution followed the Salic law and forbade a woman as ruler. Mr Heinemann had been born in 1836. But though he was a British and Hanoverian subject, he had still lost something, as he had a Christian German grandmother who had brought him up a Lutheran and he was not received by the stricter members of the Jewish Community in London; and in going into banking he had moved out of the sphere into which his family had been eminent for more than a century. Mrs Heinemann was amiable and well-mannered, and my mother could never imagine why she had married this harmless but uninteresting man; particularly as she had her own fortune.

Their problem had appeared insoluble. They had two, or it may have been three sons who were dark-eyed and graceful and pleasing to the eye; but they had two daughters, Emily and Clara, who were extremely unattractive. Emily was plain and pale, and heavily built, and Clara was like a little monkey. The Heinemanns, who were kind-hearted, realized at once that they would find it difficult to give their daughters the sort of youth that naturally fell to better-looking girls: nobody would want to dance with them, or go in a boat with them, or ride with them. If either married, the occasion could not be wholly happy. The bridegroom would, simply by being that, have proved himself mercenary. In any case, the time of waiting, of inevitable hope that this need not be so, was passing drearily, with Emily and Clara gaining little enjoyment from the party-going, when a peeress confided to Mrs Heinemann that she had suffered a great misfortune. She had lost her 'musical governess'.

Mrs Heinemann had never heard of such a person, and felt some curiosity. The European upper classes, she knew, rarely supported any institution that did not pay its way. Well, it emerged they took 'the gels' off their hands. (They all had 'gels' in those days, though none had boys.) A musical governess gave the girls lessons in singing and piano playing and whatever lessons were appropriate to their charges' natural gifts, and organized musical parties.

Mrs Heinemann felt a stirring of hope when this fact of English social life was revealed to her. She herself detested opera, saying, with a smile at her own ineptitude, that it always seemed so unnatural. She remembered that dark young woman who had played *Carnaval* in the Edinburgh drawing room. She had remembered the name of the hostess, and sent her a note to be forwarded. And now that my mother had been deprived of the home which had been hers since birth, and the company of her own mother and the servants whom she dearly loved, and the rooms where she had been together with Joey, it seemed to her apposite that Mrs Heinemann came from the Deep South, where slavery had been practised.

❧

My mother suffered a moment of blinding rage at this offhand disposal of her future. But it was no time for such luxuries, and she faced the silly old men with the obvious impracticability of the arrangement. What would her mother do, she asked, about selling the flat and the surplus furniture, and moving what was left into a new house on the other side of the city where they had no friends? Was this not an extraordinary programme to impose on two elderly ladies, one a chronic invalid? But the lawyer said, 'Tee hee, tee hee, Miss Isabella, you exaggerate the gravity of your family's change of residence. After all, Mrs Mackenzie and Miss Isa are not going to live alone, they'll be leaning on the strong arm of your brother Willie.'

'What?' exclaimed my mother, aghast. 'Is Willie going to live with them?'

'Ay, ay,' said the idiot pair in idiot unison.

'It's not right,' protested my mother.

'Why, Miss Isabella,' came the idiot answer, 'surely nothing could be more right and proper than that your poor mother, who has had such grievous sorrows, particularly of late, and her good sister, who has borne her sorrows as if they were her own, should have with them the last child that's been spared to their hearth?'

There floated visibly on his remarks the idiotic Scottish belief that any woman was the better for having a man in the house, no matter if he were no better than a sponge soaked in alcohol. My mother shut her eyes and prayed to the darkness – 'Oh, God, let my mother and my aunt not have to live alone in that house with my wretched brother' – but the voice of the idiots to whom God seemed to have handed over his authority droned on.

'Oh, Miss Isabella, I think you're looking through dark glasses at your family's future. Duncan Street is no palace but it's commodious enough. Duncan Street offers most handsome accommodation, there's ample room for your mother and your aunt, and your bonny self when you come back from this grand experience in London, and your good brother.'

My mother rose from her chair to put on her gloves as a preparation for departure, but could not get her trembling fingers into the leather. 'And foreby,' a voice whined on, 'there's a nice wee shed in the back garden where your brother can get on with his paintings.'

'Built of wood?' said my mother in a sudden terror.

'Ay.'

The domestic history of Scotland was illumined by fires started by cherished male alcoholics. My mother saw the wretched shed performing its national destiny, shuddered, and said, 'I will have to talk this over with my mother.'

'Oh, dear, Miss Isabella,' bleated one of the servants of hell, 'I'm afraid you are a day ahint the fair. Your mother's exercised all her legal rights about the flat on Heriot Row, and she's told Mr and Mrs Heinemann to expect you when you've been able to help your dear mother with the removal, and then you'll be on your way to London on some date early next month.'

When my mother got back to Heriot Row she found her mother and aunt sitting in the drawing room, the malt whisky and some savoury biscuits set out, and Willie spruced up and sober: an ensemble which meant that some possible purchasers were coming to inspect the

property. She was about to break out into an angry enquiry as to why
her future had been settled behind her back, when she was struck by
something unaccountable in her brother's manner. It was as if he had
meant to leave the room as she came in, but some second thought had
made him realize that he need not take that trouble. He had put his
plan into execution and there was nothing she could do to upset it.

Standing in the doorway, she said, her voice cracking, 'Mother, do
you really want me to go to London and teach those Heinemann girls?'

The moment the words were uttered she regretted them. The two
elderly women looked at her across the room as if in fear. Up till now
they had always seemed in all circumstances to have the upper hand,
but that was now over. My grandmother said, 'I think that would be
agreeable to you, now that nearly all the others have left,' and Aunt
Isa said mechanically, 'You should be grateful to your mother, Eedly.'
Something had beaten them to their knees and it was not for my mother's
power to raise them up, because their defeat had occurred somewhere
else, in some place unknown to her which she could not enter.

❧

The next few years were in a sense the most brilliant my mother was
ever to experience. She found in London a household which was ready
to be subjugated. Mr Heinemann was suffering from the surprise,
always touching to witness, which overcomes dull people when they
find they have produced dull children. Mrs Heinemann was hardly any
happier, though not being dull herself, she perfectly understood why
her children were dull.

The situation was at its most painful, for the two girls were going
out to débutante parties and were realizing with some bewilderment
that they were not having such a good time as other girls did, and they
could not think why. They were like all females born into the middle
or upper classes, in any European country at that time, exposed to
fierce competition so far as marriage was concerned. Their parents'
banking accounts (which shall be called x) and their looks (which
shall be called y) were what brought them satisfactory husbands: and if
x were a large amount then y could be ranked at a lower level, but x
could not approach anywhere near zero, though y might. But Mr
Heinemann, though rich, was not rich among rich men, and his

daughters' looks were in sight of zero. Their only exceptional endowment was musical talent, which had been encouraged during the year or so before my mother's arrival at the house in Eaton Square by a cousin – younger than they were – called William Heinemann. William was the son of a father who had shared in the benefit of being a double Hanoverian national, though he was not so rich. He had worked for a time in England but had returned to Germany, where William had been attending the famous *gymnasium* at Dresden. There William had shown himself a very clever boy indeed, but he was distracted by a violent desire to be a musician, which my mother said was a reasonable ambition, for he played the piano extremely well, but was likely to be frustrated by his variety of interests in the other arts.

Emily and Clara were not on the same level as their young cousin, but he had for the time being turned the house in Eaton Square into a sacred grove. The girls and William could profit from my mother's experienced teaching, and they were by temperament at ease with her: they shared the Mackenzie devotion to romanticism in general and Schumann in particular, and they lived the by-pathos that ran through their section of the sacred grove.

* * *

I do not know in detail what happened to my mother after she had spent two or three years teaching Emily and Clara Heinemann how to fill in the interstices of their empty lives. To put it in general terms, she learned that rich gentlemen are apt to marry rich ladies. It was humiliating that circumstance should have thought fit to teach her this, for she was the least mercenary woman in the world. The subject should never have been raised, it belonged to a different order of beings.

I know nothing about the man who brought it into her ambience, and I do not know how he had the heart to do it, for my mother's appearance should have inspired tenderness. She looked like the women in Tissot's pictures: slender, with long arms like branches of some delicate shrub, a well-shaped face, a soft curling fringe over her forehead, and something too delicate to be called dramatic that gave the place where she was – a garden or a room – the status of a stage.

There are many drawings of her by friends of the family which nail down for ever the cruelty of fate in making her suffer. At the time she was living in Eaton Square she must have been enjoying an advantage she had never enjoyed before (and was never to enjoy again), for Mrs Heinemann gave her all the dresses she needed to make it no embarrassment for hostesses to entertain both the Heinemann girls and their musical governess. She also learned to make herself acceptable by limiting her conversation with men to petitions for enlightenment. Any exchange of opinions was only permitted to married women, and the extent of the female participation varied with rank and wealth. But of course some men were to break the pattern in her case, as soon as they heard her agreeable voice and her original turn of phrase. It was inevitable that some man should fall in love with her and that she should fall in love with him.

I have only two sources of understanding: one of them some vague and embarrassed remarks of Mrs Heinemann. She gave me to understand that my mother had had the misfortune to attract and to be attracted by a man of superior station in life to her own. His family would not hear of the match. Later I was to hear that the situation was even more difficult. The man would have had no opposition from his family, who were aristocratic but not rich, if he had married Emily or Clara, for the Prince of Wales's liking for Jews was working on society as a whole. But the young man had never thought of either of the girls; he was obstinately in love with my mother.

The Heinemanns behaved very kindly to my mother, as, I remember her saying in another connection, she would always expect Germans to do.* Usually, they oscillated from spring to autumn between Eaton Square and their country house, which was on the downs near Eastbourne overlooking the Channel. It was a fairly large eighteenth-century house which had been derelict for some time for a curious reason. At the beginning of the nineteenth century there was a railway contractor who was a first-class civil engineer, had a way with bankers, and handled his navvies with a new humanity; and his success was such that he found himself building railroads all over Great Britain. He was a man who liked his home comforts and would not put up with country inns, and as he grew more successful he fell into the habit of buying or leasing any vacant house in the area of his current enterprises and sent for his wife to move in and set up a household, for the duration of the enterprise. He was so busy – he built railways all over the world, in France, Italy, Austria, Canada, Australia, India and Argentina – that when he had finished one enterprise he often moved with great haste to another, and often left his temporary home incompletely dismantled and, for some long period of time, unsold. This house on the Channel cliff had been among those incompletely dismantled, which added to its charm and to its usefulness as a home for a family with young people.

The decorations were faded to a vagueness of dreams; one might find a pediment or rusted surveying instrument or some beer bottles hidden behind the folds of a marble goddess's gown. It was tacitly understood that when the eldest son married all its glories would be repaired, but for the meantime it was a perfect home for a young family, and indeed it was specially so that summer. Never had the Heinemanns abandoned themselves to such a happy and informal summer. They spent little time in Eaton Square, they asked English and French and German friends and relatives to visit them, they hired a yacht that took them round the Isle of Wight and down to the West, they gave parties with wonderful music, and all this general kindness was a particular kindness to my mother, who was kept permanently busy. In this and in many other matters Mrs Heinemann's conduct to my mother showed great understanding, so great that my mother wondered if Mrs Heinemann's curious marriage was not to be accounted for by some such sorrow as her own.

But this merciful frivolity suddenly came to an end. In the main rooms of the house gas had been installed but its upper floors were still lit by lamps. One night, when the men were still up, playing billiards, and the women had gone up to their bedrooms, a sudden gale blew an old tree against the house, so that it smashed a window, and soon a room on the top floor was ablaze. Two servants gave the alarm, and all the people in the upper floors ran out along the corridors and down the main staircase into the hall. As my mother and the two girls ran across the hall to the open front door, some fine fleck of danger drifted down, a scrap of some curtain or tapestry, looking like a large leaf of flame, and rested on my mother's head. The butler was running by with a pail of water in each hand, and emptied one of them over her head and shoulders, and someone else beat out a flame that had started to devour her dressing-gown. My mother dropped to the floor and was instantly asleep. She was in just that state. She slept for two days, while the doctor talked about catalepsy, but it was simply natural sleep, a necessary flight.

She was calm and not at all astonished when she awoke in an undamaged part of the house. When Mrs Heinemann came in my mother thanked her for the care that had been taken of her and told her, 'I must go home.' Mrs Heinemann said, 'You are at home.' My mother thanked her but repeated, 'I must go home. To Edinburgh.'

'But that's a long way,' said Mrs Heinemann. 'Hadn't you better stay here for a few days, and I'll send for your brother?'

'My brother?' asked my mother. 'Your brother Alick,' said Mrs Heinemann. 'He's the eldest, isn't he? Wouldn't he be the one to send for?' My mother said in that Scots-dictionary-trained way of speech, 'No, it would not be appropriate, I want to go home to my mother.'

My mother had never returned to Edinburgh since she had become part of the Heinemann household. My grandmother never suggested that she should, though she and Aunt Isa wrote to her fondly and regularly, and sent her presents which were quite lavish, parting, indeed, with nearly all their jewellery. Every year my mother had gone to spend a few days with her sister Jessie at Newcastle, where she seemed to have settled down very placidly with her very successful husband, and she often spent at least a fortnight with Jessie Watson Campbell, now inseparable from the adoptive French parents, the Rollands, to whom she had gone years before as a governess.

This my mother thoroughly enjoyed. The Rollands' house, half château, half farm-house, was in a village a few miles out of Orléans; and though it was not very large and the Rollands were not very rich, it contained an entrancing number of servants. One did nothing but trim the lamp-wicks and keep the oil at the right level; another went around the salons mending the splits in the Aubusson carpets, which were over a hundred years old; another spent most of her time in the dairy making butter with her bare hands, and a particularly good creamy cheese that looked like rolls; and the housemaids had a daily chore that struck my mother as nearly a magic rite. Camille, the Rollands' only son, had been killed in the Franco-Prussian War, and his bedroom was kept exactly as if he had returned alive. The furniture was polished, his books were taken down from the shelves and dusted, and the sunken inkpot and the plumed pens were on the *escritoire*. The sheets on the Empire bed were changed daily, and the towels and sponges, soap and shaving-brush were ready for use in the *cabinet de toilette*, and the clothes in the wardrobe were regularly brushed and pressed. That was a custom among old-fashioned people, Jessie Watson Campbell said; and my mother remembered some very rich people in the Ruhr who kept up such a custom for an uncle who had died in the Napoleonic wars. Long afterwards, in the 1920s, I encountered the practice again in a Kentucky town: a Jew of German origin kept the room he had shared with his dead wife exactly as it had been in her lifetime, down to her elaborately fitted dressing table, which was still stocked in her favourite scents and creams. This custom was no eccentricity nor was it a custom: it was a muted cry of pain. I wished my mother could have made some such expression of her grief at losing the man she wished to marry.

She must have been choked with grief when she travelled up to Edinburgh. Her brother Willie was supposed to meet her, but did not. I can imagine the early autumn evening made of cold, cold blue clouds scudding across an amber sunset to which there adhered, like a thrown coin, a pale round moon, which she saw as the cab took her over the North Bridge, ashamed, not because she had been jilted, but because she was going to a home that was in Newington and not to the New Town of Edinburgh. She did not tell me of the acute suffering that this had caused her until long after, so intense was her emotion. It had nothing to do with snobbishness. It had to do with history.

But it had its points. Duncan Street* was a line of handsome but narrow houses, four storeys tall, with long strips of garden in front of them, and when my mother arrived there it was just past the hour at which thoughtful people put a match to their gas-jets in the hall; and the light showed through the hansom. The sitting-room lights were already on behind the drawn curtains; it had for some time been too dark to read without them. There were four dim lights, one above the other, which marked the staircase; and above that the starlit darkness.

My mother's heart expanded; she laid her hand on the gate, but she had forgotten something. There is, or was then, an ingenious arrangement in Scottish towns whereby garden gates remain closed to the visitor's touch until someone in the house, having looked through a glass aperture and seen that the visit will be welcome, presses a lever which releases the gate. In an instant my mother felt cast down, rejected, homeless. She longed to be back with the Heinemanns. But the gate clicked, the front door opened, and let out a broad ray of light which showed her a paved path bordered by two beds of rose trees, and at its end two of the three servant-maids that had been part of the Heriot Row household, calling her by name in their beautiful Highland voices, and opening their arms to her. And when they drew her into the lighted hall, there was Aunt Isa, who said, 'Eedly, Eedly,' and bent to give her a tremulous kiss, an agued kiss, an anguished kiss.

My mother's emotion was intense. It shot through her mind that Aunt Isa had in fact chosen to walk out of the comfortable house where she was born and leave her father and mother to be with my grandmother and her children, simply to help them, and that she must be forgiven everything, she was so loving a creature. She realized also that to this old woman, whom she did not even like, her absence had been a source of intense grief; and that she herself must repay her love. But there was something else which was distressing her, and that was the extraordinary cap she was wearing. Her dress was as my mother would have expected, well made, designed to hide her hunched back, of good material – though, now she looked at it, shiny about the seams. But her cap was dreadful. It looked like a green helmet worn by a soldier who had refused to be measured for it. No cap so ill-cut had ever left my grandmother's lace shop in George Street: and the material was a coarse linen used in houses where there was no care about such things, for the maid-of-all-work's use.* This puzzled my mother even while she responded (with an honesty she would have thought unlikely) to Aunt Isa's vacillating embrace and her sobbing welcome. 'Come in, bairn, come in, you'll catch your death. Oh, your mother'll be out of her mind at seeing you, since noon she's been watching the clock. No, not up the stairs. She canna manage stairs. She's in the back room, aye, in the back room . . .'

She was there, looking small in her armchair, though it was small. 'Eedly,' she said out of a round mouth, 'Eedly,' and held a steaming cloth to her right ear and jaw. When she saw my mother at the open door, she dropped the cloth into a bowl of hot water on a tabouret beside her, and held out her arms. As my mother was to learn later, my grandmother was suffering not merely from neuralgia, as Aunt Isa had often mentioned in her letters, she was also a victim of that agonizing variation of neuralgia known as *tic douloureux* which changes the face to a clock which keeps time with pain. When my grandmother put the cloth back in the bowl there was a terrible contrast between the soft mash of her face and the still lovely and springing forms of her hands and her forearms. But out of this muddle of defeat and inviolability came a welcome that was nothing else, simply pure welcome, that ignored any defeat she or they might have met. Nothing disagreeable managed to survive. They laughed aloud: her pain-disturbed mother, her aunt, born deformed, still deformed, the servant-maids fresh as coast winds on a mild day, my mother herself – who, I suspect, thought nothing good would happen again.

NEWINGTON

My grandmother, of course, divined my mother's humiliation, but showed it only by asking, in what might have seemed a brusque and heartless way, the name of the man concerning whom, she understood from Mrs Heinemann, there had been some talk of marriage. Out of Victorian obedience my mother quietly gave the name. My grand-mother asked her nothing more, but a week or two afterwards a call was paid on my grandmother by an elderly lady, with whom our household had an odd relationship of an antique sort. It was then the custom of the holder of any title of reasonable antiquity and state to visit all his or her kinsmen once a year, either in his own person or by deputy of some member of his near family. The elderly lady who now appeared in Duncan Street was the sister of a Highland duke, and we were included in her round because of a relationship which was tenuous indeed. (I looked it up out of curiosity in my later life and found that the only link was a marriage in the second quarter of the eighteenth century.) On this occasion the deputy stayed half an hour and was gone; but a letter was brought by hand. My grandmother sought out my mother and said, 'I mentioned the gentleman's name you gave me. She says you are well out of it. His family might well have condescended to you.' That was the last word that ever passed between them on that subject.

For some weeks or months, I do not know which, my mother tried to start life afresh in Newington, with no success at all. Nobody whose family has not fallen to pieces can realize how such an accident reduces their own value; they are worthless, a fragment of broken china. Yes, her piano playing was remarkable, London had made her quite sure of that. But what had made her life pleasant at Heriot Row was not simply her own love of music, it was a blend of my grand-mother's good looks and handy character, of all that Joey and Johnnie were, of the servant-maids' good humour, of Willie's brighter moments, even of Aunt Isa's Partan Bree and cold buds with rowan jelly; and all the bright faces of their friends, their good will, the men's familiar compliments, the women with their familiar jewels. Tears came into her eyes when she remembered a small but exquisite diamond always worn by an elderly lady, the widow of a flautist, whose reverberant music was perpetually present too; they belonged to the same order of pleasure. But there was nothing in Duncan Street to join with her music to make something coherent like a Meissen plate. Willie painted less and less, one could not even give a party to show off his latest work, though of late he had become enthusiastic about the Frenchman Courbet. And there were no guests, it was too far to expect friends from the New Town to make the effort to come all the way to Newington, and she received few invitations. If she was asked out for the evening, it might well be to play card games, whist or this new thing bridge, with people older than herself.

Her only real distraction was to cross the main street and stroll in the park below Arthur's Seat and Salisbury Crags, distant about half a mile, and approached by a suburb that was strangely and not unhappily incongruous. It had been built during the mid-century by wealthy men of the soberer kind who, perhaps because they were Radicals and disliked the references to imperial splendour made by the New Town, had chosen to build in the Italian style, which was picturesque but, as it was framed to exclude excessive heat, kept out any warmth the sun might be dispersing. Grim and grey these towers and loggias looked on most days but within the King's Park the extinct volcano, Arthur's Seat, built in the image of a *couchant* lion, and alongside it Salisbury Crags, presented a design purely abstract, yet provocative of deep emotion that mysteriously seemed to be recol-lected. As a base there is a steep slope crisped like a wave, and above that a vertical cliff and above that again a vertical wall of rock, and above that, stone flinted like the pipes of an immensely broad organ, and all set askew to the horizon, so that space in these parts seems to be doing what modern physicists all agree space does in the remote universe.

My mother would have liked both to climb Arthur's Seat and walk along the top of Salisbury Crag, but the park sloped away from the two mountains to the dark medieval slums of Edinburgh, and it was considered dangerous for women to walk alone in this suddenly desert place. So she used to walk no further than a seat on the lower slopes of Arthur's Seat, well within view of the gates and the houses beyond, and try to think of what she must do if she wanted to start teaching again; but her mind indolently returned to the harebells that coursed delicately through the rough grass at her feet, or to the faraway fresco of the Pentland Hills in the distance.

But one day it was all solved. She found herself standing in the drawing room, before her mother and her aunt, both looking more like themselves than they had done for some time. Her mother was giving orders as she used to do: and Aunt Isa was again aggressive in the grand manner, which had made Joey say that she was like a vinegar bottle made by a quart glass-blower. For an instant or two she went on thinking of him: silent and that should not be, it was not his nature. Through her marvel that anyone, God or man, should have thought of anything as wicked as death, she heard her mother say, 'Would you mind if you do not go back to teaching? Would you mind going away again?' As soon as she had heard and understood, she answered, 'Not at all, not at all.' She divined from the length of their silence that they were hurt by her answer, but her mother continued at once. 'There is a way you could help us.'

There was sincerity in her voice. My mother enquired, 'Yes?' and thought, 'Why, they are afraid, they are throwing themselves on my mercy, they must be desperate.' She stared at them, and it was so. Their attitudes were hieratic. My grandmother was sitting in a chair made, it was said, by William Kent; the arms rested on lions' heads and, my mother said, it was as if Van Dyck had borrowed a model from Raeburn, and Aunt Isa stood behind her chair like a lady-in-waiting.* 'Yes?' my mother said again, her heart bleeding for them.

My grandmother then unfolded a plan which I find it shocking to contemplate: a quite reckless disposition of a young woman's life. But when I think of the alternative – the only alternative that these women were permitted to consider by the society in which they lived – I am not sure. The mercilessness of that society can be shown by the certainty that my grandmother and Aunt Isa felt that if my mother stayed in Edinburgh she might, for no fault of her own, have become an outcast. So glibly my grandmother explained that Johnnie, who had seemed to be getting on well in Australia, had found his first good luck had gone from him. With a pang of guilt my mother realized that she had not received a letter from Johnnie for some time. She had not worried, his first letters had been so confident that Australia felt a personal affection for him. Everywhere he had been he had found Scotsmen hungry for their music, and many of them, particularly the miners, would pay anything to hear it, so when he had hastily knocked together a Scottish concert party the money had started rolling in.

But he had fallen ill, so ill that he had been for several weeks in hospital, first in Ballarat,* and then in Melbourne, at each place for some weeks. At the moment he was better, but it was feared that he might yet have a relapse.

Faltering, my grandmother proposed to her daughter that she should go to Australia and see how Johnnie was getting on, and, if it were the right thing, to bring him home. This was a most astonishing suggestion. It was unthinkable that a young woman should make such a journey alone. Why should she? If she could pay for a ticket, she surely had a husband, or a father, or a brother, or widowed mother or aunt, who could accompany her. If she had not, then of course there was a risk she might be disreputable. (Can there really have been so many disreputable women in the world last century as is suggested by the universal fear that any solitary woman who appeared reasonably well off was seeking whom she might devour? If so, such a huge number of men must have consorted with prostitutes that the society which set up these values must have been such hypocrites as to make the moral codes a humbugging bit of nonsense which ought to be ignored.) And who was to take her in in Melbourne and give her a respectable background? Not the prosperous father of Jessie Watson Campbell and her sister: the intransigent had ceased to write to my grandmother even at Christmas time. It would be all right if she could take Johnnie straight out of hospital and put him on a steamer for England, but she doubted she would be able to do that.

Always when my mother's path seemed uncharted she thought of Ovid's *Metamorphoses*, of people being changed into animals which did not die, or into trees or rivers. How odd that the ancients did not realize that vegetation also had, in time, to breathe its last, that springs lost their heartbeat and were still. She saw herself and Johnnie as exiles in Australia, frozen by their fate, never making any home for themselves where they could eat or sleep in comfort, or have friends at their table, or get into a tram or hire a cab to take them to the docks to any ship that would take them back to Leith or Liverpool. She was suddenly carried away by hallucination, and thought that it was not Johnnie, but Joey she was going to bring back to England – but then she felt the deepest shame for having put Johnnie in second place, he was so loving and innocent. She grieved that she was not beside him already, and cried out, 'The only question is, how soon can I go?'

Yet at the same time her heart was hardening against the situation. She recognized the helpless nobility of her mother's expression as a sign that she had, once again, been wasted by the male. Johnnie might be ill in Australia but the real reason my mother was having to go out to bring him home was that it suited the convenience of one of the family doctors or lawyers. 'Shall I stay here and defy these old boors and get them to show their hand?' she asked herself. She answered, 'No, they have the upper hand. They always had it. They have it everywhere. I can do nothing. And the first thing is for me to help Johnnie; nobody can stop me trying to save him. And what am I to save him from home?' And something told her 'Willie is behind all this,' but she disliked feeling suspicion.

And she felt there was no reason for suspecting Willie of anything unworthy. It seemed often that, if he had a part in the plan to get her out to Australia, he was even proud of it. That was oddly noticeable when he showed her a painting in oils he was about to send down to the annual exhibition of the Royal Scottish Academy: a canvas that made her exclaim with pleasure, it was so like his earlier work. It was a still life which really was still, which really spoke of silence undisturbed by speech or animal noises. It showed some everlastings in a glass vase, the ghostly flowers standing above their own ghostly reflection on the highly polished surface of a round table, set in a broad and high window. My mother said, 'You got it all down,' and saw that the view through the window was ghostly too, for the rain was falling and making a diffused ghost of the failing light, and praised him for detecting the variety permeating the monotony.

Willie nodded his acknowledgement and 'Ay,' he said, 'last week I stuck by that window till the last drop of drizzle had gone clean down the panes, and that was for five days.'

'So it was,' my mother said. 'How lucky I am to be going to Australia.'

'Ay,' said Willie with something of a smirk, 'you'll have the sun to your heart's content.'* Now what could he mean by that? It was as if he were looking forward to her undertaking a journey that must be embarrassing and shadowed from its start by the fear that death might await her at its end. She could not understand this satisfaction.

PORTLAND BILL

Now my story becomes more difficult to tell. Up to this point I have been covering white paper with a mixed medium composed of my mother's memories and my recollections of the things we had both seen: the harebells in the King's Park, each dancing on a single thread, and my adaption of my mother's account of people with my own, much later memories of them. This makes my descriptions of Edinburgh easy writing but it is harder work when I tell of my mother's travels in Australia, for I have never been there. She left me no impression of the years she spent there, only the blazing flower of light, the changing colours of mountains and great waters and grasslands, the shock of extreme joy or grief. When she came to actual description of scenery she bewildered. Can she really have meant that a gentle stream making its way through pastoral lands by gentle cascades in the neighbourhood of Ballarat recalled the Lake District to her memory? And she described to me as hovering at high noon just such a sun as I have seen from a plane over Africa: a sun that looked blind, as if it had cataract, but still retained its mesmeric power. All these impressions which lasted in her mind so that she could pass them on to me unfaded and still electric owed their survival to the quality of glory and violence which they shared with her recent experience of love. But for the rest I see her without a background, but with a foreground that was crowded from the minute she got on board the steamer at Liverpool.

Some of the passengers were always drunk (and these were not bums since it was in the respectable classes the recognized technique for getting rid of undesirable members of the family to send them to the Antipodes). But of the others most were charming, and that could be said of some of the social rejects, of whom one was the best company conceivable to my mother. This was Lord William Somebody, the son of an English peer, who had recently left prison after serving a sentence for fraud and embezzlement. My mother thought not much less of him for that, for his trial had taken place when she was with the Heinemanns, and she had heard them talking of him and saying that his crimes were due to a kind of mental aberration. The initial trouble was that he was given to what are called games of chance, though anyone who has ever watched play at a casino knows that games of malice would be a better name. The immediate trouble had been that he had been cleaned out of all his available funds at a gambling hall (as they were called then) only a few days after he had been told by the family lawyer that he could expect no more help from his relatives; and he had then resorted to fraud of a kind so elementary that it amounted to an example of prodigious innocence rather than guilt.

It happened that very soon after the ship set out to sea my mother heard the young man playing Chopin quite creditably on the Broadwood in the lounge, and for the rest of the voyage they happily read scores and played accompaniments at ship's concerts. They got on very well, so well that he presently confided in her with schoolboy laughter that as he had served his sentence in Portland Jail his younger relatives now insisted on calling him 'Portland Bill'. When my mother first heard this little joke she was deeply shocked, and said to herself, 'The English are cold fish. Scotsmen will never make a mock of a thing like that. But then, he doesn't seem to mind,' and she remembered that a couple of his relatives had come to Liverpool to see him on to the boat, and had seemed to be taking care for his comfort.

There was enough music on board, what with the pair of them, and a girl and her brother who had sung in a choir, and an old man who was a fair violinist. My mother was drafting a programme for the hymns for a Sunday morning service, when a man walked by her and said, 'Beautifully as you play the piano, leave it alone tomorrow. You must see Tenerife tomorrow. It is not good weather. It should be worth looking at.' He was a man of just over or just under forty whom she had noticed because he had brilliant black eyes, which were not in harmony with the gentleness he showed when he spoke to women and elderly people. She wondered who he was: he was often with a pale, slim woman of the Pre-Raphaelite type and a boy of sixteen or so. Indeed one might have thought them a family, but there was no easy conversation between the man and the woman, though the man and the boy might have been father and son, or at least uncle and nephew. The man seemed often to be teaching the boy some foreign language; they had a slim volume that might have been a textbook, and what looked like a dictionary and a grammar; they laughed a lot over their studies.

The woman, whose name my mother could never remember, sent a note to say that if she wanted to see Tenerife, they would come and fetch her, as soon as they could verify that the sight was likely to be as scenic as was being foretold. That it was. The sea was composed of fragments set at acute angles, which were tilted this way and that before the winds, some bright as diamonds, others grey, chocolate brown, purple, and dimmed huckleberry, and sometimes turned to uniform bronze by rays from a sun low on the sky. The sky was an inverted bowl of bad weather, violet-blue gleaming here and there with clouds glazed with silver. At a distance that was not exactly calculable, the light was so strange, the Island of Tenerife looked like the base of a mountain ascending into a mist streaked with shining layers of pale almond green and the purest silver. Thus any terrace suddenly became streaked, like brushwork in an oil painting, and then shredded into flakes of pale green, leaving naked a peak that, with the assurance of stone, rose high, high as the noonday sun on the equator, to an ultimate height.

All day long, the island and all around changed its dimensions and its colour, and one or other of the party would exclaim, 'Extraordinary, extraordinary,' but there was nothing extraordinary about what they saw. The sky and the sea take all sorts of colours. What they meant was that the form of matter they had seen all their life was suddenly assuming aspects of which they had never dreamed, which astonished their sight and seemed to be demonstrating that the universe in which it was taking place was quite different from the everyday appearance of the world. It struck my mother, as she described it to me once or twice, as resembling life as changed as Tenerife had been from ordinary mountains. All over the world millions of babies were born, and their births were ordinary events, incapable of causing emotion, and millions of men and women fell in love, and it

was of no consequence, and then suddenly, as she looked on the
mountain and its seas, it was as if one couple had started moving
through space vertically instead of horizontally. Birth and love and
death seemed to have been subject to alchemy and changed their
substance and their uses. When it was quite dark it seemed sensible to
go below; sleeping or walking, what she might see or hear would keep
its pre-mythic quality.

And so it did. The Southern Cross was oddly frail for its great fame,
floating on its back as if it had not learned the equivalent of swimming
in space which keeps other constellations better balanced and able to
cry to each other. She would break off and say, 'I cannot explain, but
though the stars make no noise they seem to be calling to each other,
like young people bathing, and the Southern Cross seems to be too ill at
ease ever to cry for help.'

And then there came the morning when they found themselves
encircled in a great land-locked bay, and stood on deck and looked
into the white eye of a sun staring over the curved saucer of the hills,
while the passengers, even those who had not exchanged a word
throughout the voyage, behaved like a close company of explorers,
and laughed as if they were approaching territories which would
belong to them by right of conquest, so that all that they found
of value would be theirs and would feed and clothe them till the day
they died.

My mother was chilled by this. There was nothing in this country
which would cure the wound she had suffered in England. She went
downstairs, and lay on her bed and slept, but Lord William, the good
Portland Bill, came to knock on her door, and told her she must come
up on deck, they were moored in the port of Melbourne: and presently
there she stood, blinking into the rays of a queer sun, coloured like a
buttercup, yellow-lined with a sobering glaze of silver. The ship was
travelling slowly down a channel of rocking water streaked with
reflections of this buttercup yellow, which was criss-crossed by some
row-boats that were striking out for the sailing ships, their masts
giving them a look of so many minute plantations in winter, further
out in the bay. Here long steam-ships rested at anchor, by contrast
without character, like huge dull fish. There was a babble of noise,
sirens shrieked and exhausts hissed and whistles screamed, the people
in the row-boats shouted, and when at last they drew alongside cranes

groaned, chains rattled and there was the puffing of a train not far off. She heard the porters who came aboard calling to each other in an accent unlike anything she had heard before and that, according to her, we will never hear, for it was her opinion that during her lifetime the pitch and vowel sounds of the Australian accent naturally changed. For some time such small changes entranced her; such small changes, yet they altered everything but were not frightening, because the peculiar light made so strong a promise.

But as the day went by she was engulfed by the rage and depression that comes to all travellers when they realize that leaving a ship is among the most disagreeable experiences in life. One is shut in a cell of false time with a non-existent grief: and this time the incarceration lasted all day and all night because of an accident, which made it impossible to unload the passengers' luggage. She and William played duets and accompanied volunteer singers in the salon after supper; she felt dazed, and thought she saw instead of heard the voices of the singers, the shallow line of William's amateurish playing, and the notes that came from her own fingers (her wrists were stiff). She was alarmed to the pitch of panic because Johnnie had not sent her a note to say that he was waiting for her.

The next day she was standing with the passengers on the quay waiting for Johnnie. He did not come. Presently the dark Englishman and his son came and stood beside her. They had been saying goodbye to the Pre-Raphaelite woman, who was now going down the gangway with a porter who was carrying her hand luggage. The Englishman turned to my mother and asked, 'Haven't your friends come for you?'

'Not yet,' she said, smiling insincerely.

'You let them know in time and gave them all the details?' he asked.

The Pre-Raphaelite woman turned and smiled up at him, waved her hand, and said, 'Goodbye, goodbye.' Mr Fairfield returned her gesture and echoed her goodbye, but quickly and without interest. My mother noticed this but attached no importance to it.

Then Lord William appeared with two men who had been sent by Government House to meet him, and kissed her hand, and told the two young men what a wonderful voyage she had contrived for him at greater length than they found interesting. It was extraordinary how people of that class, at any age, knew at once if one was not of their class. At last they left, and my mother said to Mr Fairfield, 'Please don't bother about me, my brother will certainly be here before long,' but he told her that he and young Nicholas had all the time in the world to get to their destination, which was in the heart of Melbourne, and they would not be happy if they got there without knowing she too had a roof over her head. So there they stood, and many of her fellow passengers stayed to thank her for having made their voyage so pleasant with her piano playing, but again and again they ended by saying, 'But haven't your friends come for you? Can we help?', and again and again she found herself saying, 'No, no, don't worry about me, my brother will certainly be here soon, he is always a little late, but in the end he always turns up. No, I don't know his address. He has just come back from the country. I have only to stay just here and he'll find me,' while the sickness of misery kept rising in her throat, and her smile became more and more a contest with agony, a thing that ought to have happened at the dentist's.

LIZZIE

At length the three of them found themselves alone. The land had taken all the passengers to itself. 'The sunshine is beautiful,' my mother said, smiling into the light with a wooden affectation. Mr Fairfield, who had been silent for some moments, asked her, 'Would your brother be alone?' and she answered, 'I would think so,' absently, because her eye had been caught by a curious waggon painted tartan, the Mackenzie tartan she recognized, and drawn by a pair of horses with a harness bedizened with bells, which was stationed up on a road that ran parallel with the pier.

A man and woman were standing by the waggon and they might have been waiting for someone, but the man was not Johnnie, and surely Johnnie would have picked neither of them as his friends. The man was coarse, and as she said the word to herself she pronounced it 'coorse' as her mother and Aunt Isa would have done, if they had been talking in their own house. He was heavily built, his neck pressed outward against his collar, his wrists and hands were thick with curly hair, there was a round curl flat against his forehead, and in the scarlet tie which was knotted over his tartan shirt was a diamond pin so large that it might have come out of a Christmas cracker. He had a fairground look to him, and so had the woman. The great chignon on the nape of her long neck was in its way as prodigiously yellow as the Australian sun, and her dark plum-coloured dress was cut so tightly that it might be a special sort of dress, made for her convenience when she climbed a pole or swung between bars high in a tent. On her breast she wore a huge gold brooch, such as a high priest might have worn in the Old Testament, but in that case would have lain more easily on the more level surface.

Mr Fairfield told my mother crisply, 'It is all nonsense, you hanging about like this. Nicholas and I are going to a hotel kept by friends of a relative of his. We will take you there and we will leave directions with the proper people here to say where we are, and then we will send someone to hunt down your brother. Come on. Not another word.'

When my mother got to the bottom of the gangway she paused to dry her eyes; and when she put her handkerchief back in her reticule she found that she was standing not so far from the man in the tartan shirt and the woman with the gamboge hair.* They had walked slowly to the bottom of the gangway and were staring up at the last dribble of descending passengers; and my mother was now so near the man that she could hear him softly whistling.

'Oh, hush,' she said to Mr Fairfield, greatly surprising him. For she spoke with reverence, and came to a dead halt.

Serious musicians take whistling with more respect than the laity, for they often practise this odd art, as it enables them to make sensational contributions to parties. There are all sorts of technical tricks one can play, such as whistling two notes at the same time, and thus perform strange duos. But this was the art in its glorious purity. What stunned my mother was that this man was giving a superb performance of that loveliest of laments, the elegy for the Jacobite dead called 'The Flowers of the Forest'.

> I've heard the lilting at the even milking
> Lassies a' lilting before the dawn of day
> But now they are moaning in the green loaning
> The flowers of the forest are a' wide away.

My mother calculated that if there was anything as good as this whistling happening in the town where Johnnie lived, Johnnie would know of it. She stared into the man's gross face, which could no longer be gross to her, since she had heard that pure small stream of sound. 'You're from Johnnie?' she said, and he answered, 'Och, you'll be Johnnie's Isabella. I tell you, we're deeved to death* hearing all about you.'

Secretly she thought to herself, 'Why, he'll be from the Glasgow slums,' and said aloud, 'Ay, I'm Isabella,' and the lady with the lemon-coloured chignon said from the background, 'And we've heard all about you, and how wonderful you are,' and completely floored my mother. In those days many Australians spoke a dialect in no way resembling what is called Strine today, but very close to the language Dickens puts in the mouth of his Cockneys, even to the substitute of 'v' for 'w'.

'Ye ken this is Lizzie?' the Whistler asked my mother.

'How do you do, Lizzie?' said my mother, at a loss. 'I am very pleased you've come to meet me. But where's my Johnnie?'

'He'll be here,' said the man in the tartan shirt, 'he'll be here. Dinna worry.'

'Don't worry,' echoed the woman with the gamboge hair. 'Oh, the sly thing, Johnnie, the sly thing, he never told me you were the slender sort, you might be the Princess of Wales, you've such a shape, and I've been thinking you'd be a great big raw-boned Scotswoman and that I'd have an 'orrible time fighting for my rights when we got merry on a Saturday night.'

'But where's Johnnie?' said my mother. She spoke as if she were about to faint, and pulled herself together. 'Women like this, they understand about death, they're at their best about it,' she thought, and said, 'I must see Johnnie. Losing Joey, you know about Joey, it makes me feel I want to be sure that Johnnie's all right.'

'All right, yes, he's all right, he just has a sore head, all my blokes here had sore heads this morning, they drank your health last night, and we dropped him on the way here to buy a dram, the house hasn't a drop left in it of anything except the vinegar.'

'We wished ye sae well, Miss Isabella,' said the Whistler from Glasgow, 'that we all had sore heads this morning.'

'And he'll take his time,' said the woman with the gamboge hair, 'when he goes on an errand he takes twenty-four hours; for whatever he sees that he hasn't seen before casts a spell on him like the hypnotists at the fairs, he just stands and gapes.'

'You're aye picking faults off him since you married him,' said the Whistler from Glasgow, and my mother's heart struggled in her breast like a gun-shot bird.

'Look, I said our Lizzie lied about him! He's across the way!' The Whistler cleared his throat and shouted, 'Step up, dandy! Your wee sister's here and we think she's awfu' neat!'

My mother watched her brother cross the road. She thought, 'Oh, God, how ill he looks.' Then an icy shudder ran through her, and she said to herself, 'No, he is not ill at all. He will live to be eighty.' (And so he did.) 'But he looks like Willie. He has gone the same way as him.' And then she wanted to weep in a room with a locked door. 'He has been out here all alone, he is not steely under the silk like Joey. It is only natural he should go to pieces.'

She realized from various minute kindnesses that Mr Fairfield and Nicholas were producing in her service, concerning her luggage and her music-cases, that they were profoundly shocked, not least, she imagined, by Johnnie's attire. In Edinburgh Johnnie would not have borne a bottle of whisky naked round the town, and it was even less probable that he would have gone about such business wearing full-dress Highland costume. All his brothers had their kilts, of course, but they were worn at ceremonial occasions and within a strictly drawn geographical barrier.

My mother was by now enfolded in Johnnie's arms; but she cried out and freed herself, lest these kind strangers, Mr Fairfield and Nicholas, should break their hearts on her account. 'For dear's sake, Johnnie! Why are you wearing the kilt? You'll no be telling me that Australia's north of Stirling?'

There was a second's silence and then Johnnie said with some shame, 'Oh, never heed, they don't know about that sort of thing in Australia.' My mother would have ended the whole thing in laughter had not the Whistler, for some obscure reason, taken offence. 'What's all this about?' he asked, looking at my mother. 'What ails you with Johnnie's kilt? Do you want him to go bareleggit down the Melbourne streets? And what's all this about Stirling?'

'Why, you must have heard that nobody's supposed to wear the kilt south of Stirling,' said Johnnie.

The Whistler shook his head and said, 'Nobody's ever said about that in Glasgow. And with Jack on the box in his kilt, it's a good advertisement wherever we go. And the van's necessary, it takes the upright piano. But it's the kilts give us quality. We're known and we're doing well. Oh, I'm well content.' He tapped his diamond pin. 'This is real and so's your brother's.'

'Ay, ay,' said Johnnie, 'and now we must think of the ladies. Lizzie's not had her wedding present yet. Isabella, did you know we were married?'

'At last we've got some good looks in the family,' said my mother, and kissed the woman with the gamboge hair.

Mr Fairfield watched her thoughtfully, took out a notebook from his pocket, wrote something on it and gave it to my mother, saying it was the address of the hotel where he and Nicholas would be staying for some time, and they would be glad to do any little service for her that she should require till she had settled down. They kissed the hands of my mother and of Lizzie, and wished the bride and bridegroom long life and happiness, and were gone.

A silence had settled over the port, the sun was like a burning glass. They would have liked to have stayed there for a little, it was so quiet, but the men had to get the porters to carry the luggage to the van; and Lizzie introduced my mother to the two horses, saying she liked the white one better of the pair, he was almost human.

My mother realized when she settled down in Melbourne that all her suspicions were correct, and Johnnie had made no attempt to follow his serious musical career. He had found it much more profitable to set up one of the companies, made up of instrumentalists, singers, dancers, comedians, who travelled round the mines and gave variety shows, often with a nationalist bias to suit the origin of the men who worked at particular mines, particularly the Welsh, Irish and Scottish. It had been possible for a number of these companies to make a lot from their audiences, which were composed of miners who might be getting rich, but were often bored to distraction by the isolation of the camps, and willing to pay heavily for any amusement. The rewards were not so great by this time, because the delirious days of the first boom were over, but Johnnie could make more money than other people. He was lovable, his audiences liked to see him often, and became familiar with his easy character. Also he could keep a company in a good temper, and he could, being utterly unselfish, help all his performers to use their gifts on appealing and memorable material. But only the desperate would care for such a life; and Johnnie, my mother perceived, because of Alick's desertion and Joey's death, and because of his exile to Australia, was desperate. She also instantly recognized that Lizzie had the power to alleviate his symptoms, and so, though it seemed the end of her life, she joined the concert party as a pianist in order to give help to both her brother and her sister-in-law.

It was of course an imbecile idea. As a result of the combined effort of herself and Lizzie she succeeded in cutting down Johnnie's consumption of spirits, but he was still sober only on Mondays, and less so on Tuesdays, and mounted by steps to offensive, injurious drunkenness at the weekend. This was the routine of most of the other men, and some of the women, and many people in the audiences, and these last would hang around after the performances and stand them drinks, and some of them would vomit. This debauch was not always insisted upon: but the occasions when it was so were loathesome, and ate away Johnnie's capacity for disgust. My mother grew ill with a sickness that was only partly physical, and her only comfort was the goodness of Lizzie, who did something for her that was like lifting her up and carrying her. It was Lizzie who put an end to the brave and foolish experiment and sent her back to Melbourne.

My mother was to love Lizzie all her life long. When she was dying she told me to burn all Lizzie's letters unread, and I obeyed, but I read two of them. It was enough. I copied out two passages from the correspondence which might have been written by a mother superior of a strict order.

Don't blame yourself for not staying with us. It would have done no good. You would just have got mixed up with the rest of the mess. That might have made you feel good, but it wouldn't have helped me much and it wouldn't have helped Johnnie at all. Your getting out made it clear to him that there are still people living as he and I and the crowd don't live, and it reminded him of what he had been.

Look, you mustn't fret because you went away. Much as I loved you, it was a blessing in disguise. I have always been able to quiet Johnnie down in his bad times by saying, 'Johnnie, Johnnie, your dear sister was so fond of you she came all the way from Scotland to see you, she could not stand the life you led, and we lost her.' When I tell him that he often settles down for a bit.

I correct her errors of spelling and punctuation, because they seem to me to falsify her image, which according to my mother was enhanced by her beautiful singing and speaking voice, as melodious and classical, my mother said, as Ellen Terry's, provided that her listeners made allowances for the Dickensian-cum-Australian twang.

I would not have been born had it not been for Lizzie, for when my mother fell sick on the tour the company was at an isolated mining town, brand new and highly productive, and by this time squalid. A year or so before it had consisted of a central square containing a bandstand flying the Union Jack, a Catholic Mission hall, a Presbyterian Church run by lay preachers, a general store, and a farriery kept by a discharged convict who had been in a cavalry regiment before his misfortunes and was an excellent shoesmith and vet. Up till then the place had existed to serve the trading needs of a scattered community who farmed clearings in the forest, where there was water. But now that gold had been discovered in and near the streams that ran through the woods to the rivers and the valleys, there were whole areas of the forest that looked as if a dentist had been at work among the trees.

The mining went on either in the streams that ran down the defaced slopes or in holes that the miners dug in the flat poachy ground in the valleys. They dipped deep iron pans either into the streams or the waterholes, or they used cradles, which were troughs mounted on rockers with a perforated bottom; they packed the cradles with the wet earth and shook them back and forwards, and the fine particles of gold fell through the perforations on to a canvas screen backed with transverse bars of wood. The miner who got his gold in this simple way performed half a dozen monotonous movements again and again; and sometimes his rewards were great.

So the central square looked different now. The Catholic Mission, discouraged by a sudden influx of Scottish Presbyterians, had sold their hall, which had been converted into a place where theatrical companies (including Johnnie's concert party) could give their shows, and such festivals as St Andrew's Day could be celebrated. A hotel had been built, very draughty but very showy, with plenty of balconies and a tower, and an attached eating house, decorated with stuffed animals. It was the proprietor of this hostelry who had given Johnnie and the Whistler their diamond pins. Money was flowing from hand to hand, and casual liking was the occasion of handsome gifts. A single mine had yielded sixty thousand pounds worth of gold in two months.

But this opulence was at once beautifully real, as precious metals alone can be, and an illusion. Some miners made a fortune in a few days, but some made nothing at all, and many made no more than the average industrial wage of the time; and the exceptionally lucky miner, the miner with run-of-the-mill luck and the failed miner alike found it difficult to obtain what makes life agreeable. The eating-house offered little food except huge slabs of ill-cooked beef or mutton, and a heavy kind of bread. There was a notable shortage of milk, butter, and vegetables, for the reason that workers of all sorts laid down their tools to go and work at the mines. This gold rush also meant that the miners deprived themselves of a number of other necessities, such as railways, which simply stopped being built and could not be manned if they were, so that many people reached or tried to reach the mines by carriages or carts and drays or on their own feet along unmade roads, which did not provide adequate shelter or food for man or beast, with the inevitable result that a great many of them never reached any destination but death or permanent invalidism.

It was impossible to see how this situation could have been avoided. It was inevitable that many Australians and many people who came from other continents subjected themselves to all sorts of hazards to find a substance which was only of use to exchange with commodities; and that the steps they had to take to find this substance destroyed the commodities they wanted to buy. But my mother was not too unhappy during her involvement in this curious crisis. If she could keep Johnnie more sober than he would have been if she had not been there, it counted as a victory. She was fond of Lizzie, she liked the Whistler. But of course the place was scaring. It was like nowhere else, she said, and when I pressed her as to how it had been scaring, since there were no bushrangers in the district, she answered, 'It was like Coleridge.'

She explained that at night, when she looked from her bedroom window in the hotel, she looked down on the stage where the drama of the place was performed, where a stream and its lode wound down to a gentle incline, the water and poachy earth strewn with cradles and pans so that they looked like part of a kitchen dropped by invading troops and here abandoned, perhaps because of attacks from soldiers in the spectre-coloured canvas tents which stood close-packed on the low hills all around, among the mutilated trees. These were simply the miners' temporary homes but they suggested an unimaginable army bivouacking the night before a battle for some incomprehensible cause. 'It was like *The Ancient Mariner*,' said my mother, 'or *Christabel*.' Certainly she was not unhappy: she was doing something that nobody could do in helping Lizzie with Johnnie, and she was in a strange and beautiful place, abounding lakes that were unflawed mirrors, reflecting shapely trees, and mountains coloured like the rainbow but more gravely.

But suddenly her condition changed. She was not frightened, indeed she would not have wished things any different, but she was certain that she was about to die, and quite soon. She lay still on her bed, and Lizzie and the other members of the company went in search of a nursing sister who was said to have stayed on in the town after the Catholic Missionary hall had been turned into a variety theatre, but nobody could find her, and they brought her instead an ex-convict who had been an orderly in a naval hospital and had managed to keep possession through a long and troubled life of an old-fashioned thermometer of great size. With the aid of this he pronounced that my mother was very ill indeed, and should be taken at once to a hospital a week's drive away.

My mother begged nobody to prepare such a troublesome expedition, for she was certain she would die on the journey, long before she reached its end. But presently Lizzie and the hypnotist-cum-conjuror of the company arrived and told her they were both expert drivers and were starting almost at once, and she felt the open air on her face, and a complaint from a horse that seemed to express clearly that he did not know what all this was about, and he did not believe anybody in the goddamn place. It seemed to her natural that the horse spoke English with an Australian accent.

She was tossed about as on the seas, often weeping from pain. She slept and woke in a strange room: she had certainly never seen before the coloured print of the Duke of Wellington receiving the mother of Napoleon, who was represented as having fallen on her knees before him, begging him to show mercy towards her son. She was listening to a conversation between a male and female voice as unfamiliar as the room, the female speaking slightly incorrect English, overloaded with two accents, one Australian and the other, she guessed from a recollection of a Swedish violinist in the orchestra of the Theatre

Royal, Edinburgh, some Scandinavian language. The man and the woman were complaining about something, or rather (for that sounds unhandsome) grieving over some misfortune, and Lizzie, her big, jolly voice dimmed with the hoarfrost of fatigue, was trying to convince them that whatever had gone wrong was of no importance at all.

My mother supposed that the strange people were inconvenienced by the presence in their house of a dying stranger, whom she recognized with detachment as herself. She was trying to suggest that they could put her anywhere; if they could put her back in the van she would probably be as well out in the yard as in a house, it could not make much difference, particularly as she fully realized she must die some time. But a few phrases revealed to her that she was not playing a determining part in whatever was happening. She was simply present at a tragedy of the type which was being enacted all over Australia at that time.

The man and the woman were Swedes who had left their country some years before to claim an inheritance left by an uncle, a prosperous timber merchant, and had bought a farm in a district where mixed farming was possible, with sheep as its mainstay. They had found it easy and profitable to run with the help of their son and his wife, and a few hired hands, and they had been entirely happy till gold was found in the district. Then their hired hands left them, and though a number of people had applied for the vacant jobs these were people who were on their way to the mines and had run out of money on their journey, and they left as soon as they had put by a few weeks' wages and could face another stage of their journey. What was peculiarly disrupting was the way that as the gold rush spread and drew more and more men from the industrial and commercial workers, this help was more and more unskilled. They would go back to the road by night, and it would be found in the morning that something dreadful had happened to the lucerne; and when employers grew cannier and took on hands for a trial job, the gold rush men had grown cannier too, and had taken a few lessons from agriculture workers who had left their farms, in the performance of the jobs they would be most likely to perform as a test of skill. Ultimately the fraudulence would be detected, but by that time the fraud would be on his way.

In the end the farmer's son and his wife could bear it no longer, and the old people woke up to find a note saying that they were going to try their luck at the mines and would be back with their fortunes made. But they had not heard from them since. They were left with one old man as their sole employee.

The old people were not thinking of their sorrows at that moment. All that was troubling them at the time was that they thought my mother would die if she did not have some fresh milk, and in a robbery a few days before some thieves had wounded the sole remaining old labourer, and taken with them all the cows except one that had been frightened and would let nobody come near her. The only reason that the farmer and his wife were lamenting was their conviction that my mother might die for lack of what they could have given on any night but this.

My mother, on the contrary, saw what had happened as something she would have easily been able to prevent if she was allowed. She realized that she could not stand, but it seemed to her reasonable to demand that she should be propped up and taken to the side of the disturbed cow, which she would certainly be able to milk. 'I can milk a cow,' she kept on repeating, and this was true. The children at Heriot Row had often spent their holidays on a farm and helped the women with their work, and my mother was excellent at dairy work. Utterly confident, she struggled to get out of bed, saying in the accents of one anxious to control a number of hysterics to common sense, 'I tell you I can quiet down most cows in no time, please make no more fuss, I realize I can't stand but if somebody will prop me up and take me to the poor creature, I will manage.' But hands kept on pressing her down, and she fell back into the darkness, and after many dreams woke in another room, with Lizzie beside her bed. My mother cried in anger, 'Pull yourself together, take me to that cow, it may be in real pain,' but Lizzie answered, wiping away her tears, 'Oh, you poor silly little bugger, that damned cow's twenty miles behind us.'

It turned out that while my mother was lying unconscious in the Swedes' house, a neighbour had visited them and told them that a religious teaching community a few miles distant had imported two nurses to deal with sickness among the gold seekers, and as these had just arrived and set up a ward they might be able to take in my mother; which happily turned out to be true, so that she was to live for many more years – during which she was, strangely enough, to repeat, not infrequently, Lizzie's remark, 'Oh, you poor silly little bugger, that damned cow's twenty miles behind us,' as a lesson in the proper attitude to misfortune. This she was able to do because she never knew the exact meaning of the word 'bugger', except that it was improper, but only, she thought, to the same degree as the word 'damned', and could therefore be whispered behind a forefinger pressed against the lips.

People with acute hearing sometimes looked surprised, but how right was my mother's regard for the remark. It is a perfect admonition to those who insist on nourishing ancient griefs; it takes away the malice of memory. The remark must have seemed for quite a long time a magic spell which routed the ill luck at that time dominating the life of herself and all the members of the Heriot Row household, which was perhaps the work of Uncle Alick, or his wife Mary Ironside. But I would be more sensible to ascribe my mother's temporary protection to some spell exercised by Lizzie, whose personality was made clear to me by the letters exchanged between my mother and my cousin Jessie Watson Campbell.

&ᴉ&

Jessie had a special affection for Johnnie, so my mother had felt it safe and desirable to tell her what she never told me, the full story of how he had found his way to the management of a Scottish variety company touring the gold mines. It appeared that he had found very easily a position in a Melbourne orchestra, and had even started giving lessons, but was put off his balance by an accident which had revived his great grief over the death of Joey. The General's son who had been his companion on the voyage from England benefitted not at all from the change of climate, and died suddenly of pneumonia. At that Johnnie had started drinking, and was one day dismissed from his post in the orchestra. Walking the streets that night he strayed into a bar, where he drank himself into a stupor, and presently picked up Lizzie and the Whistler, who were themselves perfectly sober, but were in the company of a rich young man who was even more intoxicated than Johnnie, and who had attached himself to them because he had heard them at a concert and kept telling them over and over again how much he had admired them.

Lizzie and the Whistler were embarrassed by this admiration; they were tired and wanted to go back to the hotel where they and the other more important members of the troupe were staying. When Johnnie also attached himself to them, they became seriously worried, but the rich young man told them that he had been lent the house of some relatives, which was completely empty, as they and their family and their servants had gone to their country house. Lizzie then said she must get her sleep and asked him to take them all there, so that they could lie down on whatever beds and sofas were easily available. He could trust their honesty, she said, for Johnnie was carrying a violin, and what criminal would embark on an evening's crime accompanied by such an identifiable object? But the rich young man said he was only in the bar because he found that he couldn't open the door of the house with the keys he had been given. The Whistler said that was all right: he could open the front and back doors and windows of any house that had ever been built; he'd learned it from the other boys at his school in Glasgow.

They then all went along to the house, got in without any difficulty, and each chose a bed, and slept soundly. In the morning over break-fast Lizzie asked Johnnie how he lived, and what allowance he got from his family at home; and on learning that he was no remittance man, she and the Whistler asked him to play to them. When they had heard him they told him that if he liked he could have the post of musical director and manager of the variety company to which she and the Whistler belonged. He had simply to walk half a mile or so to the home of the impresario who owned the company, and was also a ship's chandler, a minor horse-breeder and a land speculator, and the job would be his, if only because the impresario was a homesick Jew from Dalry in Edinburgh (then most markedly a Jewish quarter) and smart enough to recognize competence. Lizzie then ironed his suit and soon they were all three on their way to the impresario's office.

What was interesting in this exchange of letters between my mother and Jessie Watson Campbell was the success with which my virgin mother managed to communicate to her virgin cousin that Lizzie was a prostitute, and without making any reference to the existence or nature of prostitution; and her cousin, while preserving a similar reticence, managed to convey that she perfectly understood what was being communicated. What was also surprising was that my cousin managed to convey that if marrying this prostitute was the only way by which Johnnie could be prevented from going to the dogs, it was good news that he had done so. I was also surprised by my mother's comment on what had struck her as a disingenuous statement by Lizzie regarding her and her friends' slightly scandalous use of a stranger's house. She had found, she told my mother with a show of indignation, that though there were several servants in the house, they had left some parts of it quite filthy, notably the kitchen and scullery and larder; and to pay her debt to the owner of the house Lizzie represented herself as having given these tainted quarters a good clean and even specified the number of cakes of soap she had used. My mother had been delighted to note this artless assumption of innocence, for Lizzie's expression reminded her of the sanctimonious look on the faces of the pictures of Mary Magdalene which she and her mother had seen when they were in Italy. 'She looks too cheerful,' my grandmother had once said. 'Far too cheerful. Considering.'

My mother sometimes laughed at Lizzie, and her terrible misuse of her beautiful voice: 'She sings Bach, even Bach, and makes it sound like a barrel organ, and tells me not to bother, it would never catch on.' But how sweetly Lizzie made the effort, for she wholly misunderstood the object of the exercise; she thought my mother was seeking to provide her with something special for a Burns Night. And how sweet it was that it was she and not my mother who kept the slip of paper which that kind Mr Fairfield (who had sat with her while she clapped her hands at the sight of Tenerife, and who was so kind to her at the docks) had inscribed with the name of the hotel at which he was going to stay. My mother, disconcerted by the tartan bed van, had dropped the slip of paper on the floor, and Lizzie had picked it up and put it in her purse.

True love has not, so far as I know, been compared by the poets to the bulldog; but it has the same sort of grip. The reason why Lizzie put the slip of paper in her purse was because she had already seen that Johnnie, for some reason connected with the death of Joey, had fallen off the world into the half-world, where people were never ashamed to be drunk and therefore rubbed shoulders with the drunk and the ruined and the cruel. She would not for that reason leave Johnnie; but she knew it would be shocking to ask my mother to share his life. She had perceived that Mr Fairfield was a gentleman; he would be certain to take his son to a respectable hotel, and unless he was a widower, they would probably be joining a wife who would be a real lady like my mother. But probably the whole family would be gone by now, either to a house in the town, or to some other part of Australia. Even if that were so, the hotel would still be a good place for my mother to go when she was released from the hospital, given its respectability and its situation in a suburb of Melbourne said to be very pretty, named St Kilda.

PART THREE

THE FAIRFIELDS

ST KILDA

I can describe St Kilda as it was then, for I own a watercolour painting of it which several people have attempted to buy from me under the mistaken impression that it represented a coastal scene in the West of England by Edward Lear. The foreground shows a clear and delicately blue sea lying cupped in a bay with a narrow beach of rosy grey stones, from which, only a few yards from the fragile line of surf, scattered trees, sturdy and trim in foliage, rise from the close turf, and are assembled as a dense wood along the summit of a long low hill. In the middle distance there is a rosy cliff, surmounted by houses, extravagantly large, looking out to sea, and behind them a village spreading over a hill softly as smoke. From its centre rises a square church tower, giving the scene an English look. In the far distance the hills rise and mingle with the clouds.*

I hear that St Kilda is brick-bound today. Then it must have been heaven. My mother was to love it, and for a time she was glad that she had no friends there. She was content to be alone; she was almost happy, if it had not been for a feeling that she had mislaid her future, as people who lose their memories mislay their pasts. She was fascinated by the hotel itself, the premises.* Then its core was a one-storeyed house, said to be one of the oldest in Australia, containing several rooms, the largest of which was, by the time she saw it, the communal dining room; this was flanked by two blocks of two storeys high, not nearly so old, built to give protection from the heat, with verandahs and balconies at every point where they could be constructed, all encased in wire netting which supported flowering creepers that sometimes, because of the bright substance and fantastic forms of their blossoms, seemed to be strange beings looking out of the shade. She could be happy for hours in the garden, or walking about the adjacent roads, stopping every few minutes to look at the marvellous gardens, or going down to sit on the beach, where often there were children and their nurses in a curious faraway allusion to English middle-class life.

It made her smile to think that this lovely benevolent place should be called after those isles which shiver under the gales west of the Outer Hebrides, made by the harsh hand of a volcanic eruption. It was odd that that St Kilda and this St Kilda should exist in the same world. The light here was not just light, it had a bloom on it, tender as the bloom on a peach; and the bay was only half water, it was half light as well, and related to the diamond. If the heat was too much for her, she could go back to the hotel, and either lie on her bed and read some of the good novels which Australia was already producing (she was a great admirer of Marcus Clarke's For the Term of his Natural Life*); or she could play the upright Broadwood in the recreation room, which she could do without fear of disturbing the other guests, for nearly all of them went up to Melbourne to work, most of them, oddly enough, for societies which bore names that suggested a charitable purpose, but seemed to have no connection with each other.

That was indeed characteristic of this hotel, which had its mystery. The rooms and the corridors were spacious, but they were sparsely furnished, and seemed swept clean by some arcane preoccupation, in the manner of religious institutions. But there were no obvious links with any form of belief. The proprietors, Mr and Mrs Mullins, who were a middle-aged couple, sometimes asked her if she would mind sitting at table next to some guest who had just arrived in Melbourne and might be feeling lonely away from home, but seemed to be making the request as a form of patronage, as if to give her some sort of status. This might or might not be a sign of some institutional affiliation which obliged them to make it clear that all their guests were respectable.

She was wondering which it was, with not very urgent curiosity, while she sat at the piano after she had been playing Schumann, when Mr Mullins came in and gave her a copy of a Melbourne newspaper, saying he thought it might have an interest for her, as it contained an article by somebody he thought she knew. It was on such a serious subject that it might not interest a young lady, he said, but he had a feeling that she and he had been seeing so much of each other, coming from the Old Country, that she might like to see it.

The appearance of Charles Fairfield's name on that article was no surprise to my mother, because she had thought he was going to draw cartoons for the paper.* He was evidently very clever. She wondered if he would answer the letter Lizzie had sent him. She hoped so. She thanked the proprietor, who went on to say that Mr Fairfield had been a very pleasant guest when he had briefly stayed at the hotel; and my mother asked whether his son had been with him. Mr Mullins answered, 'But he has no son.' It was a peculiarity of the proprietor and his wife that they talked as if speech was something not to be indulged in as a mere gratification of human volubility. A dose of so many words might be uttered, and not exceeded.

'Oh,' said my mother, 'he was with a boy on the boat, and he treated him as if they were father and son.'

'So he does,' said Mr Mullins, 'but that is only from the kindness of his heart, which is why we are glad to know him.' He went on to ask my mother if she had noticed a house, almost as old and out of fashion as his own hotel, a couple of hundred yards along the street. It might have caught her eye, he thought, because its verandah was smothered by a huge creeper bearing large crimson flowers; and indeed my mother had often stood still to admire it. The flowers were always dark as if they were in the shade, even though the sun was full on them. The house, Mr Mullins stated, still giving only the bare bones of the thing as it had been lived, was owned by a man named Foster, son of the man who had built it, a naval officer remembered for the part he had taken in Australian exploration in the 1820s. The family was now rich, having land in the centre of Melbourne, and having been lucky in ownership of a coal mine, and the present owner had sent all his three sons and three daughters to England to be educated.

One of the girls – 'the most . . .', the proprietor's wife, who had just come into the room, began to explain, but it was not bare enough to meet her spiritual demands – she found 'beautiful' or 'pretty' too lush. Her husband solved the problem that pretends to praise but becomes denigrating as it is uttered. 'Comely,' he said. (What woman on earth could want to be called that? my mother wondered.) Well, the most comely of the three girls had suddenly telegraphed that she had met in London the son of an American, known to her father by reason of his not very impressive involvement in the precious metals business in his own country and in Australia. The two young people had fallen in love, and the telegram was to announce their engagement, and more than that, their almost immediate marriage. The rage in the St Kilda household was extreme. 'It was not only that it was from a worldly point of view not a good marriage,' said Mr Mullins, 'it was that nobody actually put in black and white that they were sorry for marrying into St Kilda's royal family without permission.' His wife added in a flaying tone of forgiveness, 'But some people cannot help being hasty.'

'Oh, the unhappiness that followed,' the proprietor continued. 'I have often thought that a devil must have installed himself in that house. I have passed it a hundred times and looked up at that creeper and wondered if it were not commanded by the Lord to flourish and mark for all eyes that a devil was enthroned within that house.'

My mother asked, 'What, do you believe in devils?' Mr Mullins demanded, 'Why, do you not?' and my mother, anxious not to prolong an argument that could not be settled, answered 'Yes and no.'

Mr Mullins nodded as if she had wholly agreed with him, and went on, 'It must be remarked that he had nothing against the young couple or their parents, against whom also there was really nothing except that the father had been unwise to be so exclusively interested in silver, which is not as stable as one might wish. All silver is quick silver, as I used to hear them say in the market places which I have now abandoned. But had his daughter and her husband taken to evil living, our neighbour could not have cut them off with a sharper knife than the hatred he felt for them and endlessly, slanderously expressed.'

Mrs Mullins said to my mother, 'His poor wife was endlessly complaining of her husband's stiff-necked refusal to forgive. She would come in even on my baking days.'

'Do you know,' said Mr Mullins, 'that our neighbour was so stiff-necked that when a cable came telling him that the Lord God had approved his daughter's marriage by causing her to give birth to a son, he would not tell them he was glad? Of course he was subject to great temptation, for his other children had married and been fruitful, and having been given that assurance of divine favour he was able to disregard the Lord's sign of pleasure displayed in the birth of this son. So he kept silent. But all was not well.'

'Mind you,' said Mrs Mullins to my mother, 'I have to say I think it was a bit hard.'

'About a year ago,' her husband continued, 'our neighbour got a letter from a stranger, from this Mr Charles Fairfield. He said he had been manager of a silver mine not far from the town of Pueblo, Colorado, in which town this girl and her husband had gone to live some years before. They had been his closest friends, and he now regretted to have to tell them that both husband and wife had been killed in a stagecoach accident on a mountain road. He was careful to say they had suffered no pain. But the husband's father had died, and left not much money. I was not surprised, he had made some mistakes that nobody can afford to make if one has gone into silver.'

'Not now, James,' said his wife. 'Not now.'

'No, indeed, my dear. Only I get carried away. What that man had lost, and no need for it. Well, there was really no relative who could take the couple's child over: so, Mr Fairfield, who had intended to go home to the Old Country to attend to some business and then to come here, to Melbourne, offered to bring the child to his grandparents. Who have never renounced the Gospel. Who therefore had no alternative but to say that he and his wife had a place ready for the boy at their hearth.'

'He would rather have stayed with Mr Fairfield,' said his wife.

'But his place was with his own blood,' Mr Mullins told her very gently, in a most interesting way. 'You have often heard it explained why this should be so,' he chided her, and with a marked increase in hostility, 'in places where they spoke with authority.'

The proprietor's wife bowed her head in acceptance of the rebuke, or near-rebuke, or ritual rebuke, whatever it was, and changed the subject. 'It does us all good to see Mr Fairfield,' she said. 'Why do we not go and see him some day? Miss Mackenzie would like to see him again. And he lives in a very nice place. He is working for the newspaper now, and spends half the week in Melbourne, but the rest of the time he spends at a country hotel, about seven miles away, on a river, we know the people who keep it. A Mr and Mrs O'Brien. They like him very much. Indeed Mr O'Brien is very glad to have him there. His wife is troubled, gravely troubled. She has been much better since they have had Mr Fairfield with them.'

'We will go over to them for supper,' said Mr Mullins, benevolently, as if he were not proposing to enjoy the hospitality of the O'Briens, but offering to be their generous hosts. 'It will cheer you up, Miss Mackenzie. It is a blessed place, particularly towards the end of the day. One can sit there and watch the evening come down on the distant mountains and the forests and the pastures and the waters, and it is as if God's way of working wonders was shown before our eyes.'

'I always think morning is the reminder to us of the Creation,' said Mrs Mullins, and her husband said, 'Yes, my dear, indeed any time of the day, if it comes to that. I often think there is something about the moon. Ah, well!'

My mother often wondered what sect it was that had left its mark so deeply printed on the Mullins' conversation. They reminded her of a Scottish expression, 'borrowed light': which signifies the light in an inner passage or room, which shines through a window in one of its walls from a room or passage that has the benefit of access to daylight or artificial light. She saw the proprietor and his wife as having been exposed at some time to moving rituals and penitential sermons, and the repetition in full faith of creeds not credible, and understanding nothing of the proceedings except the hieratical position of the persons who performed the rites. It was not that they were cynical infidels, it was that they had simply missed the point of all religious institutions, as worshippers are usually conscious of it. The one and only part of it that they had understood was the authority of the clergy, which they had assumed as if they had been truly elected Bishop and Abbess. As both of them were naturally kind and self-denying no harm was done, but the effect was often grotesque, as it had been, indeed, in the conversation I have just reproduced, when the couple had made the day and the night a huge award of good-conduct medals to be pinned on the bosom of God Almighty. But they were not absurd or presumptuous when they saw to the well-being of such of their boarders who seemed of late not to have had what they needed, even when their conception of the unsatisfied need was at fault, as it was when later that evening they served my mother with a pound of underdone beefsteak, and shook their heads when she could not finish it.

The next few days, as it happened, were so busy that my mother had less time to be sad. Mrs Mullins had bought some dozens of new hand-towels, which my mother volunteered to embroider with the name of the hotel in scarlet cross-stitch. Like many women pianists of that time, she had special soft finger-guards to protect her fingers when she sewed. But she had to lay this task aside because Mr and Mrs Mullins had arranged that they should drive on the following day to the O'Briens' hotel, where Charles Fairfield was staying; and she had some trouble with Mrs Mullins over the preparations she should make for this visit. My mother had adopted the fashion of wearing her hair short while she was working for the Heinemanns, and she looked indeed as Manet or Renoir liked their young women: but when Mrs Mullins suggested that she should go to a hairdresser, it appeared that she hoped my mother would buy a switch. 'Didn't you,' she asked in amazement, when my mother declined, 'have it cut off in hospital when you had fever?' No, she had had a beautiful haircut from Lizzie, who had started life as a hairdresser in Melbourne. Mrs Mullins looked puzzled over that and also over the dress my mother produced for the occasion. It was very simple. 'The truth is I've never seen a dress quite like it,' she said, and without doubt this was true, for the Heinemanns had given it to her, and it was made by Worth. She read in Mrs Mullins' expression deep sorrow that an unmarried woman should have been brought up among people who had no idea of fashion, and liked her still more.

AN AUSTRALIAN
EXPEDITION

They started on the expedition in a hooded waggon and followed roads deep in fine dust, through air cooled by sea breezes. (I cannot give the name of where they went, for I never heard it.) The landscape spread out all round them, the ground colourless and brilliant, looking much the same where it was bare and where it was grassy, because of the glaze painted on by the sun. On the shimmering distances there grew trees quite unperturbed by the heat, then dark, dense foliage, looking heavy as if it were soaked with rain. The woodlands on the summits of the downs were shade itself. On the high horizon the strong light burned mountains to the transparency of clouds and the meridian skies to sheer light. On the right of the road more lagoons and then the open sea, in streaks of blue and silver, here and there divided by black lines.

The waggon turned away from the sea and was in a village, as it might be in the North of England or the Scottish border, with a church in it, and a chapel, and houses like old houses but with an amateurish look, and gardens spilling over with flowers and shrubs, and children playing, blonde sunburned children, and hay barns with sleek cattle and horses; and then the road took another turn and they were back in the Antipodes, and jogged along a road that cut across a swamp where dried and crepitant reeds grew out of a soup of mud, and my mother heard strange bird-calls.

Then there was a line of trees, and as they drew nearer they found the road ran beside a river which flowed wide and black: black but bright as ice, transparent as nothing could be that was not clear, and so very bright that it hurt the eyes to look at it. The Mullins said that this was due to a bed of minerals through which the river had to find its way near its source in some hills nearby: but it had an artificial air, partly because large stick-shaped white flowers lay in patches here and there on the black water, and there were sometimes families of black swans opening orange beaks in perpetual argument. Then the river broadened, and piers ran out into it, and moored boats slept full length in the water. On the landward side the by-road offered access to a low hill, perhaps an artificial mound with a flat top, on which was built a replica of an old English inn, actually a famous Thameside house, I think on the opposite side of the river from Greenwich, but roughly and rawly built.* The hill below it was covered with a garden planted with flowering shrubs, growing here in the open and rowdily healthy on it, though in Great Britain they were only to be seen under the lovely glass domes where gardeners moved with the solemnity of vergers, knowing they were about special business. Through these splendid flower-beds, impudent in their own natural home, there wound zigzags of steep pathways and flights of steps, with here and there crudely carpentered garden seats painted a wild colour.

My mother's description of the place has left me with an odd composite picture hanging on the wall of my mind: a high and narrow picture, divided into three parts. The lowest third was in the style of a Japanese silk painting: it made plain the differences between the river's blackness, which was hard as a black diamond's, and the enigmatic blackness of the swans' plumage, which gleamed under the strong light; the slight but delicious difference between the swans' orange beaks and the orange of the wild flowers growing at the water's edge; and the peculiar impression given by the sombreness of the foliage of the trees, which suggested that they were thick with moisture they had secreted everywhere, even to the veins in their massed leaves, in case this continent should betray them and leave them thirsty, tortured, dead. The second part of the picture should be the garden, with its realization of the wildest hopes ever raised by the cover of a seedsman's catalogue, and its shout that a feast is far, far better than enough; and the third was this curious reproduction of the Thameside inn on the hill's summit, which suggested an admiring attempt by someone who could not draw at all to copy the apparent simplicity of a Rowlandson drawing.

The stables were on the road. Mr Mullins stayed with the driver to help care for the horses, and Mrs Mullins and my mother opened a swing gate into the garden, and began to climb one of the zigzag paths. Soon my mother paused by a shrub which threw up a green fountain of branches on which there balanced smiling heads of innocent multi-coloured dragons set on long sinuous necks, and asked Mrs Mullins if she knew its name. There was a long silence, after which Mrs Mullins opened her parasol (which was pure white and looked like some kind of church furniture) and answered, 'No. No. I cannot say I ever heard it called by any special name.' She continued to mount the path, with just a trace of embarrassment: 'I think perhaps we are coming to an age when, if one must speak of our dear growing things, we are content with all the beautiful texts in the Gospel that speak of the flowers of the field.' After that she strolled on with a more confident manner, found another seat, settled herself down again, indicating that she wished my mother to stay by her side instead of wandering off among the flowers, and took a pastille out of her reticule and put it in her mouth, saying, 'Repeating is my cross. I am grateful it is nothing worse.'

A silence fell. My mother listened to a noise like a ticking clock, coming from deep among the rich branch and blossom of the shrubs. 'Is it a bird-call or some insect?' she wondered. 'I am on the other side of the world, everything is different. I do not know the names of the flowers or anything about the small things of nature. It is all, all different. I wonder if my life will change.'

Mrs Mullins spoke through her pastille, scanning the view below. 'They have a very nice property here. They own all the land to that bend in the river. Where there is a little hill with thin trees on it. But possessions are not everything.' She stated this as a fact. She was not implying, as many people would have been had they used the same words, that the O'Briens were putting the possession of land and money before more spiritual and intellectual riches.

'I wouldn't think,' my mother said, 'that any of your friends would attach much to money or property. I have seen something of the world. I have met people who seem charming, oh, utterly delightful, and in the end money and property turned out to be what they cared for most. But I have watched you and your husband, and see that – and it is only natural – you want your hotel to be a success. But I have seen also that you both want all of your guests to be happy. It is delightful to see how much you wish them to be that.'

'Oh, it is only natural,' said Mrs Mullins, 'for the saved to give help to the saved.' She shut her eyes, turned her face upwards to the sun, nodded approval and said, 'It grows a little cooler.' She went on to say, 'But the O'Briens are in a difficult position. I do not think they will ever be able to extend their property past that little hill. The one with the three trees growing on it. The wives of the owner's sons are quick breeders. Of course the O'Briens will succeed to our position in our Church when we die. But they are not much behind us in age. I doubt that they will live long to enjoy the privilege, though it is a matter of indifference to my husband how soon we are called.'

My mother had never before asked the name of the Church of which the Mullins were members but now she put the question. She was told it was the Church of the Special Connection between God and Man.

Looking down the slope, she saw Mr Mullins' hat bobbing along between a gap in the flowers, and suggested that Mrs Mullins should go into the house, which would be cooler, and that she should wait for him, but the offer was received with kind amusement. 'No, no, that is out of the question. Dear child. It is the custom that the leader of the congregation and his wife always make the entrance to any gathering of the faithful together. It is a custom designed to make it clear that I can act as my husband's deputy in case of need. Occasions which mercifully are rare.'

They sat in contented silence. The light was liquefying, and as my mother looked down the steep garden, with its layer upon layer of flowers and leaves as bright as if they were made of paper that had just been coloured with paint that had not had time to dry, she said, laughing, 'Oh, Mrs Mullins, look at your husband's hat!' It was all that could be seen of him as he made his way up along the steep zigzag paths, sometimes moving to the right and sometimes to the left, sometimes taller than the flowers, at other times showing nothing but the bobbing crown and brim of his Quakerish hat.

Mrs Mullins stood up. 'Miss Mackenzie, please go down to my husband and tell him not to walk so fast. He is keeping up a ridiculous pace for a man of his age.' My mother called to him, to get the business done more quickly. But Mrs Mullins had another idea and said, 'No, go to him, calling to him does no good. If you would not mind.' She was still standing when my mother brought her husband back to her, and said in a low tone, 'Never call to my husband. It is not that he is deaf, but he is not very good at hearing. He has, as yet, no defects.'

'And now, John, come and let me tidy you up before we meet the flock.' She passed a handkerchief over his face, which was indeed beaded with sweat, and brought into clearer view a lock, whiter than the rest of his hair, which lay across the forehead, a slight rearrangement which gave him a more spiritual look, and corrected the fold across the back of his coat which had ridden up as he sat in the waggon. Then she said, 'Now let us keep our friends waiting no longer,' and started on the last two or three zigzags that brought us to the house, from which there was coming quite a remarkable amount of noise, in the way of laughter and raised voices with a background of music of an unfamiliar kind – something that squeaked, but had heard of better things. Mrs Mullins put her arm in her husband's, and walked slowly through the open doors, and my mother, following some paces behind, noticed that the moment they crossed the threshold the noise escaping into the garden entirely changed its character.

Certainly Mr and Mrs Mullins had presence. They were not simple-minded people who had grasped the idea of presence and were making a continuous but unsuccessful effort to personify it. The door had led into a bar where some men were sitting drinking beer and eating sandwiches: they paused with their glasses in mid-air, with curious effect, for the door was still open and the rays from the sinking sun were reflected by their glasses, so that it looked as if they were holding huge diamonds, sized as if from Ali Baba's cave. One called out, 'O'Brien, your company's come,' and there appeared, on a level with the bar counter, what seemed to be a bodiless head. It was a head which promised delight to my mother. Among Antipodean pleasure she ranked high her encounters with people who looked Scottish, Scottish as a Fifeshire fishing village, and proceeded to open their mouths and address in a language used by nobody but the less prosperous characters in Charles Dickens novels. (I have noted before that nineteenth-century Australian was not Cockney imported, bequeathed by early involuntary and voluntary immigrants, but something manufactured by the imagination after they got there. I do not apologize for mentioning this again, because it seems an interesting characteristic of human activity. Something made the people landing in the Antipodes alter their way of speech thereafter. Now why? And how did they become united in their determination to carry out this linguistic fantasy? The rapidity with which this new *lingua franca* spread through the country makes the process more bewildering.)

While the beer drinkers chaffed Mr O'Brien in incomprehensible language, a door in the corner of the bar opened, and disclosed a number of people standing on its threshold, male and female, young and old, ten to twenty of them, dressed in what were obviously their 'best' clothes, smiling and crying out in welcome.

But Mr Mullins, who was standing arm-in-arm with his wife, commanded silence with a slow wave of his free hand, saying, 'Just a moment, my friends,' and waited – and there was silence. The beer drinkers stood up and put down their glasses, whose light went out, and then he pronounced the words, 'Peace be with us and all the saved,' in a slightly different voice, from which he had, surely consciously, removed all trace of spontaneity. He might have used the phrase again and again, until it had no meaning for him. But there was another impression which must have been very difficult to create. What made him dumb in the meaning of the words he spoke, which plainly must have been of great significance to the people, or they would not have been there to hear them? The answer was that he was not dumb so much as numb. He had borne a thousand responsibilities, of all the highest kind, in the past, and he would have to bear a thousand more before he died, and all for the sake of his congregation. Such was the dedication that, though he would not have looked out of place behind a grocer's counter, it was possible to imagine him as a bishop, a cardinal, even as a Pope.

After the blessing had been given and acknowledged with hearty cries, almost cheers, of 'Amen', and Mr and Mrs Mullins had unhooked their arms, with a peculiar leisured grace, as if they were now about to rise from the ground and float in the air, the gathering changed into an ordinary, quite secular party. A nice party, full of the kind of goodwill that my mother found was such an agreeable feature of Australia. The air was blown about with laughter, caused not by anything that could be judged funny, but by a conviction that as likely as not what was happening would turn out to be funny in the long run.

In the midst of a gust of this abstract laughter, some trick of acoustics made my mother able to overhear a dialogue between the Mullinses, who were standing a little distance from her. 'Our little girl,' Mrs Mullins was saying, 'is looking very white and tired.' 'So she is, bless her,' said Mr Mullins, 'and I hope your feet are not hurting.' 'They are agony,' replied Mrs Mullins. 'Oh, my poor dear,' said Mr Mullins, and my mother saw out of the tail of her eye that he squeezed his wife's hand. And soon Mrs Mullins was by my mother's side, accompanied by Mrs O'Brien, who was another example of a pure Hibernian type speaking with a Dickensian accent. 'We are to be shown what our wonderful hosts have been doing with this marvellous place.'

Shortly afterwards it was revealed that the Rowlandson inn in which they were standing wore the usual hotel accommodations down its back like a pigtail. One opened a door in the bar, which was in the wall opposite to the door by which one had come in from the burning slope bright with tropical plants, and looked down the corresponding but cool side of the mound, and over this were scattered a number of buildings resembling those built by the first colonists in Australia: wooden bungalows with sloping roofs, set on verandahs, raised above the ground. They were of different sizes: the bigger ones included a dining room and a kitchen and a billiard room, and the smaller ones housed the bedrooms. They sprawled down the hillside in a double string, all brown, differing in shade according to their age and the way the different woods used had weathered. Most were the colour of spices. Beyond and below, the country was spread out like a map, but of a miraculous nature. My mother was looking at the country through which she and the Mullinses had just travelled from St Kilda, but that seemed impossible. Surely the highest range of mountains had lain further to the north, and surely there had been more villages and large farms scattered over the plain; and what river was it that she had not seen, though it looked even broader than any of those she had crossed? But Australia was the place of changing landscape. She had been told that often, and told too that it was no illusion; it was a fact due to the peculiarities of the continent's geology, and she believed it.

It was the other side of the world, where one could break off what was happening to one and start afresh.

She was sitting on the verandah outside the kitchen, having been excused from the company of Mrs Mullins and Mrs O'Brien on an inspection of (among other matters) a new type of cooking stove which had just been installed, the same which, they had been assured, was used at the British Embassy in Melbourne. Mrs Mullins had said to Mrs O'Brien, 'Forgive me, but I do not wish, I really do not wish Miss Mackenzie to accompany us. She has been *gravely* ill.'

She said it splendidly. It was in better taste, somehow, than saying she had nearly died, and it saved time, for it would have been hardly proper if she had mentioned my mother's narrow escape from death without a certain amount of pious comment on the insecurity of human life. 'It would be advisable, dear Mrs O'Brien, if she sat on the verandah till our return.' But the tour of inspection was now over. Mrs Mullins loomed over her, and said, 'Isabella, that kitchen is like a palace. Like a *palace*. There cannot be a better one – oh, don't mention Government House in Melbourne – there cannot be a kitchen better fitted – or as spotless – *spotless* – in Buckingham Palace.'

Mrs O'Brien dropped a curtsey, half as a joke, but also with some real reverence. She told them that she proposed they should see more of her and her husband's establishment. 'I have more to show you. I have two empty beds ready for you, and you can both lie down and sleep till the rest of the guests come and we have refreshment till supper is served at six.'

Mrs Mullins and my mother uttered sincere thanks. One of the few faults my mother saw in Australia was that the population was apt to show bewilderment if anybody said they were tired. 'And there's plenty of cold water in the ewers, fresh pumped. It is a mercy we have so much water on the plot. But we have a lot of heat too. And I'm Irish! We'd rather have wet weather than this heat. I can't bear it. All that sweat!'

'Yes,' said Mrs Mullins, 'perspiration is a most disagreeable function.'

'And don't your feet hurt horribly?'

'Well, no,' said Mrs Mullins. 'I think I am saved that inconvenience because I have a narrow foot. I think it helps. All my family have narrow feet.' As her skirts swept the ground, she could make that statement with impunity.

'But before we go to beddy-bies,' Mrs O'Brien said, 'you must see the new bar, but it's more like what they have in the Grand at Melbourne than a bar, it's where the boys can have a snorter and play pool or have a game of cards. Though there's not much gambling done here, and I don't think, I really don't think, that we've got a bad name over the drinking on the premises.'

'Oh, no,' said Mrs Mullins, 'no, no, indeed. I am sure of that. Never have I heard anyone say one word about any such impropriety. In fact, some people have actually asked me if you served any drinks at all.'

Mrs O'Brien was for a moment silent, as if her conscience had pricked her, but decided not to confess to this good and worldly woman. 'Let me,' she said, as one who says farewell to an awkward subject. 'You said,' Mrs Mullins said, kindly (making amends, my mother thought), 'but may I see the improvements of the laundry you spoke of?'

'It'll be a pleasure,' said Mrs O'Brien, 'but first let's go to the lounge I've been talking about, with all a mother's foolish pride, I fear, since it was my son who did the decorations. And we'll find a nest there for Miss Mackenzie to settle herself till we are back! Sam did it, you know him, my son Sam, he's the stout one.'

Mrs Mullins and Mrs O'Brien and my mother went to another bungalow where screens had been put round the verandah, because the evening sun was edging round to this quarter, so it was pitch dark. The inner room was also dark, but Mrs Mullins put her head in and looked round at the wholly obscure walls and furniture and said, 'Princely, princely,' and then turned about, eager, it may be supposed, to take her rest. My mother felt that the laundry was not going to receive its accolade, and would have liked to see the technical finesse with which that inspection would be forgotten, and was looking round for a chair at the end of the verandah that was still in shade, when she perceived that in one of the chairs there was sitting a most beautiful girl, of a type she had not seen since she left England. I say 'England' because the type was then unknown in Scotland: there girls with red-gold hair were called 'Carrots' and abandoned hope.

The beauty of this girl was only just visible in the shadows. Through a break in the screens a ray of light had entered to discover her pale red-gold hair, her delicately blue closed eyelids, her high and fine cheekbones, fine as the bones in a small bird's wings, and the lovely curved melancholy of her mouth, that hallmark of Pre-Raphaelitism, which suggested that she realized how necessary it was for those about her to take some action regarding an element in their lives, but it was by now too late for the matter to be even named. The sunlight travelled from her hair down to the little diamond brooch pinned on her breast, and her silver shoe-buckles.

Mrs O'Brien said to my mother, 'Why, it's my daughter-in-law! It's Sam's wife. I won't wake her up. She's been very poorly till the last few weeks. Well, we'll go on our way, and you can introduce yourself when she wakes up.' My mother watched them go and made a bet with herself how many minutes it would take Mrs Mullins to dodge the laundry and approach the white sheets, and wondered at the girl's extreme beauty and the meaning that seemed to lie behind it, though it gave no indications of intelligence, or any feeling but melancholy, and indeed hardly of life. The breath that shook the narrow and dark dress flickered like the flame of a taper, and no more.

Presently, my mother heard the noise of some men entering the inner room. The lights were switched on: there was the noisy male fuss of ordering drinks, and of settling down at tables and saying 'Here's' to something or other. Then there were some moments of quietness, which were broken by an English voice saying, 'But this is the most fascinating story! Is it really true? Or are you trying to make a fool of me, because I've come from England?'

There was laughter over that. Then an Australian voice swore he had told the truth and that he had – and he had mates who would swear to it – gone to deliver a load of agricultural machinery imported from Great Britain to a remote farm in the outback, and the drivers had lost their way. They found themselves in some land that had been farmed; there were plenty of indications of that, even to ruined buildings, and many hedges run wild; and indeed when they enquired later they were told that a wholly unexpected flood, bursting from a faraway mountain, had made its way to the sea. They had pulled their waggons to a flat patch near a stream for a rest before they turned back, when they heard a strange noise, which grew louder. 'It was light and heavy, if you understand me,' the story-teller said, and his listeners assured him that they did, but the English voice said, 'I think I do.'

Then they saw a line of what they thought were ponies coming across the fields at a great rate, taking the hedges as smooth as silk, obviously a hunt of a sort, but it wasn't an ordinary hunt. The proportions, the anatomy, of what was clearing the hedges and stockades were eerily wrong. The noise got louder and louder, the mysterious animals came nearer and nearer and turned into a hunt consisting of kangaroos, which rode straight at them, neatly divided to leave them untouched, and then closed again. They were going so fast there was a sort of funnel of air they were riding inside. 'Oh,' cried the teller of the story, 'it was a ryce, it was a ryce! And I tell you there were the riders and the horses going as if they were at Flemington,* they knew as much as any jockey.'

One of his listeners asked if he'd seen the weighing-in and what a kangaroo bookie looked like, but the English voice broke in again. 'Oh, what one wouldn't give to be both horse and rider! And at a tremendous speed, you say? You couldn't guess what speed? Oh, marvellous.' It was the voice of Charles Fairfield. My mother felt extreme pleasure at the joy he felt at the idea of rushing through the air on one's own power, not helped by the winds and the air, like a flying bird, but evoking the energy simply from one's own body, one's own energy. She thought, 'Why, when we looked at Tenerife in that storm, he made me feel as if we were its equals.' She went on sitting by the sleeping girl, listening to Charles Fairfield when he was speaking, and listening to no one else.

CHARLES FAIRFIELD

Two or three afternoons later, when my mother had gone to rest in her room at the St Kilda hotel, a servant knocked on the door and told her that Mr Fairfield had called on Mrs Mullins, and Mrs Mullins would be happy if she would come down and drink a cup of tea with them. Until my mother had fully awakened she thought she had been told that there had been a mistake about Joey, and Mr Fairfield had come to tell her her brother was not dead. When the delusion passed she got up and combed her hair, noticing that a wind was blowing inland strong from the sea, and the hundreds of small white bell-shaped flowers on the creeper which covered her balcony were shaking as if they were ringing out a peal, and the long green leaves of the palm trees beyond were whipping the upper air. She went down the corridors which were quite silent; it was too early for the guests to have come back from their employment in Melbourne, and the emptiness gave the place the appearance, my mother thought, of an unusually unsuccessful but rigorously clean hospital. But she loved the place. What kindness she had received there!

She went down the sherry-coloured wooden staircase, its hand-rail and bannisters thick, as if this were an earthquake country, down the hall with the desk and the register and the bundles of big numbered room keys, and into Mrs Mullins' private drawing room, which was based on a photograph of the boudoir of a minor European royalty as reproduced in a woman's paper sent out from England. There were a few ample upholstered armchairs, and a great deal of spindle-legged small pieces of furniture, including some silver-tables, which were much more interesting, my mother thought, than the European equivalent. Looking into the silver-tables of the grand houses in

Charlotte Square she had seen her fill of snuff-boxes and housewives and *châtelaines*, but here, in Mrs Mullins' drawing room, one might stumble on a medal given to a convict who had rescued a fellow convict at the risk of his own life when a bridge had been broken by floods, or an enamel portrait of six or seven aborigines with their dark, blunt, doomed and permanently astonished faces, standing on each side of a smug-looking missionary man. Mr Fairfield had found the novelty of Antipodean silver-tables for himself, and was at that moment looking into a silver-table and saying, 'And what is the meaning of this tribal badge?'

Mrs Mullins also was occupied with the meaning of a tribal badge. It was then (in the early 1880s) the custom for gentlemen when calling on ladies to take their hats with them into the drawing room and put them down as nearly as possible to their chair-legs. My mother had sometimes seen the rite performed in Edinburgh (always in the New Town, and by Episcopalians), and she had become familiar with it when she was living with the Heinemanns; but it was obviously a novelty to Mrs Mullins. While she enlightened Mr Fairfield's ignorance of Australian aboriginal culture, her eyes kept returning to his hat, so mysteriously on her carpet. Hats are for heads, or the hooks on umbrella stands, not for carpets: and there is an abstract principle of the fitness of things, which till now she had been certain would never be disregarded by Mr Fairfield. Presently she made her excuses, spoke of a necessity to give instructions for a children's picnic to be held by the Melbourne 'God's Temple' (a name which the sect to which she and Mr Mullins belonged gave to all its churches) and left the room, to return at once with a less troubled expression and an apology for needing to absent herself for another quarter of an hour.

Mr Fairfield began, for no reason, to tell my mother how he and his brothers used to go as children to a place called Churchill on the west coast of County Kerry, a tiny village set on a wide half-moon of sound, on which the Atlantic beat down, like Liszt playing one of his compositions on a piano made to his own measure, and that measure expanded to the right geographical greatness. Their mother had a cousin who was a priest of the Irish Established Church, which is to say the Episcopal Protestant Church, and he lived in a wonderful house not two hundred yards off the gigantic surf, and defended from it by age-old trenches and banks. The wonder of the house was that it was small as a farmhouse, but had the nobility of a palace. They were not allowed to bathe unless they wore harnesses of rope which were secured to a wheel set deep into the ground, and the cowman and the driver of the haunting-car standing beside it, wearing long garments like nightdresses, out of Roman Catholic modesty: and usually one of the family was with them, indeed, large samples of the cousinage. 'Several Chutes, lots of Crosbies and Cosleys and Wellesleys. We are all cousins down in that part of Ireland.'

'Like our clans. But the net is wider with us. Only the English try to live alone,' my mother said. The men and the women she had met with when she was working for the Heinemanns were not part of their people as the Scots were. That took her back to Scotland. She found herself telling Mr Fairfield about the grudging hand with which colour was doled out in the North, beyond the Border, getting meaner as one went north and west, where one could stand and look over a black moor to a range of grey mountains, with one sheer cliff catching the light and shining white and bare. Edinburgh, too, was one grey set against another. But if one returned to the moor in late summer, the heather at one's feet was the colour of red wine in a decanter that caught the light, and the grey mountains gave up a reserve of different shades of blue that it had stored in its slopes. And if one paused in passage up the steeps of the New Town, and looked down on the northward Firth of Forth, there was no knowing what colour that twisted bar of water might not be, from blue, blue like the Australian seas, to black as steel, or white as milk. Lovely things were scattered over Scotland, and oh, the lovely things to eat. She and Jessie and Johnnie and Joey had spent a summer holiday somewhere in Perthshire, and there was a chalk pit nearby where there were thickets of wild white raspberries, sweeter than any berry that came out of a garden.

'What we loved,' said Charles Fairfield, 'was fish out of the stream. My father was a great man for that, but not so good as some of the poachers in the village.' He laughed happily. 'And we ate with them too!'

Tea was brought in by an old man called Jobson who worked about the hotel, sometimes as a boots and sometimes as a waiter, reputed to have arrived in Australia as a convict long ago. He hung about after he had set out the cups and plates, and said, smiling in goodwill at

Mr Fairfield, indicating an invisible presence, 'She's been out to see me. About the way you put your hat and gloves on the floor. I told her you were all right. I'd seen swells do that in some good houses. The ones built on mud.'

When he had gone and my mother and Charles Fairfield had smiled at each other, he said, 'Did you know what he meant by houses built on mud? I suppose most people have forgotten by now. You didn't understand it? Well, Belgravia and Pimlico were largely built on Thames mud raked up and landed on Thameside swamps and drained. But that's a long time ago.'

'I never knew that,' my mother said, 'and I've lived in Eaton Square.' She added quickly, 'But only because I was a governess to a family who lived there.'

'One family was lucky,' he said, smiling, 'and now take me to the door.'

She came back from the front door as soon as the gate closed on him and found Mrs Mullins sitting by the tray, having brought in a clean cup, which she put down with an air of one about to make an important announcement. 'I took the liberty,' she said, 'of asking Jobson about your friend's disposal of his hat and gloves on the carpet. He understands such things, he was a butler with a grand family until there was trouble over some matter. Well, he says it is the custom in certain quite fashionable circles for gentlemen callers to do as Mr Fairfield did. So there seems nothing against Mr Fairfield.'

My mother said nothing. Like all jilted women she would never lose her sense of insecurity. Mrs Mullins mistook the reason for her silence and said, 'Forgive me if I have been intrusive, but I would not like you to become familiar with an inferior.' She paused, bit her lip and went on: 'Also, I must be honest. I did not know what your friend's action meant. It was something I did not understand, and the position my husband and I occupy in the Special Connection means we cannot afford to be wrong about anything. Anything at all.' Her voice became markedly resonant, she might have been speaking from a pulpit. 'But let us look to the future, and hope that Mr Fairfield may be an agreeable companion to you.'

So he was. He came often to see my mother, and they talked of many things that were plainly of no importance, but were delightful to recall, often belonging to their childhood. He recalled an outrageous performance by himself and his brother Arthur which had led to painful consequences at the time but had, he thought, left a recollection so satisfying he would not have been without it for anything. They had a close relative who was an Archdeacon of the Established Church of England, a narrow and mean man who used his religion as a bleach to take all colours out of life, and as a file to scrape away any deposit of pleasure that formed on the day. Reluctantly the two boys were staying at his house somewhere in County Kerry when they slipped out of the house after mid-day dinner one day, when it was the Archdeacon's habit to go to his study and fall asleep in an armchair with *The Times* (sent every weekday from London) spread over his face, while the rest of the household had to preserve silence.

The two little boys used to go into the garden to play in the orchard, and there, that afternoon, they found two old friends. In those days there were a number of Russians who used to travel all over Europe with dancing bears, even so far as Ireland; and one of these and his bear were old friends of the Fairfield children. Mr Fairfield's father, who had a great love for all animals, had long made them his guests whenever they chose to present themselves at the family shooting-box up at the foot of the Black Mountains. Unfortunately the Russian bear-leader was not in a position to renew the friendship. He was lying asleep with his back against an apple tree surrounded by a rich aroma of whisky. But the bear was mindful of the friendship, and after being fed with some pumpkins and cucumbers and cabbages accompanied the two boys into the hall and up the staircase to the Archdeacon's study. It was a matter of moments for one boy to open the door and abstract the key from the inside keyhole, to shove the bear into the room, and lock the door from the outside.

The boys' suggestion that what ensued was a Fenian outrage was ill received; and anyway they would not have put it up to their father, partly because it would have been a shame and disgrace to lie to him or their mother, who were always good to them, and because they were too shocked to justify themselves. Their parents knew what the Archdeacon was as well as their children did; and it was hypocritical of them not to approve their children's act. After all, it was not as if the Archdeacon had been put in any real danger. The bear was not large, particularly considering it was a bear. It has been born in captivity, so the idea would never have entered its head to eat an Archdeacon or any other human being. Also, the Archdeacon had only to go out on a balcony and step over a railing (though perhaps it was rather high) to be on the balcony outside his own bedroom, to which he could safely retire. True, the bear had done damage to a number of sermons in manuscript and correspondence with bishops and curates, but who cared about that? Mr Fairfield was not even in favour of a Protestant Established Church in Ireland; he could tell when his own people were doing the wrong thing, and this was a wrong thing to happen in a predominantly Catholic country. But everybody else was on their side. The boys were shut in their own bedroom at home with a loaf of dry bread and a jug of water, but there was a visitor sent up by cook in the form of a housemaid, who brought some fresh soda bread and a huge pitcher of crab soup.

Crab soup? Partan Bree! That sent my mother off into accounts of infant rebellion against Aunt Isa at Heriot Row, and the similar undermining of discipline by the Highland serving-maids, who had brought Partan Bree and fresh baked baps in the interests of the higher justice. My mother and Mr Fairfield laughed together over such stories as these on many afternoons and evenings in the drawing room, or on the verandahs where the creepers that opened large flowers and screened them by large leaves against the burning Australian summer, so immoderate that it sometimes seemed there was a hugely diffused smell of toast from the browned continent. Sometimes in the cooling evening Mr Fairfield took Mrs Mullins and my mother out for a waggon ride, and Mrs Mullins had even suggested a visit to the hotel on the mound by the river that ran black. But Mr Fairfield demurred; he said that the O'Briens were in great distress. Their daughter-in-law, Norah, the Pre-Raphaelite red-haired beauty, had become the prey of a melancholy for which there was no discernible cause. Mr Fairfield said she must recover: she had no real troubles. My mother would certainly be able to visit her later, when the girl's malaise had worn off.

Presently the ship on which my mother was supposed to make her return journey to England was back from its special commission and reported as ready to make the homeward journey in a fortnight's time.

Charles Fairfield heard the news on the same day as my mother. Ever since that day at the riverside hotel, he had been calling more frequently than before at the Mullins' hotel to sit with them on a shadowed balcony, watching the sun set over the bay behind a frieze of prodigal trees growing in their neighbour's garden and drinking fruit juices which Mrs Mullins had bottled and kept in the cisterns sunk by the farmers who had first built the house; and Mrs Mullins would go and fetch my mother to join them, and she would come in, wearing a cool thin dress. These evenings must have given perfect satisfaction to my father's taste. He liked women to be of the neat and slender kind, and the fruit juices were also exactly what he liked: he hated the taste of alcohol. It touches my heart that my mother must certainly have taken his dislike for drink as proof that any woman who married him was bound to be happy. When my father entered the shaded balcony and heard the news of my mother's imminent departure, he greeted the news with an animal sound. 'He uttered one roar, like a bull,' she told us, 'I did not know where to look.'

'Why, Charles!' exclaimed Mrs Mullins, shocked and pleased, and her husband chuckled, 'That's right, Charles, show a bit of spirit, don't let a first-rate filly bolt out of the paddock.'

'You will not sail to England that day,' my father told my mother, rather as if he wished to beat her instead of marry her, which was, as he then announced, his intention.

❧❧

My father came of an Anglo-Irish family – to use the traditional term for the families who came in as a result of the English conquest and live in a state of ascendancy over the native Irish population – but the Fairfields were really Scottish in origin. Fairfoul was their name originally, and they were petty landowners in Fife, from the district of Pittenweem. There was a legend that they had left Scotland and got to Ireland as soldiers of fortune, because the women of the family had become involved with witchcraft; and there is evidence that there was a coven of witches at Pittenweem.

They emigrated in the seventeenth century, and made some good marriages: one had a wife who was a Clydesdale Campbell, and another married a Miss Cuppidge. She had an interesting ancestry, being descended from a seventeenth-century soldier of fortune called Faustus Cuppich, who is described as German, but is said to have been a Wendish Serb, that is, a member of a Slav enclave in East Germany which has obstinately preserved its language and culture, and even now, in Communist East Germany, has insisted on its identity. His genes must have been powerful, for my father was strongly Slav in appearance, with high cheekbones and bright eyes. When, as a middle-aged woman, I went to Bosnia,* I was amazed to see my father walking about every town and village, but the resemblance was not perfect: my father was well-made but not tall, and the Bosnians were a giant people.

My father's father, Charles George Fairfield, who was in the Cold-stream Guards, got the family into much trouble. He was a gambler from his boyhood, and before his middle twenties had inherited and lost two small fortunes, and it would have gone badly with him had not a brother-officer, Lord Pembroke, felt sympathy with him and made him a land agent of one of his properties which lay near Dublin. My grandfather then married one of the Kerry family of Crosbies. She had a substantial marriage settlement, and they moved from his native county of Longford to County Kerry, where he had a small estate.

After some years she died, childless, and he married Arabella Rowan, who was a Denny and a Blennerhassett, a Roper and a Massey, and much else beside, and they lived on the first wife's marriage settlement, which enabled them to enjoy a pleasant enough life on the Kerry estate and in Dublin. But when my grandfather was still a middle-aged man he died of an inflamed gall-bladder. He was then Chairman of the Committee for the Promotion of the Great Exhibition (which was set up in Dublin after it had had its run in Hyde Park) and the Committee sat and got drunk in the dining room while he agonized upstairs. On his death his widow was left with four sons to bring up, Arthur, Edward, Charles (my father) and Digby, and one daughter, Lettie (so called after an ancestress, Lady Letitia Coningsby, who married a Denny in 1700).

Arabella was an original character, not specially favourable to this situation. She was very beautiful in a statuesque fashion, and slightly mad, though not in any noxious way. After the loss of her husband she joined the Plymouth Brotherhood and passed into a state of quite noble religious mania. It is significant that my father never had any but the plainest food when he was a child, and never saw wine served at his mother's table, for the reason that every penny that could be saved was given to the victims of the Irish famine, both on her estate and in the neighbourhood. She had her absurd side. Her Dublin house, which was round the corner from Merrion Square, was plastered all over with huge notices about the Blood of the Lamb; and she engaged a French tutor for her children on the assumption that, since he was an exile, he must be a Protestant persecuted by wicked Catholics, whereas he was the famous anarchist Elie Reclus,* who had fled after having engaged in an armed demonstration against Louis Napoleon. This was an error of pure genius, however, for he gave the boys a remarkable education, and from the moment when he became fully aware of the confused lady's misapprehension he took a vow to himself never to express any opinion to the boys which their mother would not have approved. He filled the post for several years, living with the Fairfields in Ireland and at their house in St George's Square, London, and the bond between him and the boys was very strong.

Thanks to Elie Reclus, the young Fairfields did well when they went to a famous crammer's establishment in London, in Westbourne Grove, where my father and his brother Digby prepared for the army and his brothers for the Civil Service. Among the ways they passed the time was to sit for other pupils' examinations. It was not long after the modern spirit had contrived that commissions were no longer to be bought but had to be granted as a result of competitive examination. The four Fairfields often presented themselves at the examination halls under the names of their fellow pupils, with satisfactory results for the boys whose parts they played. As the examiners never saw the candidates again the fraud was never suspected.

Young Digby and my father could not afford to follow their father into the Coldstream Guards. Poor young Digby went out to India with the Royal Artillery and got cholera and was buried in the Fortwilliam burial ground, like many another English boy, at the age of twenty-five. Both he and my father had an interest from infancy in ballistics: my father was a gunnery instructor in the Prince Consort's Own, in which he was firmly planted by one of those marks of royal favour which were passed over by the family in silence.* The Prince Consort's Own was the second Rifle Brigade which the widowed Queen Victoria vainly tried to make a crack regiment with the prestige of the

Guards; and when my father got his commission Queen Victoria summoned him for a special interview, at which he was transfixed by hearing the silvery voice of a young girl issue from the pursed lips of a stout and red-faced woman. (I imagine she had a voice like Queen Elizabeth the Second.)

His military career was not a success, though he was an efficient solider and was careful of his men and popular with them. But my father was unpopular in the officer's mess; his conversation was highly allusive and imaginative and exquisitely witty, and it must have been as if George Bernard Shaw had been dropped among them. He had some interesting experiences in the army and particularly enjoyed a period his regiment spent in Canada; he saved up some leave and made a dash down to the Southern States while the Civil War was still raging, was at the Battle of Vicksburg,* and acted for a time as stretcher-bearer somewhere else for the South. But he caught some sort of fever while serving, and on the way back to Canada was stricken down as he passed through Pennsylvania, and was taken in by an Amish family, that amiable and intelligent people who do very well in our modern world, who looked after him very kindly.

When he returned to England he left the army and was wretched. He could not go back to live in Ireland for he had no place of his own. His mother was living in a small house in the country, with a very small 'domain', as an estate is called in Ireland. His father's death had meant the end of the first wife's marriage settlement but Arabella seemed at first to have more than enough to support herself and her family, and she was able to keep up a house in London and a house in Kerry. But this state of affairs had come to an abrupt end. There was talk of a twisted agent who had deceived her, a failure to persist in the collection of rents which were in arrears, one of those cases of dereliction of duty which gave nineteenth-century Ireland such a Russian air. When in my childhood incidents of this sort destroyed the remarkably delicate equilibrium of our household, I noticed that my father at once became gently hopeless.

He could write. He was always writing. But his mother had taken him in his adolescence away from Catholic Ireland to Protestant England, and she had few friends there. His brother Edward was a brilliant success in London, but in conditions which gave my father no reason to hope he could imitate it. Since Mrs Fairfield could not afford to send her sons to the University, Edward had passed straight from the crammer into the Colonial Office as a second division clerk, but his competence had soon attracted the attention of those senior civil servants who operated the system by which the Ministry created its own legal department by picking out the abler juniors with appropriate gifts and sending them to eat their dinners at one or other of the Temples. This set Edward Fairfield intellectual tasks which delighted him, and he also enjoyed the company of lawyers and Ministers and diplomats and senior officials brought his way by his work; and with some of them he had ties, because he had been at Harrow or Rugby with their relatives. But this success depended on early involvement in a closed system not to be gate-crashed by a half-pay army officer in his early thirties.

The truth was that Mrs Fairfield's religious preoccupations, insofar as they had led to the transportation of her family to London, had been a disaster for all of her sons but Edward. The effect of their segregation was to be seen in the fate that befell Arthur, the odd man out among the Fairfields. He had gone into the Board of Trade and had shown great promise in his first years of service, delighting in such technical problems as the seaworthiness of the new Atlantic liners. But he had made few friends in London and married a woman with the strange name of Sophie Blew-Jones,* for no better reason than that he was wildly interested in Buddhism and her father enjoyed showing him objects he had brought back from Asia, and he had no opportunity to meet any other woman often. She was a vulgar and malignant woman, who was to cause suffering to many members of his family for the next two generations; and the irritation of her company increased his coldness and eccentricity so greatly that in the end he was asked to resign from the Civil Service, and then left her, and retired into a curious public hermitage in an uncomfortable Thameside hotel.

My father dearly loved his brother Edward but did not want to intrude on him. He loved his brother Arthur less, but was concerned for his obviously worsening state. It came back to him that some time before he had had a letter from an American whom he had met in Canada, asking him to stay with him on his Virginian plantation. Two months later he was very efficiently running a saw-mill in Virginia. He found great happiness in running a saw-mill, and this he did for five years, during which he married a girl from a wealthy family named Allison, who knew as much or more about horses than he did. They had one son, Stephen. But to his surprise she divorced him when suddenly he felt an irresistible desire to go West.*

He carried out his intention and let her go, feeling freer without her, and again he did this and that. Somehow he became a Sheriff in Colorado, while reading the works of Herbert Spencer and entering into correspondence with the great man and beginning to write on political science, in which he had an admirable grounding from Monsieur Reclus. Then he took a journey in a stagecoach that broke down in a mountain village, and the passengers had to wait for a day or two. My father spent the time shooting in the company of another passenger, older than himself, a self-educated man who was a great reader of political science; and he was enchanted by my father's talk. He had mining interests and offered my father training and employment as a mine manager in a small and remote mine.

My father enjoyed the work and the place, and grew fond of the old man; and he lived a curiously busy and happy intellectual life teaching the old man all he knew about political concepts of the past. He was able to send to a bookshop in Philadelphia for any book he chose. He published some essays on politics and economics in American journals, and sent some home to the English press, and he would have stayed on. But it happened that a neighbour and his wife, who had become his close friends, were killed one day in a buggy accident. They left a boy of seven, and the wife had been Australian. Her relatives sent word they would take the boy, but had no one they could send to fetch him. My father felt impelled to take the child on that journey, although it meant that he must lose his position as the mine manager.

This is the journey, already mentioned by the Mullins to Isabella, which led to Charles and Isabella's meeting on the S.S. John Elder.

MR AND MRS
FAIRFIELD

My parents found the house they were looking for just a day or two after their search began in the suburbs of St Kilda,* not far away from the Mullins' hotel, close by the sea, at a point where the beach was never crowded, but was rarely so empty that swimming was venturesome. It was a pretty little house with a touch of fantasy about it and a well-planted garden that would take care of itself, and the whole thing was not beyond my father's resources nor below the standard of the company he kept. He was in a position to think he was offering my mother a future at once amusing and secure, which was a great relief to him, for when he first landed in Melbourne things had not turned out so well for him as he had thought they were going to.

He had believed that when he had handed over the orphan boy who was travelling with him to his grandparents he was to take up his duties as a caricaturist on one of the two great newspapers in Melbourne, and he had no doubt he was going to find them easy and pleasant. This was a time when upper-class children of both sexes in the British Isles got their first lessons from uncertified governesses, and these excellent women laid a foundation of sound training in all subjects to which their charges had any natural bent. My father and his three brothers had all been taught to draw from a tender age, and while none of the family had ever contemplated taking up painting or drawing professionally, they had gone through life keeping their talents in practice. When my father was a young officer he had done a course at Woolwich, and he remembered with pleasure the high standards of teaching in its art school, which had been originally determined by Paul Sandby,* who was head of the Military Drawing

Department at the Tower of London in the middle of the eighteenth century and was later succeeded by some members of his family.

When my father and Edward were young men they had co-operated in caricaturing contemporary statesmen for various comic papers slightly more free in spirit than *Punch*, and my uncle had continued to make such contributions to the colonial press, which was easy enough, as he met in the course of his duties several owners from overseas. During my father's voluntary exile in the Far West, he had kept his gift alive by drawing those of the population of the mining area as were his friends and found pleasure in receiving a likeness of themselves and their families at Christmas, whether they were white or Indian, and whether they enjoyed being teased by good-natured caricature or liked portraiture better straight. He also filled sketchbook after sketchbook with the landscape of the Sierras and the desert. He had brought back a great deal of his work to England and Edward thought all of it good, and had recommended him without reserve to the Melbourne editor who wanted a caricaturist.

But when my father had got to Australia and had attended sittings of parliamentary and lesser governmental politics, and submitted his drawings of the most notable Australians that these gatherings had disclosed to his eyes, the editor-in-chief told him that his appointment had been a disastrous error, and he proposed to annul it without delay. 'Why, you do not seem to recognize the first essential of a caricature,' he exclaimed, crossly.

'And what is that?' asked my father, humbly, for he had often wondered just what that might be.

'Why, that the subject should be drawn as if his head were much larger than his body,' said the superior authority, with supreme authority.

My father groaned aloud. He was the less prepared for the remark because he had since his arrival in Australia met one or two native-born men who seemed to be shaping well as comic draughtsmen. (I have a vague idea that these were the seniors of families who were in the fullness of time to produce Will Dyson, the Lindsays, and David Lowe.*) But before he could expostulate, the editor was telling him that though anybody with eyes in his head could see that he was singularly ungifted as far as drawing was concerned, anybody with his full complement of two ears would agree that my father could talk the hind legs off a horse. 'You're always telling us that our public finance is heading for ruin, and people tell me that what you say makes sense. Come ashore for writing leaders and feature articles and I'll pay you all you would have got as our funny fellow.'*

After that the marriage could not possibly be considered imprudent by the most cautious and conventional. All was going well for the time being; though there was misfortune, which threw a darkness over my mother's wedding, though it really had nothing to do with that, or anything else concerning herself and my father. For some time after my mother had first visited the hotel on the mound beside the black river, she and my father and Mr and Mrs Mullins had frequently returned to sit on the verandah, or walked in the steep garden and looked down on the conjunction of the sun and sea that burned through the wettish earth. After their marriage had been fixed there had been so much to do they had no time to go there, though they had taken care that the O'Briens were among the first to be invited to the wedding breakfast at one of Melbourne's best hotels. But they had received a refusal from Sam O'Brien who regretted that his wife, whose Pre-Raphaelite beauty had made my mother feel friendship towards her, had for some time been ill with what seemed like a nervous breakdown, so seriously ill that there was no use in pretending that she would be able to attend what would be a long and even boisterous party. She said that she had felt warm affection for my mother from the first moment she had set eyes on her, and she mentioned how on some later occasion she had admired her lace collar and cuffs, which had been mere modest white spider's webs, but elegant beyond anything real, like something that might have been worn by a lady in a painting in an art gallery. She said she hoped my mother would believe in her own sudden affection for her, particularly if it were to happen that they did not meet again very often.

After my mother had read this letter she said to my father, 'I believe the poor girl knows something about herself that we do not, and I am worried about her.' But my father expressed the opinion that Norah O'Brien would get over what was troubling her, sooner or later, and probably sooner. There was no reason why a woman as beautiful as she should not get what she wanted out of life. 'But we know what Norah O'Brien's beauty has got out of life, and that is Sam O'Brien, and as they are both Roman Catholics and cannot be divorced it is most unlikely, since he looks healthy enough, that there will be a second benefit coming to the poor girl,' said my mother, 'and she might well feel dissatisfied with that.' My father reflected and evidently thought my mother had reason on her side, for he looked grave and shook his head. But their talk then turned to more agreeable subjects, to my mother's wedding dress (which as the ceremony was to be at a registry office was a white taffeta afternoon dress, with full skirts amounting almost to a bustle) and the wedding breakfast, which was to comprise other things than steak, and the country house that was to be lent them for their honeymoon by the proprietor of the newspaper for which my father worked, which had a famous string of horses trained on its verdure.

'Everywhere, all the time,' said my father, 'there will be a chorus of big blonde bouncing Australian ladies, whispering to each other that you are not pretty, and of course you are not, because you are beautiful, and the two things are incompatible. Also a lot of them would have liked steak instead of what we got the French cook at Government House to suggest, but in any case throughout the afternoon, no wedding guest will beat his breast, for he heard the loud bassoon. All is going to go well.'

'How strange it is,' my mother thought, 'that I should grow up in an Edinburgh flat with two silly brothers, my Joey, my Johnnie, who made up silly songs making fun of The Ancient Mariner – there was one with such an idiotic chorus, 'I did not say I was an albatross, I said my name was Albert Ross' – and I have crossed the world to marry a man who also makes silly jokes about The Ancient Mariner.'

Charles Fairfield and Isabella Mackenzie were married in Melbourne on 17 December 1883.

My mother felt delight when Johnnie and Lizzie came in, and laughter and greetings ran through the crowd, and a number of people clapped their hands; and this welcome flowered again when Joch the Whistler came in and did not stop when he scowled from embarrassment, the laughter only grew more tender. At the end of the breakfast Joch played Scottish tunes on his fiddle, and then Lizzie sang Scottish songs and Joch rose from his chair and walked along the table till he faced my mother and whistled 'My Love is Like a Red Red Rose'; and she thought not of herself – she would not have wasted five minutes on considering whether she was like a red or a pink or a white rose or any rose at all – but of what Johnnie had been able to teach this native savage, out of his long grounding in music, that she had been tempted to think of as wasted, often and often since she came to Australia.

It was the diggers who had made the concert party's reputation so great that everybody knew Johnnie and Lizzie and Joch as soon as they came into the hotel dining room, and nobody had resisted their claim; people were studying classical music all over the place. It was a curious geographical circumstance that it seemed commoner here in the Antipodes for children to be born with good singing throats. This was part of the generosity of the place; there was more sunshine here than at home, and second chances were more generously given. When the time came for the bride and bridegroom's health to be drunk, it seemed to my mother that the lower half of the dining room was full of people who were gilded by those second chances, who had fortune and forgiveness and more shining straight down on them like the Australian sunshine, while the air above seemed parched with the celestial stuff of well-being that does not depend on the exercise of the will, either divine or human, but simply on chance-dictated circumstance of a delicious kind. Surely she and my father were going to live happily ever after, and that meant in Australia. Down the table Johnnie and Lizzie and Joch the Whistler stood very still, holding their full glasses to their lips, preparing to take a sacrament, nameless but intrinsically felt, never to be forgotten, shared with my mother and my father to the last intricacy, to be remembered in detail by each of them till death.

ALICE AND LETTIE

The little house of my parents at St Kilda was to exemplify a truth I was to learn in my time, by lessons too repetitive, and far too costly to civilization. Any way of life, if those who live it have to move out of the buildings in which it was engendered, keeps its character, even if that had seemed the result of the surroundings. My father brought fellow journalists and poets and painters and men of affairs and politicians back to his house in the evening, and there were recreated the wild evenings of corybantic argument on political and moral philosophy and history and economics that had taken place every night of his childhood in his father's house in Fitzwilliam Square, that Georgian masterpiece in wet Ireland, but anyone who came into the small Antipodean room filled with tobacco smoke and contention could not have detected the spiritual difference.

My mother was not in the same position of being able to reproduce her early life, for to these men all sound except argument was an interruption, were it music or the caterwauling of cats. She was an excellent housekeeper; she took great pleasure in bringing in food at the right times and, if a quotation came into question, finding the right book on the right shelf. She dressed well, was witty, and possessed European elegance without European arrogance. She was also admired as a musician. But she could not sympathize with her husband's friends' desire to consume, late at night, even into the small hours, thick slices of underdone steak smeared with a harsh kind of mustard, and stuck between heavy bread, which was a special offence to a Scotswoman. (The bread in Edinburgh was then as bread elsewhere was to *brioche*: home-baked or shop-baked, it was a delicacy.) She never felt happy at people drinking whisky in her house, but that could not be helped, it was something the male had imposed on the world; but she felt almost disgusted when she had to give her guests strong black Indian tea.

The one piece of bad news that came the way of my father and mother since their marriage was that the Pre-Raphaelite beauty, Norah O'Brien, had been found drowned in the black river that ran by her house some days after their wedding. It affected my mother and father more than might have been supposed possible, considering what a short time they had known her and the slight and merely social relationship they had had with her. But she was so beautiful, my mother once told me, that the degree to which they had known her had not much to do with the sorrow they felt; it was more as if a famous picture had been destroyed.*

All that was forgotten when my mother, a year after her marriage, gave birth to her first child. There were three people in the little house at St Kilda and all of them were delighted for peculiar reasons. My mother had been aghast because of her losses: the loss of Joey to death, the loss of Alick to his monstrous Mary, the loss of Johnnie to circumstance so alien that it was impossible for her to follow him into that strange land, the loss of the Edinburgh painter and the man in London who was as incapable of sharing his life with her as she was incapable of sharing Johnnie's life. It had seemed to her that she was running the risk of living in a depopulated world. Her own mother was old; Aunt Isa was an eternal stranger; Jessie Watson Campbell had been adopted by France; her sister Jessie was accessible but inaccessible, like a historial conument or a museum, only open at certain times on certain days, so deeply, it seemed, was she engaged in her marriage. But my mother had begun the task of repopulating her world by marrying Charles Fairfield, and at once had continued the good work by engaging a servant who, like many of her servants, immediately became more than that.

This was Alice, a tall and well-made girl with golden hair and blue eyes, a lovely creature, physically born to condescend, who had wept steadily through her first interview with my mother, because she was under the impression that she was so deeply tainted with disgrace as to excite the abhorrence of everybody she met. The fact was that she came of the good convict stock which contributed much to Australia's greatness, since it consisted of people who in their native England had been born into such poverty that no sane person would blame them if they tried to alter their state by practising dishonesty and making revolutionary passes at the established order of things, and in either case they proved their good sense and energy.

Once Alice's forbears had served their sentences out in Australia they had been freed, and by the time her generation had come into the world the family was known and respected. But when little Alice was a schoolgirl, and an envied schoolgirl, her father had a curious throwback to the parent stock, and proved that perhaps there was something the matter with it not wholly due to poverty. He exploited the trustfulness of some old and unoffending people, and the family history was revived.

Alice had never been beloved by her schoolfellows because she was too beautiful and fortunate and unassuming, and their revenge was barbed. Her parents' house was sold, and though her relatives were willing to pay for her education she left school and worked in various shops and saloons, changing her employment constantly because she was tainted, or thought that she was. Now she was trying domestic service for the first time and had unusual good luck in fixing on my father and mother, who were absorbed in their own glowing interests, and had sufficient dramatic gifts to affect complete unawareness of hers. 'I have heard of a new shop where they sell baby clothes. Mrs Mullins is coming too, Alice, you will enjoy it!', my mother would cry, and Alice would forget her sense of being the victim of the gods.

As for my father, his optimism was a shield to my mother's occasional fears and to Alice's sense of doom, but as an expectant father he was awaiting a sign from heaven of protection for all underneath his roof. His ancestress Letitia Coningsby was supposed to have been loving, brave, self-sacrificing, beneficent and to have shown these virtues not under the inspiration of motherhood, for she died childless, but as a spontaneous reaction to human need, wherever she saw it, though her natural disposition was to laugh her way through life. So prodigious was this prodigy that long after her death the successive generations of her family called their daughters Letitia, and when my grandmother and grandfather's eldest child turned out to be a daughter they had never thought of calling her anything else. But in the end this memorial to a beloved angel in the house proved to be a terrible misfortune. Letitia Fairfield died when she was seven years old of a mysterious ailment which was probably appendicitis, at that time unidentified.

When my mother became pregnant, my father was immediately possessed by the idea that the child would be a girl, and that it must be called Letitia. So inevitably the baby was called Letitia; and that was what she was. She was Joy, and in the classic form. Her little body was exquisite, and so was her spirit. My mother and Alice would put her in her cot and she would fold her hands and lay her cheek against them on the pillow, as if she were praying, but she was also smiling, and she would go to sleep, and only cry in the night if her nappies were wet, and once the discomfort was remedied, she would sleep again.

My father was entranced. This was Letitia descended to earth again, ministress to her descendants. My mother wondered why he was so grateful, as if for a drastic change in fate. Had not things gone very well with him so far in his life? He had had a beautiful existence so far as she could see: a boyhood with fond parents in beautiful surroundings, with brothers whom he obviously loved, though one he spoke of as being a cold fish. But there had been, as far as she could make out, no terrible equivalent of her brother Alick in either Dublin or Tralee, or the London square where the family had settled after the father's death. He had tolerated army life because the military techniques fascinated him, he had enjoyed his life in America, he was enjoying his life here in Australia. He was becoming, it seemed to her, very well known, and favourably known, as a journalist and speaker and debater, and he made friends wherever he went. He was also enjoying his marriage to her. Yet his attitude to his first-born child was not that of an ordinary man who had become a father, it was rather that of a man who had found his guardian angel, and was immensely relieved, since for lack of that angel he had suffered throughout his life long pain and suffering.*

This pleased my mother, though it seemed to her an imaginative freak; but there was really something miraculous about little Letitia and the effect she had on Alice. So far as she knew there could have been no legend in Alice's life comparable to the sanctification of Letitia Coningsby; the girl's ancestry had been the product of late eighteenth- or early nineteenth-century London, where surely such mysticism did not flourish. But the girl might have been a priestess in care of a holy baby, particularly when she took little Letitia swimming. My mother was not much use in this ritual, for an up-bringing in Edinburgh gave few opportunities for sea-bathing, and though she had learned to swim in various lochs she could not trust herself to go into the Antipodean sea with her tiny baby, particularly as there was often a rumour of sharks. But to Alice, who had swum all her life, the sea was nearly as friendly a medium as the land. Early or late, before the sun was scorching, she would walk into the waves, carrying the child in her arms, beauty enfolding beauty, and it would be as if the world had just begun and had not piled up its bad record. And they would meet the waves and rise above them, and float when the sea was smooth. My mother sometimes recalled with zest the gesture with which Alice, feeling the sun rising to burning point, gathered the child into the shadow of her arms and, loping with her beautiful long Marshal-Niel-coloured* legs over the sand to a hut, took off the little thing's wet bathing suit and rubbed her with a towel carefully chosen for smoothness, while my mother saw to the spaces between her fingers and toes, and the creases on her little neck; and then they put on her one of the beautiful little dresses that Aunt Isa sent across the world through the Government House bag, of a slightly dark material that stopped the sun's rays, made specially for the children of the great ladies who bore children in India. God help them, for too often the dresses only survived.

My mother had another child, Winifred Alice, when my sister Letitia was two or three years old, and this event had not worked out so well as my parents expected. It was something of a disappointment that the second child should also be a girl; my mother would have liked a change, she would have liked to be the mother of a tough, good-looking little boy, who would have rode well and understood machinery and tax problems and settled things by his presence. But the disturbing element in the situation was not her second child's failure to be a boy but her success in being a girl. Consider now the position of my eldest sister. People still came to the beach hut and cried out in admiration, but what they said was not 'What a beautiful baby!' but 'What beautiful children you have, Mrs Fairfield. Dark and fair and both equally lovely!' The expression which I remember as characteristic of my eldest sister throughout her life, which lasted ninety-two years, was I think impressed on her at the suburb of St Kilda, outside the city of Melbourne, in the late 1880s. She had in her infancy been the recipient of praise which implied that she was uniquely beautiful. Suddenly she was informed that she was not a *nonpareil* as constantly suggested but one of a pair, and the other as wonderful as she was. This humiliated and abased her, and I cannot see how it would not.

My mother talked to her last days with intoxication of the joys of swimming off the sandy beach with her little children and her wonderful strong servant. But presently my father forecast that there was going to be a bank crash in Australia – upon which his readers demanded that his employer dismiss him. So he and his family went back to England, where he was to draw an inadequate salary as an English correspondent to the same newspaper, which was unlikely to do him much good as he had to write under a pseudonym. It made no difference to his circumstances that presently the banks crashed as he had predicted.

PART FOUR

CISSIE

STREATHAM PLACE

My first memory would have been sad had I understood, but I saw the scene utterly detached from its significance. I remember sitting up in a go-cart pushed by somebody whom I can only identify as somebody I was fond of (which I wish I could analyse) and passing the gate of the house next to ours. The gate was open and there were four men carrying out a long box on their shoulders. Whoever was pushing the go-cart slowed down so that they were quite close to us. One of the four men had red hair. One of the other three said something to him and he laughed, and crossed the pavement to some vehicle which I did not trouble to look at. We went on to our house,* and the go-cart was put in a recess in the hall, and my nanny picked me up and carried me upstairs to a bedroom, where my mother was standing by a dressing-table brushing her short black hair. My nanny said, 'Captain Diamond' – that is how I hear the name but I think I am wrong – 'has died. We saw them carrying out the coffin.'

Before she had finished the sentence my mother flung down her brush on the dressing-table with a passionate urgency, then raised her arm and said, 'I will see to Cissie, please go downstairs and pull down all the blinds.' The gesture with which she threw down her hairbrush was characteristic in its curious combination of impulsiveness and a deliberate ritual quality. It was a quality I have never seen except in ballet dancers or athletes, yes, and in Sarah Bernhardt. This is odd because my mother was incapable of following any physical discipline, not that she rejected it, but she had been too busy in receiving impressions and commenting on them. Neither my sisters nor I inherited this curious wild grace.

I told my mother of this first recollection when I was a schoolgirl and she looked up a cutting she had kept recording the death of the sea-captain who had lived next door to us in Streatham Place, when I was under two years old. What strikes me as strange is that I was stirred and awed by the gravity of her movement and the rise of her voice, and admired them as beautifully appropriate to what had happened. Yet I did not know what had happened. I did not know what was in the box, or what my nurse meant by saying that the captain had died. I am positive of that, for it was much later that my sister Winifred explained to me that hearses filled with flowers were not, as I thought, a kind of carnival float. Plato's notion that we are born with valid ideas about reality already implanted in our minds seems to me great nonsense, yet this experience of mine seems to support it.

The house in Streatham Place was the first home I remember, and we had come there in such calamitous circumstances that I marvel I can have so many happy, even ecstatic memories of the life we lived there. Because my father had begun his writing too late, because he had made his success in Australia, because he got into trouble by foretelling a bank crash, his merits were as little recognized in his own country as if he were an exile. He got what work he could, but he was too old to make his mark, though he secured a limited fame by joining an anti-socialist society, the Individualists' League.* He often spoke for this society, and was apparently a remarkable orator. I was once told by an old man of a wonderful debate between my father and the much younger Irish immigrant, George Bernard Shaw, that lasted all night. They carried it on in the Conway Hall until the caretaker turned out the lights, and continued the discussion all over London, finding such favourable sites as the steps of St Paul's or the Embankment, always being driven on by the police, but never losing the thread of the argument. The old man said that my father had had much the best of it, and that must have been true, for when I asked Shaw if he remembered the debate, thirty years afterwards, he showed signs of anger and distress.*

But such triumphs brought in no money, and my father finally took a post as leader-writer on the *Glasgow Herald*. There the staff were dazzled by his brilliance but he wrote above the head of the readers, and in any case my mother's health could not stand the Scottish winters, particularly as she was about to bring me into the world.

So the family travelled back to London, and my mother, quite ill, and troubled by an infection of the eyes, could not face setting up a new household. In Australia she had come across the institution of the furnished house which was for rent, and she looked for one to give her shelter till after I should be born. But it was held in England at that time that nobody respectable would want to rent a furnished house, and certainly nobody respectable would want to let their house furnished, so she had to make do with a house in Notting Hill,* a curious district of large Victorian houses which had never found tenants to match their solidity.

It was a development which had been built a mile or so north of Hyde Park, to match the area of similar houses which had sprung up south of the Park, in Knightsbridge and Kensington, during and after the Great Exhibition. But it had never prospered, partly because the southern development was right on the park and it was quite far from it, and also because there was little public transport available and people who could keep their carriages wanted to live in a more fashionable quarter. It was therefore seedy from the start, and was so when we went there, and was to become more so. The side streets were the homes of successive generations of immigrants, first the Poles and Irish and later the West Indians, and in their time the house where I was born had a home-made bomb thrown through the transom of the front door, for the reason that it had become a Negro club. In my mother's time it was simply empty and bristling with 'To Let' boards, and she quite enjoyed it, particularly as the white stucco-front houses had a classical magnificence. My mother and my sister Winifred recalled all their lives how they used to go for an evening walk to a terrace facing west which used to glow with the reflected fires of the sunset.

My mother could not move as soon as she expected, for the infection of her eyes was graver than had been supposed and she had to go into hospital for treatment by her oculist, a man called McHardy.* He showed her many kindnesses, and she was deeply grateful and very fond of him. I do not think it ever crossed her mind that he was in love with her, though that was the case, as I was to discover long after by an incident of the sort that is characteristic of our family, which was perpetually finding itself led to truth by the wild lights of coincidence.

When I was seventeen I had a brief and unhappy time at a school of acting, the Royal Academy of Dramatic Art, which had a bright-mannered spectacled secretary whom I was surprised to find in a collapsed state on the staircase, with tears running down her cheeks and at her feet a jumble of objects. She explained that till a short time ago she had been secretary to the famous oculist, Mr McHardy, to whom she had been devoted. He had dismissed her a year before, and she had felt hurt, for there seemed no good reason why he should, as he said, be unable to afford a secretary any longer and she thought that something had gone wrong with his mind. And she had been right, he had gone mad and had tried to commit suicide. His closest friend had called her in to clear up the office and sort out the files and collect the personal articles that were lying about, and these were the objects that were lying spilt down the stairs.

She picked up a framed photograph and said, 'I have taken this, I don't know that anybody will want it, it was his wife who died years ago.' I found myself looking at a photograph of my mother, her favourite photograph, taken shortly after her marriage, in which she was wearing a pretty check dress. I said nothing about this, and told my mother simply that I had heard he had gone mad and tried to commit suicide. She said sadly, 'Oh, I can believe it, he used to be very odd, sometimes he seemed not in command of himself. Oh, he was such a good, kind man.'

Because of his care for her my mother was able to start afresh with her characteristic resilience in Streatham, which was then a very agreeable place, in a house much like the one I described as the home of the Aubrey family in *The Fountain Overflows*, except that it had no coach-house. It was one of a line of semi-detached Regency villas which formed one side of a charming street. Not one stone of these houses has remained, most of them were bombed in the Second World War, and all were demolished to make room for flats built on the same design as cheap expanding bookcases; and the road has been broadened into characterless motor highway.

Although the coach-houses had been pulled down, there was still an equine atmosphere, for the house had once been occupied by a lunatic who believed that horses ought to be kept underground so that they really would enjoy getting out into the fresh air, so the cellars had been fitted up as stables. (This is apparently not an uncommon delusion among lunatics, for I have come across three instances of it.)

The reason why my parents chose to live in Streatham was that it was the only London suburb which had all-night trams, and this made it and the adjacent Brixton popular with actors and music-hall artists, burglars, night-watchmen and Fleet Street journalists. I think that was the only reason, though my father's family had a vague connection with the district. One of our ancestors, Richard Fairfield, who started life as a soldier and then joined John Company,* described himself in legal documents as 'Of Streatham', and there was a family legend he had once owned a farm where lavender and violets were grown to be sold to the scent-makers, Floris of Jermyn Street, and it is a fact that flowers were bought in quantity from that district. But there is no record of any Fairfield as a landowner in that district since the six-teenth century, and then the Fairfield was a butcher who supplied the court, and had apparently nothing to do with us.

It was a graceful house, with nicely shaped rooms and a garden with a grove of chestnut trees at the end of the lawn. We had a strange bird that bounced in the air when it flew, which I learned, thirty years afterwards, was a green woodpecker, a yaffle, not a frequenter of London as a rule. Our garden was not well tended. We were too poor to employ a jobbing gardener, except very rarely, miniscule as the pay such as he got was in those days. (We were so poor that when my father was away my mother did not light the gas in the hall.) The result was that in our garden sheltered several of that weed among trees, the elder; and the first time I can remember my heart turning over not at the sight of any loved person but simply of an object was when I went out one summer evening when it was getting dark and stood by an elder tree and looked on its greenish white flowers, along the sharp leaves that are so crisp and green to the sight, as if they were going to float away with the dark that was coming down, among the chestnut trees. To this day the bitter, heavy scent of the elder gives me a feeling of mystery and joy; and the two foods that give me a mystical joy are gooseberry and strawberry jam that has been cooked with elder syrup.

My mother's houses always had a certain charm, though the signs of

poverty were blatant. We had some quite fine late Regency dining-
room chairs covered with maroon leather so worn that the surface skin
was peeling off in little rolls and exposed a friable silver and crimson
substance which has never presented itself to me since. Our towels
and bed linen were darned to patchwork, and the cleaning of our
curtains and cushions was a crippling expense that had to be planned
and saved for. We ate well but very simply, and our clothes were
painfully shabby.

But what seems extraordinary is that we always had a nurse and a
maid-of-all-work. Girls were so eager to get into domestic service that
they worked for pitiful wages. This is now assumed to be because the
working classes were then so poor that they would do anything to get
their bare keep, and it is true to some extent, but I think the
inducement was also that domestic service was a way of connecting
with a more interesting set of people than they would otherwise have
met. Kate, our servant, enjoyed the company of my parents. Bringing
me back from some winter errand to a shop, she paused as we got out
into the street and stood still and inhaled voluptuously before she said,
'Now, your Mamma will be putting on the light in the drawing room,
she will be setting the lamp ready by the master's desk and seeing to
his pens, and by the time we get back she will be back in the drawing
room and sitting at the piano, playing whatever she likes, with no
music in front of her.'

I share Kate's feeling that our house was a magical place. (I still
remember the exact address, though the place was demolished twenty-
one years ago by a German bomb, and I left it about sixty-six years ago
– 21 Streatham Place.)* And for me it was set in a magical district.
The earth in South London is very fertile. The trees cast a deep shade,
and the flowering shrubs used to cast on the pavements wide circles of
scattered petals, white and pale pink, the colour of sweets. How we
enjoyed walking with Papa, to hunt out fragrant bushes or low-lying
plants, and how we enjoyed going to somebody's farm and having
fresh Jersey milk. We were happy. I will not say that my father was not
often unhappy, but I know now it was about his debts.

We had all sorts of small treats and little games. We used to amuse
ourselves by offering my father on our fingertips morsels of any food we
thought delicious, because he had been deprived in his childhood of
all the sweetmeats that children even in our permanent state of need

were given at birthdays and Christmas: notably exquisite mouthfuls wiped off the face of the earth by two wars, called Carlsbad plums; brown-black prunes, dried but not dry, folded on each other's dark moisture, and dusted outside; also *marrons glacés*, then not sticky, their syrup a powder through and all over them. There was a historical reason for my father's ignorance of those *friandises*,* as he called them, sometimes adding that if he had had a really pretty daughter he would have called her Friandise – but, as he added sadly, that was not to be. His parents had been the kind of pious and military Anglo-Irish who had taken the Famine with deep contrition, and had eaten plainly so that they could give food away to the starving; and they and their children had had little on their tables that was not staple food of the labourers on their fields. He had never lost the sense that plain food was good food, as he had never acquired the habit of drinking wine or spirits, which were kept in our house only to give to visitors. But there was a wild delight; it all might have got out of hand, the French windows in the garden might have blown open and we might all have rushed out through the woods and over fields to cliffs and a sea that like all landscapes was not there, while we were holding our Carlsbad plums and *marrons glacés* and tips of orange jelly to him, calling 'Take mine! Take mine!' and watching him, and then crying out, 'You liked mine best!', though he would have moved somewhere else by then and be saying abstract things. 'Strange to think the orange is a winter fruit . . .'

⁂

When I look back on my life in Streatham Place the first thing that comes into my mind is a form of tribute any little girl would enjoy. If I was taken out in a baby carriage, or toddled out gripping my nurse's or my mother's hand, down the wide streets of Victorian houses standing in lavishly green gardens, sooner or later I would find myself in front of a gorgeously dressed and beturbanned Asiatic who would bend over me, his black beard split by a dazzling smile, while he murmured clucking endearments in a strange language and, after making formal gestures to my mother or my nurse, run his own fingers round the curve of my jaw or through my hair, always smiling, always admiring me. This was not the fantasy that it might be supposed.

Queen Victoria had her Diamond Jubilee in 1897, and large numbers of the Indian troops she loved were brought over to England and billeted round London, some of them round Streatham, some for as long as two years. They were all very fond of children, and I must have been one of the children who lived nearest their billets. Sometimes they would let me play with the hilts of their daggers, which were made of shining metal, sometimes etched with precious stones. I was fascinated by their strange words and the look of their hands, the palms of which I remember as being of a curious colour.

My mother and nurse were amused by this but rather alarmed. It seemed an odd thing to be happening. But my father, who was passionately fond of Asiatics, impressed on them that these were people of high civilization, that they would certainly be insulted by stupid people in this country, and that therefore we must treat them with great politeness. His feelings were strong for two reasons. My father was old to be my father – I was a child of his second marriage, and had ties with a remoter past than was likely, for he himself was the child of his father's second marriage: my grandfather was born in 1798, and the family had worked for John Company and served in the army. This meant that the attitude of the elders who surrounded him in his childhood was free from race prejudice as the English Indians were before the Indian mutiny. (It was common for English families to stay with Indian people of their own caste.) Also, India had a mystical significance for him. It was there that his adored brother, Digby Fairfield, had died; and my father deeply loved his brothers, as he had loved his mother. The best of his brothers had been taken by death there in Asia, and he wished to think that this had been the gateway to another world. But I understand my mother's uneasiness about these curious encounters.

And, looking back, they *were* curious. I was not so pretty that these soldiers should have felt special admiration for me. It is just possible that it was because in my childhood I was very dark – but surely no darker than a good many children, and certainly not so dark as them.

I came to expect these tributes: when they stopped I felt deprived, I sometimes begged to have these dark and affectionate men brought back from wherever they had gone. They did much for me, and they added to my respect for my father, for when one of them came to the house to leave a farewell present of some Indian sweetmeats my father came out of his study with his pen in his hand to ask my mother the date (a piece of information from which he averted his mind), looked at the Indian and addressed him in his own tongue. Digby had studied Hindustani before he went out to India, and it had amused my father to share his lessons. We were all as delighted as if it were Christmas. But I got another benefit from this admiration.

My sister Lettie, who was eight years older than I was, never ceased to convey to me that I was a revolting intruder in her home. If I was sent out for a walk with her she would pause in the hall before she opened the front door and look at me with an expression of utter disgust, and with a sigh of pure loathing would put her hand on my collar and push me out of the house. She was a very pretty little girl with golden hair and blue-grey eyes, an exquisite complexion, a sweet and serious voice and a gentle air which captivated adults. I have described her to some degree as Cordelia in *The Fountain Overflows* but not her capacity for sullen anger, provoked by nothing except the sense that someone other than herself was living in her house, and not the terrifying effect of her emotions on her appearance. She would look at me and grow suddenly very pale, her eyes would seem to grow lighter and in a whitish stare, and her upper lip would lift over her perfect teeth as if she were going to be sick.

When she came in from school she would hurry to whatever room I was in, stand and look at me as if to make sure that, yes, the nightmare had not passed and, however innocent my occupation, begin to scold me. If I were holding anything, no matter if it were one of my own toys, she would wrench it out of my hand with a snarl: 'What are you doing with that?' She had heard someone use the phrase 'a destructive child' and she used to repeat it to me, in a dreamy monotone, shaking her head as if she were a sibyl. 'You are a destructive child, you are a destructive child.'

This was frightening because it was such nonsense and so unjust. I was destroying nothing. Very naturally I would try to stop her by hitting her, but she would instantly run to the nearest grownup, saying with a matronly air, 'I do not know what to do with Cissie, she is in one of her tempers.' I gave up trying to protect myself by my own efforts, and learned to throw myself on the protection of my other sister, Winifred, who was always kind and was herself the victim of

Lettie's hostility in a milder form. She always intervened if she could, and if she was too late she would comfort me afterwards.

We were handicapped by Lettie's extreme ingenuity, which enabled her to give an appearance of perpetual bewilderment at the state of affairs which she was provoking, an effect so convincing that even I often could not believe my own senses and wondered if, without knowing it, I was doing something wrong. I remember going to some sort of display at the school my two elder sisters attended and watching Lettie in a painful ecstasy as she danced a solo, so lovely, so cool, so innocent, twirling about as weightless as a snowflake, her eyes set on the distance and her lips slightly parted. If she denounced me she must be right. A burning sense of guilt brought me to tears. I was halfway on her side, and the seriousness of that can be judged from the fact that my sister really saw me as grotesquely ugly, badly behaved and stupid, as abnormal as an epileptic or a Mongolian idiot.

The depth and intensity of her emotions was to be proved in the second half of the following century, in 1959, when she was seventy-five and I was made a Dame. She rang me up and crying with utterly shameless rage, demanded by what accident this preposterous thing could have happened. It was true that many others felt this, for then my light was in eclipse: my marriage had long prevented me from doing much work. But hers was simply a cry of undying hate. It adds to my resentment that she was able to carry on her hatred comfortably because of her faculty for self-deception, which enabled her to see herself as my guardian angel, never deflected from her duty by my ingratitude and wickedness, although she was fainting under the undue strain put on her youth by the unhappy circumstances of her parents' life together.

Of course her childhood role was not as she pretended, for she did not even envisage the responsibilities she said she bore in full understanding, as a child of twelve, which was all she was when we left Streatham. She could not have helped my mother to deal with the problems of her life, which if they were gross were also subtle. Indeed my sister had a native tactlessness not at all to be harshly judged, since it came of honesty, which made her unable to act as anything but an irritant. But she was not unintelligent and she must have estimated, and, indeed, by reason of a certain timidity in her nature, over-estimated the danger of our situation; which was, quite simply that we might all starve.*

MY FATHER

The detachment of my father from the consequences of his actions was almost a cause, like his anti-socialism. The whole strength of his being was turned in a direction which led him away from his wife and children. He admired my mother and was quite proud of all three of his daughters, but he felt no desire to keep us or assist us in any way. Also he was continually and frenetically unfaithful to my mother, who was in love with him, and had a taste, which showed him to be either a sexual maniac or to be idiotically rooted in the eighteenth century, for having sexual relationships with the women my mother employed, as servants or nurses or governesses, and with prostitutes.

I recall this with anger, for I know enough now to be sure that men's extravagant sexuality is an affectation. Men have nearly all such extra-marital relationships out of hostility to their wives, not that they have any personal hostility to them, but they dislike women in general, and a wife is one woman who has got the law on her side, and they punish her by denying her sexual satisfaction. I say that out of the knowledge I have gained as a mistress – a silly word, it suggests a gaiety not at all relevant – and as a wife, which suggests a stability also not guaranteed. There is no abundance spilling over, only a pointless war. The same knowledge inclines me to think that it was those relationships which made him indifferent as to whether my mother and my sisters starved or not. Perhaps these relationships also fostered his addiction to gambling. They certainly did not initiate it, for it was a hereditary trait and one that his particular environment took for granted as part of the male equipment. But I think it possible they made him less punctilious about risking our ruin.

Of course my sister cannot have known all this or even guessed it, for though she was intelligent she was not shrewd or observant, and even if she had by some miracle of precocity grasped the facts she was the last person to be able to improve the situation. But of course she had a vague, blurred, but terrifying apprehension of our state. There were a thousand signals of my father's sexuality. I remember going for a walk with him in what was then true country though not far from Streatham, with cows and sheep in the fields and long blue-green aisles of kale. He took me into a farmhouse that had a board outside saying it provided teas and explained what we wanted to the farmer's wife, a handsome black-haired woman who, as he spoke, smirked under his eyes. I had no idea of the sexual mechanism, but I identified all the ingredients of the situation and was enraged by them.

As if I had lived a lifetime I recognized that the feeling that had sprung up between my father and this woman was quite inappropriate considering that they had never seen each other before, and I noted coldly that the place was not too tidy, the word 'Teas' had straggled across the board, and a cat that ran in from the farmyard was thin. I never felt quite the same about my father again. The message was not specific but it held meaning, like the darkness in our hall. Everybody else had a light in the hall, there was no black shadow there. Mamma minded this, Papa did not. But again hatred was impossible. He also was required to suffer more pain than humans can survive, and I saw something even then of how painful his pain was, for our small house was lit up by a historical tragedy: a Dreyfus case in little.*

Looking back on my father, it seems to me that he had many Slav characteristics: no sense of time, a gift for warm immediate intimacy which might suddenly change to self-cloistering melancholy; subtlety in everything except the business of conciliating his fellow men to whom he explained his motives only rarely, and then in terms he did not trouble to make acceptable any more than the Tsarist Empire or the Soviet Union. For example, I feel sure that his professional difficulties were so great because he was too thoroughly grounded in political science by his French tutor Elie Reclus, too well informed, and too careful in his arguments for run-of-the-mill journalism. I say this out of knowledge, for later I worked alongside one of the editors who had rejected him, and who was himself being pensioned off before his time because of the higher standards of the twentieth-century press. But my father did nothing whatsoever to make his failure appear anything more than a commonplace failure to be able to hold down a job.

He was also Slav in his nocturnal habits. He belonged, as I do, to the Slav breed of happy insomniacs who are glad of the peace which falls on the world when all that machinery stops clanking, when the difficulties of applying theory no longer keep on intruding on the discussion of theory. This characteristic affected me disadvantageously because it set me up in opposition to the grownup idea that children should go to bed early. Night was the time when my father, visibly inspired, really got going, and his eloquence spread its wings over the rapt attention of his friends, and it was clear not only that they all wanted to be saved but that they knew the right road to salvation. Nursery discipline seemed to be lifting an impious hand against religion.

Often our father overawed us, not by any harshness, but by his nocturnal quality. He was at home in the night, and made it more mysterious. I remember when I was about six waking up with the darkness thick about me, and calling to my mother and getting no answer, and crawling to her bed and finding it empty. I came to the conclusion that war had broken out, some war that had escaped out of a book. I accepted that I must fight, and got down on the carpet and crawled towards the thin yellow line that marked the opening of the door, just ajar.

When I pushed it open I saw three people outside my sister Winifred's bedroom on the other side of the landing in a disordered group: my mother in her dressing-gown, her hair wild about her shoulders, our doctor in an overcoat over his pyjamas, with a stethoscope waving in one hand like a strand of creeper, and my father, dressed as he would have been in the daytime, in clothes that had a curiously Wild West look, but very neat, and self-possessed as he would have been if he had been greeting a visitor he knew but not very well. I was not at all alarmed by my mother and the doctor, who looked exactly as I expected people would who were pulled so far out of the ordinary routine as to be walking about in the middle of the night. But I was horror-stricken because my father seemed completely unaffected by the fact that that was exactly what it was: the middle of the night. He was talking clearly and persuasively, making explanatory gestures when he ought to be in bed. I shuddered, seeing him as unabashed by a law which I had, indeed, every reason to consider as sacred as any law, since it was so universally obeyed.

All day I used to long to see the doctor coming in his brougham. He was a young man, to be a general practitioner; or did I only see him as young in the light of my infatuation? He had treacle-bright dark eyes, with eyelids that were slack, and a skin that was faintly bronzed, quite dark over his high cheekbones, and very dark thick hair. He was, which was unusual at the time, cleanshaven, and his mouth was sharply cut; I was glad his mouth was not, as it were, smudged by a moustache. He was not very tall but was slender and moved very quickly; he ran upstairs lightly. He used to put out his hand and run it through my hair before he ran upstairs, while he was talking to my mother. I looked at him always with relief when he came in, because I felt sure that my sister could not, could not – whatever it was that my mother was afraid of * – while he was in the house, but that emotion did not stay, it passed into pure pleasure.

I used to follow him upstairs with my eyes, and I stayed in the hall till my mother and the doctor came down, and towering above me, went into the drawing room. I can hear his voice today, soft, clear, and at the same time blurred, and somehow or other trustworthy. The only other person I ever was to see in adult life who resembled him was the famous actor, Sir Johnston Forbes-Robertson, and he resembled him very closely, particularly as regards the eyes and the voice. But he was of the previous generation. If I had ever known a man who looked like my doctor and had been my contemporary, then I would have loved him. But I never did. A sound and logical judgment, 'this is what I would be safe with', tethered me to a man who, as far as I know, never existed.

My sense that here was a protector, and a source of happiness, was at first a guess, but it was established as a fact when the spring came, for my sister Winifred was no longer ill. She was up, she was out, she looked as she had done before, her lovely hazel eyes and her long brown hair and her white skin were again luminous, she looked again like a girl in a painting. She would recite poetry to me for hours, she was glad to hold my hand and walk out with me, which was not the way of my eldest sister, the odious Lettie, who never touched me except to push me about, under the wounding pretext that in my stupidity, my slowness of sense, I was getting not in her way (that would make it seem as if she were looking to her own convenience in her irritation) but in the way of someone else who, almost inevitably, was purely imaginary. My sister Winifred only occasionally suggested that I was doing the wrong thing and, looking back over the best part of a century, I marvel how a child so young could be so wise. She never corrected me, she simply supplied me with information regarding how things could be conveniently done, since it had not come my way.

Now I had someone to walk with who would pick me up if I fell and pluck me back if I started to cross the road without making sure it was clear. This was because the doctor had made her well. That I had been conditioned to accept without question. My mother, to take away any natural fears, had never mentioned a doctor in the presence of her children without adding the phrase 'who makes you well'. I had the doctor to thank for the preservation of the most precious human being I knew (for of course I thought my parents super-human).

And as for the religious field, I remember so well that autumn afternoon when my father came into the garden down the steps from the french window, and found me busy at a flowerbed which I had cleared from the yellow hands of leaves cast by the chestnut trees.

'What are you digging up?' he asked in alarm. (Not that he knew anything about gardening, beyond a curiously detailed knowledge of fuchsias, which had grown profusely at his home in County Kerry.)

'I'm digging up conkers,' I said.

'I doubt if there'll be any conkers in that flower bed,' he objected. 'Lettie and Winnie have been clearing them off each morning because of the spring flowers. Are you sure you're not digging up bulbs?'

'I'm sure they're conkers,' I told him. 'I buried them myself.'

'Why did you do that?'

'I am God,' I explained, 'and they are people, and I made them die, and now I am resurrecting them.'

'Oh, you are, are you?' said my father, and sat down on the iron steps and watched me, drawing on his pipe. Presently he asked, 'But why did you make the people die if you meant to dig them up again? Why didn't you just leave them alone?'

To that I replied, 'Well, that would have been all right for them. But it would have been no fun for me.'

He nodded. 'I see that,' he said, and went on sitting there, looking at me with a gusto which soon puzzled me. This was a nice enough game, but not enough to hold a grownup's attention for quite so long. I came to the conclusion that he must be watching me simply because he loved me. My heart swelled and I dropped my trowel and ran over to him and put my arms round his neck and was swung up into his tobacco-ish warmth. My mother told me years afterwards that he had repeated the conversation to her, saying that I had blown the whole gaff and he saw a great future for me rather on the lines of the atheist Popes of the middle ages.

MISS LYSAGHT

We left the little house in Streatham when I was five years old to go to Richmond.* I don't remember the moving at all. I think I was sent away to stay with relatives.

My mother's closest friends in the neighbourhood were an obscure but talented artist named Charles Lander and his wife Mary.* They were childless, and Charles was very diligent, so Mary Lander often asked my mother to bring my two elder sisters and myself to tea. This we enjoyed very much, partly because they lived in a delicious enclave by the river. First we used to go for a little walk on the river bank, for fear of being late, because we had such pitifully few social engagements that each was a challenge and we had to rise to it. Then we used to go on to the Landers' house, which was on a most delightful terrace, built on top of a boatbuilder's shed. It was called St Helena Terrace, which gives a clue to its date, and to get to it one mounted some stone steps from the grubby towing path and found oneself among the airs and graces of Bath; some of the tenants were the kind of people one might have met at a ball in Jane Austen's time. There was a balustraded walk which looked over the water to Richmond Bridge and a romantic island which still comes into my dreams quite often. It was covered with very tall trees of the aspen sort, which trembled and languished under the river breezes as seaweed trembles under the tides. To the left was a show of elegant and decorous and useful houses large enough to raise a family in, if there were no need for pomp, each with a long garden that from spring to autumn was a mass of flowers.

Among the occupants were retired people, some of them very old, and among the oldest was a spinster who lived next to the Landers. When we went there in the summer, she was always sitting on her first-floor balcony reading, and we children used to bow our heads and squint upwards, so that we could see the hands that grasped her book, which were hyacinth-coloured claws. That was all we could see of her, except for a ribbon top-knot to her cap, sometimes lavender and sometimes pale rose, and the cascade over her knees and down to her feet of the assorted textiles which old ladies wore in those days, apparently for some ritual purpose, since they hung as thick over their aged bones in summer as they did in winter.

My sister Winifred, who had the senses of a hawk, said in the hall: 'That old lady on the balcony next door is interested in us; when the door opened and we came in she put down her book and leaned forwards and rubbed her eyes as if she wanted to see us better.'

My sister Lettie said, 'Nonsense', a word she applied to almost everything Winifred or I said or did. But in the middle of tea Mrs Lander said to my mother, 'Why, it nearly went out of my mind – Miss Lysaght, who lives next door, says she is a distant cousin of your husband's, and wants you to go in and give her half an hour before you leave. And take the children. She particularly wanted to see them.'

My mother asked some questions calmly enough, and then cried out in misery, 'But the children! How can I take the children? What will she think of their dreadful cheap clothes? What will she think of my dreadful clothes?' Mrs Lander made no attempt to dispute an opinion she evidently thought indisputable, and answered comfortably, 'Miss Lysaght will see neither your clothes nor the bairns' either, for she's nearly blind.'

The half-hour with Miss Lysaght worked out so well that it lasted an hour and was the first of many visits. In one of those crowded rooms which are lived in by old people who have had to move from a large house to a small one late in life, we were received by an elegant old skeleton, who greeted my mother with something more than politeness and winked at us children and said, 'I know you very well by sight. Did it strike you that if you squint up I could squint down?'

But my surprise and pleasure at being able to catch the attention of this exotic creature was not to last long in its full strength. Miss Lysaght then took my mother's hand again in her gentle blue claw and said, 'I couldn't resist asking you to come and see me, though it's a great bore to visit anybody as old as I am. But if your husband is the Charles Fairfield I think he is, then I am his Kerry cousin.'

My mother mistook what she meant, and began talking of the Fairfields' family home at Tralee, for she had never heard the expression which is the Irish version of *cousine à la mode de Bretagne*, which indicates a relationship so remote that it would be forgotten in a less isolated district where people can pick and choose their friends. She said that she was glad of the possibility that she and her husband and her children had a charming relative that had been till then unknown to them, that Papa was always telling us about the beauties of County Kerry, and that she was always hoping he would take us there, and if he did it would be so pleasant to find at our journey's end some nice relatives.*

My mother had by now so few friends that she blossomed in the company of any interesting and responsible human beings; and my sisters and I were delighted by Miss Lysaght's appearance, for she was one of those strong-minded women who keep to the fashion of the period when they were happiest. In her case this had been in the years just before the crinoline was adopted (for she had been born in 1818) and when the fashionable woman was thought of as tender and melting. The cap, of which we had till then only seen the ribbon top-knot, was a small muslin promise of submission, and her pale grey shawl lay on her sloping shoulders like a yoke, and the folds of her dark grey skirts would have tripped her up had she moved at what was evidently, from her speech and her gestures, her normal pace. But she was not shabby like our mother, for her clothes were exquisitely kept by her maid, so she appeared not like an old woman time had left behind, but an actress punctually dressed to make her entrance on a stage set for a costume play.

She had a face that had the brooding look of a young jockey, and like a boy she used to run her hand through her hair when she did not remember something, disturbing her cap and putting it straight as if it were a specially disorderly lock. She was indeed nearly blind and she moved her face from one or other of us and made little clicking sounds of impatience, she so longed to ingest every detail of us, and hardly anything was going through her cataracted gaze.

It was delightful to have value for her, because now one saw her not humped in a wicker chair but standing straight in the middle of her pretty room. My sisters and I liked her so well we overlooked what might have been a disadvantage for an old lady wanting to make friends with children. The malady that had turned her hands hyacinth blue had also made her lips faint violet, as if she had been sucking a lead pencil, and the flushed patches on her cheeks were the colour of inkstains that soap and water have not quite moved from a napkin. We did not mind this at all. Her way of getting old was to turn blue, and there was nothing more to it.

RICHMOND
HIGH SCHOOL

Our headmistress was a slight little woman with sad grey eyes and a plangent voice, who surprised us all by occasionally prolonging Prayers by drawing our attention to minor festivals of the church in which she hoped we would participate, always with an air of appealing to us to do so before it was too late, though as her vocal chords conveyed a sense of despair, we crossly felt she was panicking, though most of us were pious; not very pious, but pious. But there was no feeling of hostility to her.

One afternoon a teacher sent me out of the room for some offence that nobody could identify; another girl and I had asked her the possible meaning of some place-names in Scotland, and she thought I did this to annoy her. While I was standing in the corridor the headmistress came along, and came to a dead stop, saying, 'Tchh, tchh!' She enquired what I had done, and I answered her vaguely, wishing the poor thing would not take on so about nothing.

'Yes, yes,' I kept on saying in soothing tones, but she replied, with increasing excitement, by warning me of the effects of such determined indiscipline as mine, which would in the end alienate me from the fountain of all goodness. Her voice broke. 'Can I not touch your hard heart?', she asked, and led me along the corridor to her own room. There she put two chairs side by side, kneeled in front of me and said, 'Kneel, child,' in tones that embarrassed me as much as if she had stripped, and when we had both turned our faces towards the seats of the chair, she began to pray that God would soften my heart.

I was outraged. This seemed the worst breach of good manners I had ever observed among grownups, to rope into prayer a person who, by virtue of being a pupil, was in many senses under the taboos one applied to strangers. I was appalled. When her prayers became so fervent that she broke into sobs, I became infantile and took one thumb back from the proper arrangement for prayer, and sucked it.

There was a knock at the door, which my headmistress did not hear. It was I who said, 'Come in! *Come in!*' It was the Matron, a crisp personality, who came in. She had been a close friend of the last headmistress, who had left us to marry a baronet. We had liked her, particularly when she had spent before our wondering eyes more and more money on lovely clothes for her handsome person. Fixing her eyes on the present holder of office, the Matron cleared her throat. The headmistress stopped her invocation, raised her streaming eyes to the Matron's face, and said nothing.

At length the Matron said, 'Can I make you a cup of tea?' Her tone reminded me that it was often stressed that she was no ordinary matron but the widow of an Army officer. The silence endured. The headmistress said pettishly, 'Amen. Ah, there you are Matron.' But she did not know what movement she could make without losing even more of her dignity. It was the first time I had ever seen a grownup behave like a complete fool. She must be mad!

I did quite the wrong thing. I said, 'Yes, do have a cup of tea. You'll feel,' I said, my voice wobbling with sympathy as there appeared before me the towers of Colney Hatch, the best-known lunatic asylum in Victorian England, 'so much better.'

She did not move, and I found myself shouting, 'Get up! Get up off the floor!' The Matron's hand lay flat on my backbone and she pushed me out into the corridor. 'You get back to your classroom,' she said, and the door was banged.

It will be understood that things never went quite well for me at Richmond High School again. I kept getting wretched about different aspects of the incident. I still felt my infant self was caught in a terrible breach of good manners by her praying for me and making me pray with her when we had what was, in our case, the purely utilitarian relationship of teacher and pupil. And that was not the end of it. She had (though I was not to understand it till later) by her breach of good manners put me into what people call, in a disagreeably imprecise phrase, 'a false position'. I really respected my headmistress because she had faith in a Being of whose existence there is no proof, and invoked that Being in order to benefit a child who was nothing to her, which really is a beautiful act. But she had looked a thorough ass when she had committed this act, and this had given an undeserved advantage to Matron, who was simply a mechanical doll, not willing to make that sacrifice, not understanding why anybody else should make it. And Matron had that advantage not only over my headmistress, but, somehow, over me. I should not have said 'Come in.' I should not have joined in that offer of a cup of tea (which I saw more and more as a subtle and belittling act). I should have been loyal to my headmistress and made a fool of myself. But surely it is, in a way, treachery to one's father and mother, to one's family, to the great family of the human race, to make a fool of oneself, to reject the reason, the gift of the unknown.

I do not mean that these were the thoughts that I was then thinking; but I would claim that the unhappy confusion I felt was the rudimentary form of such an argument, which made me very pleased to go to Bournemouth shortly afterwards. I was sent there because my family was breaking up. My father was going to Africa in a gallant attempt to salvage the family fortunes by taking on a job for which he was much too ill and rather too old; my mother was going to Edinburgh to nurse her mother, who had been stricken with a chronic ailment, and to look for a house, since my sister was about to start her medical studies at the University of Edinburgh. The other sister was expected to take an Arts degree there later. So it had been arranged that my mother should sell our house at Richmond and leave me at a boarding-school in Bournemouth, where Jessie Watson Campbell, the cousin who had been taken in by my grandmother, taught music and French.*

In view of what had happened at Richmond High School I was glad to go; and indeed in all circumstances I would have been glad to be wherever Cousin Jessie was. At that time she must have been in her late sixties, and she was a human harvest, the crops from a fertile land sown with talents and affections, but with absolutely no brilliance. She was simply a steady light by which one could feel safety. In appearance she was very like a bourgeois Frenchwoman painted by Ingres or some later French artist. She had abundant chestnut hair, dressed in smooth bandeaux, an unlined face, kept smooth by weekly applications of almond ointment; calm brows and huge clear eyes and a chaste, not to say voluntarily dowdy look from the waist down: no

suggestion that running or jumping or any other violent action could
be expected for the feet and ankles which, sometimes seen under a
dressing gown, appeared as elegant as any cocotte's. It was natural she
should look French, for she had stayed in Orléans until 1900, when
she had moved back to England, to be near her family, and had settled
in Bournemouth. She was gentle and loving, and never ceased to
spend her small income on presents for us all.

*Charles Fairfield's African venture was not a success and he returned to
England, where he died in Toxteth, Liverpool in 1906.*

My father was found dead in a back bedroom in a Liverpool boarding-
house where he had been scraping a living by copying documents. He
was totally alone in the city. He had made one last hopeless attempt to
snatch money out of thin air in the improbable locale of Sierra Leone,
and when his return journey brought him back to the Elder Dempster
docks he moved no more than a mile or two, knowing that he had
nothing to bring to his destitute home except a further item of
destitution. A year or two passed before he died and my mother was
sent for to bury him. I remember how she came home with some scrap
of paper on which he had scrawled messages that he had loved my
mother and my sisters and myself, they were found scrawled behind his
dead body, and she told us with wet eyes how she had gone into
Liverpool Cathedral after she had seen his body coffined and heard a
choirboy sing very beautifully, 'I know that my Redeemer liveth.' She
told us too how he had endeared himself to a young clerk who lived in
the boarding-house, who had said to her, 'At first we didn't believe all
his stories of great men, he talked as if he had known them, and then I
went to the Public Library and checked up on some stories, and of
course they were all true.'

My father had helped the young man with some examination he
had had to pass, which I think was in Spanish, which my father spoke
well; but the point was that he had endlessly entertained him, they
had gone for long walks together and he had talked all the way, the
clerk said, and on all sorts of subjects, on politics and philosophy and

history; there was nothing he did not seem to know. And my mother said tco that my father had nothing when he died. His watch was gone; his studs and cufflinks were gone; even his old and battered dressing-case had gone. If he had been found dead in a hedgerow he could not have been more picked bare of possessions. If he had not left his regimental badge at home when he went to Africa, we would have had nothing of him.

MY RELATIONS WITH
MUSIC

My relations with music have been abnormal because my relations with sound are abnormal. They always have been. When I was a little child there were two forms of torment which I had to suffer without the slightest sympathy from my elders, though they were ready enough to comfort me when I had to undergo suffering which seemed to me to be much less, like a cold in the chest or a bruise on the knee. One of the torments I had to face alone and unsuccoured was attendance at Church, for the reason that the sound of an organ gave me a pain as bad as acute toothache. It was a pain that ran from a point above my left ear. I remember well the direction in which the grinding screw always followed, from left to right. I still feel this distress at the sound of any organ.

The other torment I endured was the ghastly row that filled any railway terminal. For my first few years we lived in London and when we went for holidays I started to cry as soon as we got into the cab in anticipation of the assault I was going to endure as soon as I was dragged into Waterloo or Victoria or King's Cross or Euston. It was not even localized like the sound of the organ. The noise the locomotives made seemed to beat me on the head and the body indiscriminately. I used to be hauled into the railway carriage in a state of dripping misery which nobody understood.

How magical my mother then appeared to me as she sat down at the piano and evoked sounds that caused me no pain whatsoever, but instead were pure pleasure. She played Schumann and Beethoven and Mozart and Chopin, and a good deal of Mendelssohn, *Songs Without Words*, which was meat and drink to me for the reason that made them suspect to other generations: they were such pleasant sounds that they balanced the torment of the organ and the locomotive. For me there is a special value in those *Songs Without Words*. I imagine every performer on any musical instrument outside percussion wants to achieve a perfect *legato*, and how these pieces helped even me to get nearer that aim.

When I was in my late twenties I performed the unusual feat of getting pneumonia in my left ear, and my hearing altered. I used to hear the notes of a scale as going up or coming down. A note was high or not so high or lower or low, with the same meaning as when those terms refer to material objects – to the steps of a staircase, or to points on a slope. Since I had this affliction of the ear it has all been different. I cannot quite define what I hear. A piece of music is now for me something like a film representation of an island over which a sea is washing, leaving parts of it exposed, but submerging others. All is under strong light, and the exposed parts glimmer. The island is of shifting dark rich colours, the sea of shifting richer and lighter colours. But that some notes are high and that some are low never now occurs to me. I know that when the island glitters the notes are high, because of what I can see as the Queen of the Night's solo from *The Magic Flute*.* I now see: that isn't accurate. For what I am describing is not really sight. It is analogous to sight, but not the same. I live with mystery.

Music is part of human life and partakes of the human tragedy. There is much more music in the world than is allowed to change into heard sounds and prove its point. Music partakes also of the human mystery. It is something the ear contrives for its own pleasure; but my ears are damaged, and music is not destroyed for me, it seems to have an independent existence. What music means to me above all is that I can believe that on a silent globe it still might exist; and that if people go back to the moon they might quite suddenly hear something. The lifeless moon might be like Beethoven: deaf but still a composer.

My defence has been the capacity for pure pleasure inherited from my father and mother. The pleasure with which he used to paint water-colours, rather in the Lear manner, and talk of historical and political matters, say the philosophy of Burke, which made him glow; the pleasure with which she played Schumann's *Carnaval* and looked at the mellow brick and creamy stone of Hampton Court or the Georgian houses round Ham; that pleasure was my perpetual anaesthetic and stimulant, and because of it I have not had such a bad life after all.

APPENDIX

HENRY MAXWELL ANDREWS

Yesterday* I found at the back of a drawer in my study a large envelope of the substantial sort now rarely seen, the colour of lightly baked bread and almost as tough, called a Manilla envelope because it was made of hemp from the Philippines. It was full of letters concerning my husband, Henry Maxwell Andrews, in his youth, long before we were married, and for me they were loaded with historic rather than personal familiarity, since he had then quite a different self which had not survived till he met me, but the background was known to me.

My marriage was certainly the most important thing in my life, though I never understood why it had that primacy. The second most important thing was a political decision I made when I was quite young and which I still hold to, or rather which still holds me as I approach death.* My work might have been as important as either of these if it had not been condemned to exist in limbo. I was never able to live the life of a writer because of these two over-riding factors, my sexual life, or rather death, and my politics.

Most of the papers in the Manilla envelope refer to my husband as he was in the year 1914, when, nineteen and an undergraduate at New College, Oxford, he went at the end of the summer term to Hamburg with his mother, Mrs Lewis Andrews, to carry out a sad errand. He went to look after her while she consulted her lawyers as to the recovery and resale of the house where she and her husband had lived for some years before his death in 1908. It was one of the smaller residences in the lovely quarter which the nearly patrician bourgeoisie of Hamburg had built on the green edge of the Alster's landscaped basin. In its early days this suburb had looked like the German idea of a Greek city, and in the twentieth century it still composed a very handsome waterfront.

Mrs Andrews was anxious to get rid of the house without delay, for she had thought she had sold it soon after her husband's death, when she and her two young sons had gone to England to live with his bachelor brother, Ernest Andrews. But the purchaser had run out of money before he completed the payments, and had surrendered his tenure; and she wanted to resell the house before she had to meet the mounting taxes, which she was in no financial state to pay without great embarrassment. (There was money in her family, and her husband's, but not for her.) So this was for several reasons a painful return journey for her and her son.

The most obvious reason was that Lewis Andrews, who was by nature a most charming and deeply affectionate man, passionately attached to his wife and two sons, had for almost the whole of the period they had occupied this house been suffering from exophthalmic goitre, otherwise Graves' disease, otherwise hyper-thyroidism. This is a lingering malady now easily cured by doses of thyroid extract or by a not very exacting operation, but then incurable and agonizing in its final stages. For years the house had seemed to her little but a private hospital with only one patient, who slowly changed from the most intimate of all companions to a suffering stranger.

It was to exorcize this horror that in 1914 she had taken her son Henry back with her, though he was the younger of her two boys; and there was melancholy in that choice too. Her elder son, Ernest, was in disgrace because he had been expelled from his Oxford college for cheating at an examination. This change of plan was hard on Henry, who had hoped to spend the Long Vacation either with a reading party in Wales or in France with the family of a Sorbonne professor, with whom he and his brother had already spent two summers being coached in a villa outside Chartres. But he was at that time devoted to his mother, and was wholly concerned with helping her through her ordeal, which was dire. For though in returning to Hamburg she was coming back to the place where she had spent all her early life, which had been unusually triumphant, her later life in that same city had brought her little but disappointment. This she had suffered in exile. Not that she was German by ancestry. Neither she nor her husband, I discovered when I looked into the family history, had a drop of

German blood in their veins, although they seemed at a superficial glance to be bound by countless ties to the German Empire.

The pedigree of Mary Andrews was odd.* Her mother had been a Miss Chapman of Lancashire, who was alleged to be Irish in origin, kin to the family of baronets, one of whom fathered T.E. Lawrence. She was certainly related to the North Country family of clerics and academics who produced the archaeologist and Greek scholar, Sir John L. Myres, who wrote badly enough to cancel the advantage of his scholarship but produced one engaging little book on the Mediterranean.* Nobody knows how this Miss Chapman came to take a Lithuanian husband, but she did, and her husband was probably the only member of the Hereditary Order of Teutonic Knights to be married in Manchester Cathedral. His name was Chavatsky, and he had a father of beautiful appearance, with a high forehead and deepset eyes and a delicate mouth above a pointed beard, who was long remembered for his tactful and pacific work on the Riga State Council under the Tsars. His son, Mary's father, was a civil engineer, thus bowing to a Baltic States' tradition binding younger sons to an occupation approved by Peter the Great, and he was to be cruelly betrayed by time. He specialized in the construction of tramways when these were supposed to be the final and ideal form of urban transport. He went to Hamburg and built their tramway system for them, which then gave him a certain chic, and even stayed on in his later years as the manager of the system. But by the time that Mary Andrews became my mother-in-law in 1930, she no longer mentioned that fact.

She was beautiful in a Brunnhildish way: over six foot tall, with masses of glossy black hair that fell to her hips, and immense black eyes; and she had a reasonable dowry, so that she got engaged at eighteen to a young officer. But he contracted consumption and took ten years to die, and it would have been contrary to a strong sentimental German convention for her family to break off the engagement, so at twenty-eight she went to the poor boy's funeral in the character of an old maid. She was saved a year later when she met Lewis Andrews. He had come to Hamburg to visit his father's relatives, who lived there though he and they also were not of German blood.

The Andrews family was partly Scottish and partly Danish. That combination had been improbably effected by the circumstance that a

Danish baron had visited Sir Walter Scott at Abbotsford under two erroneous suppositions. He thought that Scott was a Jacobite in his sympathies and that he believed the poems of Ossian to be genuine. Sir Walter, however, received him politely and left his illusions as they were.* Well content, the Danish baron went on his way back to the port of Leith, across the Border country, and somewhere near the Tweed and the Till passed a field with some attractive yearlings in it. He stopped and sought out the owner, who was a laird in a small way, named Andrews, bought three of the yearlings, and seeing that there were six Andrews about the place, suggested that one of them might care to bring the horses over to his home in Schleswig, settle the horses in and have a short holiday before he returned. The middle lad took on the chore, and thereafter came home only as a visitor. He married a Danish girl with some Jewish blood in her, and after that it was only to put their children in Scottish schools that he visited his native land. Most of these children stayed in Scotland, whence one or two emigrated to Canada and India.

In the latter half of the nineteenth century there were only about three or four Andrews in Schleswig, where the original Andrews emigrant had established his home; and so this line of the family ceased to be Danish after the German War of 1865 and the annexation of Schleswig-Holstein. All of these men were fairly successful horse dealers, and one of them was doing well at another trade of which I had never thought until I married his grandson. In countless nineteenth-century Continental novels characters overtaken by strong emotion in the town of J, K, L, M or N, left one spot for another by hailing a droshky, but few readers ponder on the ownership of these vehicles. They could belong to their drivers, one might suppose, but too many of them were drawn by healthy horses, and were bright with new paint and had clean cushions, to make that supposition likely. The owners were in fact capitalists who invested in fleets of droshkies, and among them was my husband's grandfather, Mark Andrews, who owned livery stables in several towns in Denmark and one or two in Germany.

He was according to family legend, both bad and mad. He would have died in the gutter had it not been for his wife, the child of a mixed marriage between a Danish merchant and the daughter of a Polish Jewess and a Danish civil servant; who looked out of her photographs with a fixed stare and a set jaw and no wonder. Her husband was a spasmodic drunkard and would desert his home to spend his days in beerhalls and his nights sleeping beside his horses in the livery stables. He was also a gambler, and it was said that he had once gambled away his silver tableware and his English china; and it was then that his wife ostentatiously took in washing. She did it, they said, not to keep her neighbours' clothes clean, but to teach her husband to keep his nose clean; and he was never so crass a sot again, though he could never have passed as a teetotaller.

For the rest he carried on the Andrews tradition. His sons – Lewis, Ernest and Willy – spoke English, Danish and German indiscriminately about the hearth and were sent across the North Sea to get their schooling, not in Scotland by this time, but to some endowed school in the City of London. At the end of their schooling Willy returned to work in a distant relative's factory in Germany, and Lewis and Ernest Andrews stayed in London; they went first to a Commercial College, and then into a famous firm known as Wallace's, which was in the import-export business in Burma, as clerks, and were quickly raised to more responsible positions.

By some process not easy to understand, these three brothers became immensely prosperous before they reached middle life.* At first I thought their reputation for wealth must have been a figment created by family pride, for the three of them were said to have been worth more than four million pounds between them at the beginning of the twentieth century; but after my husband's death I found letters and bank statements which confirmed that they had had that or more. Even so I could hardly credit my eyes, for the only one of the brothers I knew, Uncle Ernest, had never quite got the hang of worldly affairs and was baffled by such everyday matters as buying a car. In the early twenties he set about doing just that, and fell into the hands of a demon salesman who persuaded him into having a car built for himself at vast expense, so monstrous that if it entered Bond Street it could not turn up any side street and was forced to go on till it got to Piccadilly. But certainly the memory was there, and when Lewis and Mary went out to serve Wallace's in Rangoon they lived on a scale impossible to have been financed by his salary. They started living in a commodious flat over the firm's offices; but not so many years after their marriage they had earmarked a residence, horrible in its elaboration and costliness.

I keep by me several weighty photograph albums showing this projected home as a tasteless architectural riot which could justly be described as 'an expense of spirit in a waste of shame', to use a phrase which Shakespeare threw away on a more commonplace routine.* The drawing room and the dining room are like twin gymnasia, and are lit by massive standard lamps resembling those on the Thames Embankment; and the rooms are dotted with little tables and light chairs, suggesting that in a country where there are many elephants rickety furniture may have its special elegance. Everywhere there are versions of the jade and ivories and porcelains and *cloisonnés** that the East could easily spare for its Western invaders: one piece I can recognize, having often been called by my mother-in-law to admire it in her Kensington drawing room – a lily with petals of ivory and coral stamens, pale jade stalks and dark jade leaves, set against black velvet in a three-foot high Burmese silver frame. A photograph of the staff required to maintain this curiously mistaken residential tribute to the East shows what looks like the population of a small village winding in procession round a canteen block or a municipal wash-house.

A few years before the date fixed for Lewis Andrews' retirement he and his family returned to Europe for a holiday, to visit their relatives and choose a house for their retirement. They travelled in luxury, with an English nurse and a German lady's maid, and approached Hamburg by a line drawn from the port of Naples to Hamburg through a number of beauty spots. They stayed at a hotel on Lake Garda, at the Danieli in Venice, and at a famous hotel in Zurich, the name of which I have forgotten, though I visited it when it still retained some of its glory. It was a romantic assemblage of towers and balconies in the Hans Andersen tradition, where there were only the finest linen sheets in the bedrooms, enormous bath towels and hand-sewn face towels in the bathrooms, and the guests all came down to dinner wearing full evening dress and, if not their best jewellery, at least some of their real jewels.*

Arriving at Hamburg they stayed at a hotel and, at their leisure, looked for a house. This was not to be their principal residence. That, for these people who were dogged in their determination to remain British, had to be in London, probably in one of the Bayswater terraces overlooking the Park, or in Eaton Square, or possibly near Ascot or Guildford. But what they were looking for in Hamburg was a German pied-à-terre, which they could use themselves and lend to brother Ernest who, after a Burmese apprenticeship, was still working in the head office of Wallace Brothers in London. They found exactly what they wanted in this villa on the Alster, which was one of the older buildings in the quarter, and Mary Andrews rapidly furnished one floor so that they could live there for the rest of their leaves. Her husband had been complaining lately that he found the hotel intolerably noisy; he was almost irritable when he pressed his wife to buy curtains, carpets, furniture without delay so that they could move in and get some peace. Once she had made her purchases, he often made her send them back and change them: carpets had to be thicker, curtains more opaque and more subdued in colour, armchairs and sofas more deeply padded.

He was not nearly so easy to please as he had been. Formerly he had been plump, a great present-giver, and slow to lose patience; now he was irritable and sleepless, and his eyes protruded in an angry stare. It was soon obvious that he could not return to Rangoon and as his wife, big and healthy, complained, the villa was slowly injected with the hush of a clinic. He had been an exceptionally playful and comradely father, but now he could not bear his sons' chatter or the sounds they made in running about the house. He had always liked to have his wife in the same room, day and night, but now he would ask her (and his doctors) to let him sit and lie alone. He became unjust, insisting on the sudden dismissal of quite dutiful servants, and he criticized his wife's clothes and management of the household. It is a tribute to his character that everybody around him interpreted these changes as a sign that he was very ill.

He died in 1908, and his widow was to discover immediately that she was left in comparative poverty. As I have said, I have never been able to understand how the three Andrews brothers became so rich in something like thirty-five years, and I understand no better how Lewis Andrews (and indeed his brother Willy) then suddenly became poor while only Ernest remained rich, but not nearly so rich as he had been. Neither did Mary Andrews understand this abrupt change of circumstance, and she was appalled. Her prime consideration was not financial. The villa was worth some money, she had inherited a certain sum of money from her Lithuanian grandfather, and Ernest had said that he would give his brother's wife and children a home. She was also not too immodest in thinking that she might remarry, for though she was in her middle forties her hugeness and her brooding expression, which made her look like a comely elephant about to trumpet an aria from the *Ring*, was exactly what German men admired at that time. She also felt no fear of being unable to gratify her more expensive appetites, because her ignorance of the world prevented her from learning how much easier it is to lose money than make it come one's way a second time. She was, many years later, to tell me that it was one of her most cherished hopes that my husband, her son, should do so well that she could keep her carriage again, although carriages by then had vanished from the face of the earth.

But in spite of this optimism she had, even in 1908, her fears. She was doubtful whether she would be able to give her two sons an expensive education, and she knew that for a time at least she would not be able to give such expensive presents to Uncle This and Aunt That and the Cousins Other as she and her husband had joyfully and carefully chosen for them during the years of their marriage. I do not think that these regrets did her discredit. My mother-in-law resembled an elephant far too closely but she was one of the most innocent of human beings.

❧❧

Mary's sons were never able to understand the coolness of the reception that awaited them in London when they arrived with their mother to accept Uncle Ernest's invitation to his home. First of all, the boys were sent to an unsuitable school. It would have been easy for their uncle with the aid of his colleagues in Wallace's to enter them at one of the famous schools, not too far from London. Ernest had the money and these boys would have been welcome pupils wherever the tradition of learning was alive and adventurous. They were already polyglot, and their Latin and Greek were good for their ages; they were extremely musical and Henry had a remarkable mathematical gift. Moreover, both were athletes, though Henry was to lose his advantage in a year or two through a deterioration of his sight. But Uncle Ernest deposited them in a school recognized as belonging to the 'outer ring',* which was situated in the Midlands and at that time drew for its pupils on upper middle-class families not used to or tolerant of the cosmopolitan world. The Andrews family had no connection with any members of the staff or the parents of any of the pupils, and, adults and adolescents alike, they were put down as rich German Jews of no importance who were using the school as a step on the ladder to social advancement. The resulting chill was noted by the boys and puzzled them, for all their lives they had seen their parents and relatives treated as people of consequence who were also very likeable.

Indeed, the conditions of life now imposed on Mary and the boys were altogether most unsatisfactory. Ernest had given up his correct and comfortable bachelor flat near Berkeley Square when he realized he had to house Mary all the year round, and the boys for their holidays, and he had prepared for their joint life two remarkably unsuitable dwellings. One was an early Victorian mansion slightly north of Finsbury Park, which had been a district favoured by City merchants and bankers in the past, but not in the first years of the twentieth century. If there was any local society in which Mrs Andrews could have joined, its members would have been elderly and strangers would have found it hard to form bonds with it. Also, she had no transport. This meant that if Mary Andrews wanted to go anywhere a woman of her sort would want to go, say, shopping in Bond Street and Regent Street, or to a matinée or to drink tea at Gunter's,* she had to take a long journey by omnibus or by district railway, very destructive to the elaborate dress of the period. When she went to see her sons at school, the journeys and the temperate reception she got from the staff were as disconcerting, and nothing softened the asperities. Usually Uncle Ernest was too busy to accompany her, and she had to explain away this to the boys by telling them that he was forced to work very hard in order to make more money, so that he might pay for their school fees and their clothes and the house in the country. That was somewhere in the home counties, with a garden consisting largely of rhododendron beds, and therefore dark and flowerless for most of the year. There too, the family knew no one.

Though Mary Andrews was intensely unhappy the boys were not. Henry was entirely happy with his education. So long as he could read history and improve his classical languages and play the games of mathematics, he wanted nothing more. His brother was also happy. He could always make people laugh, he was an impressive boxer, he sang like an angel and played various musical instruments. Soon he could not have been more popular. They were biddable, too, in a way that made for happiness. Their mother assured them that Uncle Ernest was making great sacrifices for their sakes and that they must always be grateful to him and obey him; so they took it that that was their duty and did it. Mary was indeed a noble liar; but she did not leave her task at that. She sold Uncle Ernest the idea that the boys should go to France for their summer holidays and study with the same Sorbonne professor who had taught the children of one of the staff of Wallace brothers; and it opened Heaven to her children. Henry laid the foundation of the knowledge of French literature which made him unique in his world, and often made him look distinguished enough among my world of writers. I have seen him make the best of Bloomsbury blush, though without intention, for his malice was of the mildest brew. His brother had other advantages from these holidays. He worked hard at the piano and learned many new songs; and there were pretty girls of the family, dashing boys, a rising painter who was in love with one of the girls. Friendships started there that were to last forty years. And for Henry it was all enclosed in solemnity, for the professor's little country villa was near Chartres; he knew early that road across the plains which at a certain spot runs forward and up till it seems to meet the base of the cathedral spire and climb up it and be unified with the sky.

Mary made her appearances there at times, but hurried off to Hamburg where she was always being called on to help her husband's relatives and her own (for she had a sister who had married a German) through illnesses and other crises. She went back there quite often during the boys' term time, particularly when they went to Oxford and were even happier there than they had been at school. It was surprising to Henry therefore that she showed such grief over her return to Hamburg in 1914. He sat beside her on a bed in a small hotel and rocked her in his arms as she wept, her eyes red and blind, her massive body so shaken by her tears that her enormous coiffure of glossy black hair slowly tumbled loose and slid over her shoulders, and she became as pathetic as a small woman. He learned with astonishment that she had a longstanding hatred of the place which she thought of not as her home (and her son had always believed it was just that, her home) but as the place which had abducted her from her true home; and that, to his surprise, was Lithuania. There she had lived in a house that was white not only because it was painted white but because everything in the district was clean; and the garden and the forest round it smelled clean. In Hamburg she had been enclosed by a close-pressed city threaded with blackish canals on which there trembled the reflections of ancient houses, fit dwellings for the witches out of the Grimms' terrifying fairy tales. Why did the Germans force on children such horrible stuff, she sobbed, and went on to complain that the blackened waters and the bending lines of blackened houses led as if attracted to some place that would be beautiful, that would make up for this squalor, but landed one in a dirty port crowded with dirty ships, which in the night howled through their fog-horns like hungry dogs in the backyards of the slums.

It was not her home, she said. She had never had a home. Hamburg had not been her home, had not been kind to her when she had to live on and on as an unmarried girl while poor Franz had died. He himself had said, 'It is no use waiting for me,' but there she had been stuck. 'I had never been married, but I was like a widow at all the balls.' And then there was the awful funeral. Then it seemed that the spell was broken, and Lewis had come and had carried her off to Rangoon, but there too she never really had a home. Millions of brown people infested the forests, the jungle, the streets, the houses, in one's own house also; sometimes more of them than one knew were in one's house! And out there the white people too were strangers, they were not German, they were English. Well, so was she. But she was also Lithuanian. Nobody knew the purity of Lithuania. The cold in winter was frightful, but it was so pure. But then again Lithuania was Russian, she was not Russian, she had nothing to do with Russia. She really had no home. The house where a woman lived with her husband ought to be her home, even if he were lying in the grave. But even if someone gave her the villa on the Alster and she had the money to live there, it would not be her home. There had been an interruption of her husband's tenancy of the place. It became clear that the angry skeleton who had lived with her there in the end was so unlike her Lewis that she did not think of him as her husband at all.

Mary's son was astonished by her grief and the fortitude she had shown in not giving way to it before. But there were other things on Henry's mind. He had his own case against the Alster villa, which was not known to his mother. During the last two summers of Lewis's life he had constantly imagined that he could hear his sons shouting and banging drawers and whistling in their playroom and in the passages. This was a delusion. The boys' quarters were behind a padded door and were at the opposite end of the house and on a higher floor; and they were now too old to play with drums or whistles. But Lewis would not believe this, and insisted that they should go out into the garden to play, and went to his window to see that they were obeying. This was annoying and humiliating to the boys, who were often forced to go out of doors when they had already done enough exercise for the day, by bicycling or practising cricket and boxing with an English diplomat's son who lived nearby, and they would have liked to spend the rest of the day preparing their lessons for the tutor who came three days a week, or drawing and painting; and it was particularly irksome when they had to turn out on one of the days when the North German wind stung like acid.

This routine had imposed an unhappy image on Henry's mind. He was haunted by his father's day nurse, who used to turn the boys out of the house: a tall, thin woman, with pale blonde hair, pale blue eyes, and pale lips, a member of a religious community, clad in a uniform of stiff greyish material with a grudging cross at her corded throat. When she had hurried the boys out into the garden, holding the door open by not an unnecessary inch, so that she could close it at the first possible moment, she used to say in a flat voice, so soft that it had the unaccountable authority of a whisper: 'Keep as far from the house as you can.' They would turn their backs on her and walk away and come perhaps to a bench in the garden, and sit down. The flat voice, raised to something like the cry of an unusually controlled and malign gull, would reach them: 'Go further from the house.' They would go further, and again the call, unaltered: the barest diagram of exclusion.

'Go further from the house.' The words had no special effect when they were uttered aloud. But Henry had only to remember them in later life, as this woman uttered them, to start the symptoms of migraine.

The villa on the Alster had another maleficent memory for him: but what was remembered had not been wholly maleficent when it had happened. As Lewis Andrews' illness became worse the two boys were not allowed to enter the villa at all except for hushed meals in a basement room with their pale and anxious mother, and they spent most of the day and all night with the coachman and his wife, who occupied a lodge outside the garden gates. This was a pretty little building, originally a folly, in the miniature park of a more pompous dwelling pulled down some years before. This boarding out was not so much a hardship as might seem, though they missed their mother, because the coachman and his wife were unusually attractive people. Cousins, they were very much alike, dark-haired, blue-eyed, with a sort of slippery grace, who had some Baltic blood, though they had been brought up on a stud farm towards the Prussian border. They had about them a vivacity not at all North German and on another count remarkable, since they were middle-aged.

The boys missed both their parents, but the coachman and his wife were childless against their will, and all four were natural musicians. The coachman played a clarinet, and had a fair baritone, his wife played the harmonium, and both sang not very well but not badly either. The two boys' voices were still unbroken, they had absolute pitch and preternatural musical memories. This made their evenings warm and glorious. The coachman and his wife had worked for a time in Bremen and there they had been recruited into the ranks of a sect which called themselves Christian Scientists but would not, I think, have been accepted by Mrs Eddy.* Its worship was almost exclusively choral, and used a vast hymnody gathered from the churches, orthodox and heretical and schismatic, of the Judaic-Christian tradition. The net had been cast so widely that one of their favourites was The Glory Song, which was spreading through the United States and Europe, after the tours of two American evangelists, Torry and Alexander, just about this time. Every evening the coachman and his wife and the two boys sang hymns for an hour or two, ecstatically though softly, in case the sound reached the villa. The boys were enchanted.

It unfortunately happened that the sect had done two other things beside sing hymns. They offered up prayer *extempore*, that is to say inspired, for life everlasting: for the perpetual joy of standing by the throne and contemplating the shining Source of Life Eternal. They also offered up another kind of prayer: for the indefinite postponement of that supreme bliss. There was certainly an inconsistency here: they poured out their souls to God in an effort to persuade Him to raise them to Heaven, as soon as could be, if possible at once, but they also, at the first news of the sickness of a relative, or any friend, or even any respected figure in the community, of whatever age or condition, had to pray that the invalid might continue to live, if possible for ever. It was held that this prayer was bound to be efficacious provided the petitioner was not tainted with sin, or had refused to empty out his spirit to the last drop in his supplication. Henry, young as he was, detected the inconsistency. But he was very fond of the coachman and his wife, and he was sure they were telling the truth when they told him that by their prayers they kept alive their grand-aunt, resident near Bremen, who had been pronounced a hopeless case of heart disease fifteen years before. He and his brother had asked the coachman if such prayers should not be offered up for their father, and the coachman and his wife had made tentative offers to Mary Andrews, but she had assured them that her husband was not in any danger of dying.

But one evening the gardener came hurrying down to the lodge and called the coachman to speak to him in the lane outside; and he came back and put his arms round the boys' shoulders, and told them that the doctor said that their father was dying and how they must set about saving his life by prayer. '*Schnell! Schnell!*' ('Quickly! Quickly!') cried the coachman's wife. She pushed the boys down on their knees on the floor and, sometimes in turn and sometimes together, they asked God to save their Papa, first in German and then in English, because Papa was an Englishman. The tears were running down their faces and the sweat was running down their foreheads, and all the time the coachman's wife was clasping first the one child's head to her bosom and then the other, shaking them as if she were trying to shake the bees of ecstasy out of them as she sobbed '*Mehr! Mehr!*' ('More! More!') Their common frenzy mounted, the coachman and his wife joined in, there was babel in the little room, the boys' voices cracked in their tired throats, but they gasped on.

Suddenly it appeared that the coachman had at some point left the room and the cottage. Neither of the boys had noticed this, they only knew it for the reason that as he came back into the room, he must have been out of it. He said to them, 'Stop!' They obeyed and looked up at him with resentment. Though they felt as if their bodies were stretched like elastic and were about to snap, they had also been enjoying such a sense of power as they had never known before, that Henry was never to know again. A fluid was travelling through their veins, cool in the midst of all this fever, delicious as something that is tasted. The coachman said to his wife, 'Get them to bed.' They fell asleep at once and when they woke next morning they found their mother sitting beside the beds. She told them that their father was dead.

It was partly because of Henry's recollection of this scene (of which he and his brother never talked to each other) that he had not wanted to accompany Mary Andrews to Hamburg in 1914. He had, indeed, been brought there from time to time after the death of his father and the removal to England to visit the company of Uncle This and Aunt That and the Cousins Other, which struck him often as rather too numerous for comfort. Why did he have to have so many Germany relatives when he was English? But he had always cut such visits as short as he could, and in this his Uncle Ernest supported him. 'Better,' he would say, 'spend your time at the Grand Hotel at Folkestone and breathe that splendid air, there is nothing like it. And the food is lighter.' It was also on the cards that this present trip to Hamburg was going to be the most inconvenient visit of all. That he had not realized when he had left home, though it was the summer of 1914. Other people in England might be talking of impending war with Germany that summer, but Henry had paid very little attention, for the reason that the reverence he had been taught to feel for his Uncle Ernest was as yet unimpaired; and it was Uncle Ernest's opinion that neither Great Britain nor Germany would make war on the other because peace was essential to the well-being of each. (I was to come to know Ernest Andrews well in the future. I marvel to think that this man who was without the power to reason trusted two unwieldy states, true specimens of Leviathan, to keep the peace by their capacity for logical thinking.) But since Henry had arrived in Hamburg it had been plain to him that war between Germany and Great Britain was exactly what all the Germans in the cafés were talking about; and he had the most curious feeling when the manager of the hotel where he and his mother were staying had hesitantly said to him that perhaps he should be going home. Henry had answered as hesitantly. He knew that his mother was passionately anxious not to go back to England till she had sold the house and cleared herself of any obligation to pay taxes in Hamburg, but the reason for her intense feeling on this subject was not clear to him. As he pondered, the manager said kindly, 'You are of military age, you must be careful.' Henry was a beautiful shot, so had had his successes. But this activity had not till that moment seemed to have any relation with the phrase 'of military age'. Two separate worlds slid together and coalesced.

He was not frightened. I have known six or seven men of great courage and I place him among them. They all had the same reaction to danger. One was to carry out a process something like putting. Fear was the ball that lay on the green. They produced their courage and the ball ran towards the hole and dropped into it. Henry could do that, and his courage certainly took him over at Hamburg in 1914, but there was another force working on him. He felt quite well able to take care of himself in whatever circumstances were now to surround him. True, he took one conventional and commonsense way of meeting the crisis. On the boat from Harwich he had met a fellow undergraduate from New College, on his way to Hamburg to spend a few days there with friends before he went with one of them on a walking tour; and he had mentioned that his father's cousin, who was in the Cabinet, had promised to send him a coded telegram of warning if official circles thought war imminent; and Henry had asked him to drop him a note if the telegram arrived. It was the only precaution Henry took. He had the same feeling that he had felt on the night he prayed for his father; the same conviction of power, that was not proved empty by the death of his father, for that, he had often reflected in his adolescent years, must have been the will of God. He was prepared to experience another such victory.

The message from the Cabinet Minister never arrived. I have often wondered if this was an example of the same poor eye for politics which made him not dot the i's and cross the t's on more than one occasion in Parliament, or if he simply disliked his nephew.* So one day Henry helped his mother to pack up some possessions which she had left with a German bank, consisting mainly of a large amount of eighteenth-century English silver of considerable beauty and value. (It had been bought by the Andrews grandfather who kept a livery stable and a fleet of droshkies. In the eighties such silver was common on the Continent, though never cheap in Denmark because the prosperous Danish merchants of the eighteenth century had done much of their shopping in England.) All these Andrews possessions were taken to the American consulate, for the United States was the 'protective power' named to look after the interests of enemy aliens. The consul was one Harry Hays Morgan.* He was very kind to Mary and Henry Andrews, who at that moment must have looked like people of no importance unlikely ever to become important.

Henry's father, Lewis Andrews, had been careful to make both his sons British subjects like himself. As soon as they were born they were registered at the British Embassy in Rangoon. Their mother, who had been born with Russian nationality, became British when she married Lewis. It therefore seemed possible that Mary and Henry Andrews were integers in a wholly British family and had simply to wait till the Germans made arrangements for the repatriation of enemy aliens, and they would be home for Christmas. But suddenly it became known that the British refused to recognize as a British subject anyone, even though the title to such status was unquestionable, if he or she had been domiciled in Germany when the war broke out; and Mary Andrews appeared to the official eye to be in just that situation, because the purchasers of her villa on the Alster had not completed the transaction by 4 August 1914.

This was an utterly incredible reversal of her world. Her husband had been part Danish, and to him the rape of Schleswig-Holstein* had been still an outrage after half a century, and also he was fractionally British by blood and wholly British in spirit; and she was half British and half Russian, and Germany was now attacking Denmark, Britain and Russia. Why, the German troops were by then deep in the Baltic provinces; her beloved Lithuania was in danger. She had to seek refuge in an alien country, and waited in Hamburg while her London lawyers and her dead husband's English friends worked at getting her recognition as a British subject, and arranged for her flight to a hotel in Amsterdam.

Henry had to stay in Hamburg for good; and I cannot make out how long his mother was able to stay with him; both knew he would certainly be interned, as he would not be allowed to return home and fight for his country. At that moment his position did not perturb him, though it soon became certain he was to be interned in Germany for the duration of the war. In the last weeks before Mary's departure her emotions had seemed like an incurable disease, and he had hardly any opportunity to consider his own. This gave him a feeling of deprivation of which he was ashamed. The truth was that his state of happiness was persisting; he had only to concentrate on his own thoughts to be in a state of ecstasy. All his faculties seemed magically enhanced. He abandoned himself to an orgy of reading; he could not have enough of Plato and Shelley, he became infatuated with the now almost forgotten French religious writer, Charles Péguy,* whom he had started reading in the last years at Chartres. He wrote much poetry, all of it bad, but throbbing with emotions which might have produced poetry had he not had the tin ear for language which is sometimes the penalty for being a polyglot, and was therefore unable to recognize when a word has been edged into a position where it loses its virtue. He took singing lessons from a choirmaster in the town, and piano lessons from an aged pupil of Clara Schumann, and both thought well of him. And nobody said him nay. He ran about the town as he liked, pursuing academic knowledge, and finding it very happily, in the person of a mathematics tutor, who perhaps was the best discovery of all.

But not long before Christmas this odd holiday time ended. Henry had a note of warning two days earlier, and he was packed and ready, but that had happened twice before and nobody had turned up. He was reading the daily paper, and suddenly looked up to find two elderly private soldiers looking down at him with an expression of bewilderment. They asked if he were Henry Andrews and when he said that he was, they went over and spoke to the porter and pointed at him and got an answer, shook their heads and came back to him; and then they led him out into the street, and round the corner took him into a beer-hall, where he bought them some drinks and they nodded over the foam and told him that there was certainly a mistake somewhere, and he would not be long in camp. He might, they mentioned, be back in his hotel by nightfall.

Henry took this simply as evidence of good feeling and most likely baseless, and treated them to some more beer, and then they all went on their way and in the course of time, with more incomprehensible reassurances, his companions left him at some barracks. As they got to the entrance hall he asked them to wait a minute while he read the notices that were stuck up on boards all over the hall. These confirmed the surprising impression which had already been given him by the crowds standing around him. There were some German non-commissioned officers and other ranks, and these were the only white men; all the others who, like him, were not in uniform and were carrying their hand luggage, were black, brown or yellow. This was indeed an establishment of the sort that had been described in an American newspaper shown to him by Mr Hays Morgan some weeks before, as having been planned by the German Foreign Office. It was a camp for the natives of British colonies, who were to be trained as propagandists and guerrillas, so that they could return to their native lands and lead their fellow tribesmen in rebellion against the tyranny of the Union Jack.

It puzzled Henry that he was not thrown out immediately. He was already over six feet tall, and though his hair was dark, he had an exceedingly white skin and very blue eyes, and thus presented an appearance which did not fit in with the standard Burmese physique. But it was at once obvious that this was to be a sybaritic camp where the Asiatics were to be seduced into changing their loyalty by delightful conditions, including liberal and spicy meals. One was served to him soon after the doors of the establishment closed on him. He therefore tried, but not with much hope of success, to fox his observers by never speaking German if he could possibly speak Burmese, which he had learned to speak as a child, and he was accustomed to speak with his mother and his uncle and his brother, since it was taken for granted that both the boys would enter the service of Wallace Brothers. He was surprised to find that the officers in charge seemed entirely convinced by this linguistic fraud. Even when he asked for permission to go out to change his books at the Hamburg libraries, and had frequently got it, his captors seemed to retain undisturbed an impression that Burmese was his only, or at least his chief language. He was to learn twice in his life that war consists in equal parts of sometimes highly intelligent and sometimes imbecile military action and the complete suspension of thought regarding non-military problems.

He also discovered that though his letters from his mother were always written in English, and were read by camp censors, that too caused no incredulity regarding his Burmese origin. Only once he saw doubt rising. A spectacled old man came up to him and took his measurements and compared the result with some tables in a hand-book; and shook his head. Then he shut the hand-book and addressed Henry in English, German, French and some Slav language, and a number of Oriental languages, including Burmese, which (and it alone) brought a cascade of response from Henry. The spectacled old man and a colleague looked at each other, and walked away as if in deep grief. They were disappointed at more than their failure to resolve the mystery of Henry's ethnic being, he reflected. The hand-book must have outlined a system. It had not worked. This, for a German, would be a tragedy.

But the world got greyer. They were into winter when a party of men, all with deeply lined and tanned faces, came to visit the establishment; and Henry was called into a small room to speak with one of them alone. On the way from the compound Henry polished up his monkey tricks, but when he was face to face with his inquisitor forgot them. He had an odd feeling that he had often seen this man, long ago; but the name that was on the tip of his tongue never came clear, though to the end of his life he felt he knew it. The stranger said, in beautiful, rather old-fashioned German, 'I knew your father and your mother in Rangoon and in Zurich. You are not Burmese and you are not English either. You are German, and I will give you an oppor-tunity to fight for your own people.'

Henry said, 'But of course I am English. My father's name was Andrews, and he came from the Lowlands of Scotland.' The stranger said, 'That is a strange way to be English. The Scots detest the English. They are a recent conquest and they will be free in our lifetime.' This made Henry smile. 'But,' said the stranger, 'let us get back to essentials. You are German and it should be your pride and your glory to fight for Germany.'

'Fight for Germany?' repeated Henry, and smiled again. 'I would end up in the Tower.'

The German said disagreeably, 'Here too we have towers,' and glared at him.

Henry had learned at school the myopic's trick for frustrating the reproachful gaze. He took off his spectacles and polished them, blinking as out of a fog, blinder than blindness, and smiling, as if he would give anything to be able to see this nice person who was somewhere about. Amiably he said, 'I would rather die than betray my country,' and was answered, 'It will not come to that. For one thing you are useless to us as a soldier. What could we do with a young man who is blind as you and who is deaf?' Henry thought that this was a curious mistake for him to make. His sight was poor, but nobody had ever found anything wrong with his hearing. 'But you might have done your duty to Germany in Burma in other ways. However, if your feelings against your true country are as they are, you can stay here in safety till the war ends. Your legal status, though not, I think, your moral status, is unquestionable. You are a civilian prisoner of war and you will be interned till the end of the war, and then, as Germany is a law-abiding country, you will be released and allowed to go where you will. Back to a vanquished England.'

'Right,' said Henry, and they bid a civil goodbye.

Some days later Henry was taken by train on a south-easterly journey to Spandau, a town not far from Berlin, in the Prussian province of Brandenburg. It was then best known for the moated Julius Tower in its disused citadel, which contained what was known as the German War Treasury, gold reserved from the indemnity of six million pounds paid by France at the end of the Franco-Prussian War, and it had been placed in the tower so that it could be used to finance the next war.* This must have already become, in the eyes of the gods, a pathetic antique. It was the equivalent of £6,000,000; which even in 1914 would hardly have kept a European army going from breakfast till teatime. The camp which took Henry to itself, just before Christmas, 1914, was a converted racecourse lying on a wind-swept heath, not far from the meeting of two rivers, and was called Ruhleben: Peaceful Living.

NOTES

PART ONE: THE CAMPBELL MACKENZIES

p. 16   RW (Cicely Fairfield) was born on 21 December 1892 at 28 Burlington Road, Westbourne Park, Paddington. Her husband, Henry Maxwell Andrews, whom she married in 1930, was born in Rangoon in 1894.

p. 17   In *Cousin Rosamund* (London, 1985, p. 105), Mary consults her 'Scottish Family Bible' 'that had Mamma's people in it up to her great-grandfather, who was born when his parents were on the run after the rebellion of 1745'. This Mackenzie ancestor belonged to a Forfarshire Militia Band; his son John, RW's great-grandfather (1797–1852), was a violinist in Aberdeen and Edinburgh.

The Jacobite uprisings of 1715 and 1745 followed the union with England in 1707. In 1745 Bonnie Prince Charlie (Charles Edward Stuart, 1720–88) raised his father's standard and rallied 2,000 Highlanders. A year later his army was routed at Culloden and he fled to France. The defeat was followed by mass evictions of Highland crofters.

*   RW's grandfather, Alexander Mackenzie (1819–57), was a violinist, popular song-writer and editor of *The National Dance Music of Scotland*. He also wrote an operetta, *The Provost's Daughter* (1852). He succeeded James Dewar as Leader of the Theatre Royal Orchestra in 1845, taking the band on annual visits to London and actively promoting recent European music. His death at 37 left his wife Janet with six children to raise: Alick (b. 1847), Johnnie (1849), Willie (1850), Jessie (1852), Isabella (1854) and Joey (1856).

*   Karol Jozef Lipinski (1790–1861), Polish violinist, conductor, composer and teacher, from 1839 Royal Konzertmeister at Dresden.

*   Prosper Philippe Catherine Sainton (1813–1890), a Frenchman, was professor of violin at the Royal Academy of Music, 1845–90. Later, in the 1860s, Alick also studied under him.

*   The 'technical achievement' of James Ballantine (1808–77) as a painter was in reviving the art of glass-painting; he executed the stained-glass windows at the House of Lords. He also published volumes of poetry.

p. 18   William Henry Murray (1790–1852), actor-manager and character actor, managed the Theatre Royal 1815–48; Thomas (Tom) Moore (1779–1852) was the poet who was responsible for destroying Byron's memoirs, editing his work and writing his biography. He was married to Bessie Dyke, sister of Murray's first wife; both were actresses.

* William Murray's grandfather Sir John Murray (1718–77) had been too ill to be present at Culloden but was later arrested and taken to London where he turned King's evidence. Support for RW's notion that William was still victimized by staunch Jacobites is given in *The Annals of the Edinburgh Stage* (1888), where James C. Dibdin recounts how an old Scotswoman who actually remembered Bonnie Prince Charlie and his 'ungrateful traitor' of a secretary spat at William, '*Curses* on the *name!*'

p. 19 (Sir) Alexander Mackenzie's (Alick's) reputation, as both composer and musical administrator (he was Principal of the Royal Academy of Music from 1888), was and remains substantial. After 1885 it was achieved largely in England, where from 1892–99 he was the permanent conductor of the Philharmonic Society's concerts. Knighted in 1895, he was created KCVO in 1922. He is conventionally seen as having, together with Parry and Stanford, set the late nineteenth-century revival of British music on a firm footing by the transmission of contemporary European techniques.

As source material for her account of life at Heriot Row, RW has drawn extensively on Alick's autobiography, *A Musician's Narrative* (London, 1927), though their interpretation of events is often markedly different. In exercise book 13a RW describes him as 'repulsive in his coldness'. Apparently when her mother Isabella was dying she asked to see him but he refused to make the short journey. He came to her funeral in 1921 but left after 'a hasty handshake'.

* The principal of a town band was more commonly known as *Stadtmusikdirektor*; other titles for German musicians in civil employment include *Stadtpfeifer*. These paid employees in areas of high musical culture had to struggle to preserve their monopoly, especially in the atmosphere of increased freedom and competitiveness which followed the French Revolution.

p. 20 Alexander died on 10 August 1857.

p. 21 Eduard Stein (1818–64), pupil of Mendelssohn, friend of Liszt, who founded the reputation of the *Lohkonzerte* in Sondershausen.

p. 22 Here as elsewhere RW conflates the stages in a complex pattern of musical development. When she describes Alick as belonging to the same generation as these composers she is referring to the spirit and ideals of the music played in Sondershausen, particularly the nineteenth-century Lisztian school. In fact, Mendelssohn and Schumann were both dead by the time of Alick's arrival at Sondershausen, and it was Wagner and Liszt who were, in the third quarter of the century, identified as the foremost composers of 'new music'. Liszt's mature orchestral style was formed in the twelve or so years after 1848 – even closer, that is, than RW implies to the time of Alick's arrival.

* Liszt's symphonic poem *Mazeppa* was first performed in Weimar in 1854.

p. 23 Probably the 'Scottish concerto' of 1897. Ferruccio Benvenuto Busoni (1866–1924) was a German-Italian pianist, composer for piano and opera, and an influential music critic.

p. 24 Jean-Baptiste Greuze (1725–1805), a genre and portrait painter whose best-known works include 'Innocence' and 'The Broken Pitcher'.

* *Carnaval*, composed 1833–35, published in 1837 as op. 9, by Robert Schumann (1810–56), perhaps the major early influence on Mackenzie's style.

p. 25 The involvement of the family lawyer was possibly more substantial than is suggested. In *Rebecca West: A Life* (London, 1987) Victoria Glendinning suggests that Janet's father in fact set her up in her lace shop, installing her as manager, and also helped support the household at Heriot Row, one of the smartest streets in Edinburgh.

p. 27 Chapter 2. RW also refers to this conversation in *The Strange Necessity*.

* Merchant Maiden's was founded in 1694 by Mary Erskine and a company of merchants in Cowgate. From 1857–71 it was on the site of George Watson's Hospital.

p. 28 *berthe* = a deep (usually lace) collar on a low-necked dress.

p. 29 footpad = unmounted highwayman.

p. 33 In 1873 Alick became conductor of the Scottish Vocal Musical Association.

* Alick became precentor of St George's Church in 1870.

* In the Established Church the use of the organ was illegal up to 1864, though the law was sometimes flouted.

* There is a conflation here of ecclesiastical and secular traditions. RW probably means the 'new music' of the European instrumental composers with whom Mackenzie's early training had made him familiar.

p. 34 The music dealers and publishers Paterson and Sons specialized in standard editions of Scottish songs.

* Frederick Niecks (1845–1924), German musical scholar and author, Reid Professor of Music at Edinburgh University from 1891–1914. He was in fact two years *older* than Alick.

p. 38 In another version (exercise book 23) RW describes cousin Elizabeth as 'the notoriously sulky Flora' and gives an alternative account of her abrupt departure from Heriot Row, in which she runs off with a Glaswegian bookie, marries an animal trainer in America and ends up as the wealthy wife of a Boston Irish policeman. Fifty years later Flora/Elizabeth is supposed to have said to her cousin Jessie: 'Year after year I waited for your mother to say just once that my father was a lousy bastard for deserting my sister and me, and the words never came . . . Anyway, your mother gave us girls the leftovers and she spoiled the boys rotten, and there wasn't [one] who had a decent streak in him except that poor Joey. Why should I forgive your fool of a mother for all that?!' It seems likely that the two versions are equally fictive.

p. 40 Dr Letitia Fairfield (1885–1978). See note for p. 202.

* The hedgehog incident is in *Sunflower* (London, 1986), pp. 253–55.

* 'Greenhouse with Cyclamens', *A Train of Powder* (London, 1955, Virago reprint 1984, p. 255). Puhl was a Reichsbank official who gave evidence in the Funk trial at Nuremberg.

p. 41 Alick also tells the Chantrelle story in his autobiography.

p. 43 Her name was in fact Mary Melina Burnside (in public records and in private family trees) but RW recast her as Ironside. In a document owned by Alison Selford called 'The Mackenzie Tree' RW wrote that Mary was 'the daughter of a gardener at the Rosslyn Estate near Edinburgh, and the village minister sent her to Alick with a letter of introduction to him. She had sung in his choir, and had taken a job in some office or shop in Edinburgh.'

248   NOTES TO PAGES 49–91

* The ability to sing a specified note without preliminary playing, or to identify a heard note unseen.

p. 49 Samuel Smiles (1812–1904), social and political reformer and author of the best-selling *Self-Help* (1859), a didactic work promoting thrift, hard work and self-improvement.

p. 51 Irvingites were revivalists, members of the Catholic Apostolic Church who believed that the second coming of Christ was imminent. The doctrine was in part inspired by the Scottish minister Edward Irving (1792–1834).

p. 52 Keelie boys = members of an Edinburgh street gang.

p. 54 RW more likely means Schumann's chamber works involving piano.

p. 60 gey large = pretty large; eident = keen.

p. 63 bawbees = coppers.

* weans = young children.

* havers = nonsense.

p. 64 gey and low = pretty low.

p. 67 Sir James Simpson lived at 52 Queen Street from 1850–70.

p. 70 This is the Manet painting used on the jacket, now housed in the Staatliche Museen, Preussischer Kulturbesitz, Nationalgalerie, Berlin. RW possessed a print of the picture, given to her by the critic Alexander Woolcott and now owned by her friend Gwenda David.

p. 71 *Ancestral Voices* (London, 1975), p. 28. The entry for 28 February 1942 reads: '. . . Rebecca West speaks in a high, rolling, not unaffected voice which somehow does not become her, and does not give a right indication of her essentially masculine mind. She is handsome-plain, of big build, with uncouth legs and hands. And she is big enough to brush aside and defy all conventions that are a hindrance.'

p. 72 Alick may have known all four musicians. He met Hans von Bülow (1830–94), German conductor and pianist, in 1877–78: von Bülow performed his overture *Cervantes* in Glasgow in December 1879; Anton Gregor Rubinstein (1830–94), composer and pianist whose playing was said to match Liszt's, frequently toured Europe; Joseph Joachim (1831–1907), violinist, composer, conductor and teacher, visited England annually from 1862; Clara Schumann (1819–96), German pianist and composer, regularly played in England after her husband Robert's death in 1856.

p. 74 Some of these operas Isabella would have seen later, in London, and the memory of them has been transposed.

p. 75 Robert Henry Wyndham (1817–94), Scottish actor-manager, manager of the Theatre Royal at a variety of sites from 1853–75. Sir Henry Irving became a member of Wyndham's company in 1857.

p. 81 stramash = commotion.

p. 84 *Ruins of the Palace of the Emperor Diocletian at Spalato* (1764) marked an important stage in the 'Adam revolution'. Charles-Louis Clerisseau (1722–1820) was one of the architectural draughtsmen who accompanied Adam to Spalato (Split) in Dalmatia to study the palace.

p. 86 Since Isabella died in 1921, this passage can be dated to the late 1970s.

p. 90 The 1967 Sexual Offences Act decriminalized male homosexual activities in private for adults over 21, excluding the armed forces, in England and Wales.

p. 91 In another version RW implies that Joey was the scapegoat for a hushed-up scandal, and writes: 'It is said that Robert Louis Stevenson had been at the party, and that this brought to a climax his unhappy relations with his family.' Perhaps RW could not resist spinning a tale around the fact that the Stevensons also lived in Heriot Row, that RLS was a contemporary of her uncles (he was born in 1850), and that he and his student friends were well known for their defiance of the prudish, self-regarding New Town, preferring to spend their evenings in the company of prostitutes and criminals. Jenni Calder (*RLS: A Life Story*, London, 1980) refers to a fierce confrontation between RLS and his father one night in 1873, which RW might have known about: the timescale in this chapter shifts back and forth during the 1870s.

PART TWO: ISABELLA

p. 98   John Bidgood, who took the photographs of the young Fairfields in the 1890s.

p. 99   Tramontan = a wind coming from beyond the Alps.

*   The strathspey is a slow Scottish reel, which usually either leads into or is led into by a foursome or eightsome reel, without a break.

p. 113   The Heinemanns' kindness to RW's mother continued: they helped her out financially when she lived in London with her young family in the 1890s. They appear (as 'Kastner') in 'A Visit to a Godmother', *Writers on Themselves*, ed. Norman Nicholson (London, 1964).

p. 116   The Mackenzies had moved to No. 5 Duncan Street.

p. 117   The awful, symbolic hat is reminiscent of Hedda Gabler's relationship with her husband's Aunt Juju.

p. 121   William Kent (1685–1748), architect, interior decorator and furniture designer; Sir Henry Raeburn (1756–1826), a leading Scottish portrait painter who specialized in recording the likenesses of lawyers, scholars and the bourgeoisie: he drew straight on to canvas with his brush.

p. 122   A former goldfield district 73 miles north-west of Melbourne. The city of Ballarat is now a major country town.

p. 124   Willie's last words in this book are reminiscent of Osvald's in *Ghosts*.

p. 132   gamboge = a gum resin from Eastern trees which gives a bright yellow colour.

*   deeved to death = up to here (literally, deafened).

PART THREE: THE FAIRFIELDS

p. 149   Perhaps RW's watercolour, now owned by her nephew, was indeed an English coastal scene: according to its Historical Society, St Kilda has never been a pebble or stony beach and the shoreline is very flat, apart from some esplanades built in 1860.

*   Almost certainly the Royal Hotel on the corner of Robe Street and the esplanade, quite close to Acland Street, where the Fairfields later set up house.

p. 150   Marcus Clarke (1846–81) was a sheep-farmer and journalist known for his stories and plays about Australian life. His famous book *For the Term of his Natural Life* (1874) portrayed life in an Australian penal settlement.

p. 151   The *Melbourne Argus*, which was first published as the *Argus* in 1846. It was an influential paper whose origins could be traced back to the first newspaper in the settlement, the *Melbourne Advertiser*, published in 1838 by John Pascoe Fawkner, one of the founding settlers. The first issues were handwritten.

p. 157   The Yarra River divides the city, and ferry posts were built to traverse it, usually with inns nearby. This inn must have been near one such river crossing point, possibly at what is now the Punt road bridge. RW was fascinated by waterside inns and their proprietors and used both in her fiction, often with a religious connection.

p. 166   Flemington racecourse was established in the suburb of the same name in 1840, and the famous Melbourne Cup race, with its week-long carnival, is held there annually.

p. 174   This was the journey through the Balkans for *Black Lamb and Grey Falcon*.

p. 175   RW sometimes refers to Elie (Michel-Elie Reclus, 1827–1904) by the name of his more famous brother Elisée (Jean-Jacques-Elisée Reclus, 1830–1905), but Elisée's pamphlet *Elie Reclus 1827–1904* mentions Elie's tutoring 'une famille irlandaise', and refers to Digby by name. Elie was involved not only in the republican movement of 1848 but in the 1871 Commune. He wrote a study of *Les Primitifs, études d'ethnologie comparée* (1885) and collaborated on many books with Elisée, who was also an anarchist, active in the Commune and the Siege of Paris. The brothers were members of the revolutionary circle of intellectual refugees who congregated at the British Museum in the 1850s.

*   Elsewhere RW implies that her grandfather (Charles Fairfield's father) was the illegitimate son of a Royal Duke.

p. 176   July 1863. Vicksburg was a Confederate stronghold impeding Union control of the Mississippi River. Greatly outnumbered, the Confederates capitulated only after a siege.

p. 177   RW's niece, Winifred's daughter Alison Selford, believes that her loathing of Sophie Blew-Jones (see intro, p. 5) derived in part from a remark of Sophie's that it was RW's affair with H.G. Wells that killed her mother. Such 'betrayal' was unlikely ever to be forgiven. It is to Aunt Sophie's credit that she started Lettie off on her medical career, though that is probably not how RW saw it.

p. 178   For a plausible interpretation of RW's account of Charles's young life, his first marriage and the birth of a child, see Victoria Glendinning, *op. cit.*, pp. 12–13.

p. 179   26 Acland Street, St Kilda.

*   Paul Sandby (1725–1809) was Drawing Master at the Royal Military Academy, Woolwich from 1768–97. He was a watercolour painter, engraver and caricaturist, and a pioneer of topographical art. He was draughtsman for the survey of the Northern and Western Scottish Highlands.

p. 180   Will Dyson (1880–1938), a cartoonist and native of Ballarat, son of a mining engineer, moved to London after his marriage to Ruby Lindsay and became chief cartoonist at the *Daily Herald*; the five Lindsays, children of a Ballarat country doctor – Percy (1870–1952), Lionel (1874–1961), Norman (1879–1969), Darryl

(1889–1976) and Ruby (1885–1919), were all celebrated Australian artists and thinkers; David Lowe (1891–1963), a New Zealander with whom RW collaborated, was cartoonist on the London *Star*, Beaverbrook's *Evening Standard*, and many other papers. His father was a pharmacist.

p. 181 From 1884, Charles Fairfield wrote for the *Melbourne Argus* as 'Ivan' on a variety of subjects from economics to art to the position of Jews and women in society.

p. 185 Elsewhere RW implies that the Pre-Raphaelite beauty committed suicide because she had been having an affair with Charles Fairfield.

p. 187 In a letter to her daughter 'Eedly' (Isabella) written soon after Lettie's birth, Janet Mackenzie sent greetings to Johnnie and Lizzie and wrote: 'Many thanks to Charlie for his letters — he puts me in mind of the Italian gentlemen who were so fond of their Babies.'

p. 188 In 'Greenhouse with Cyclamens', *A Train of Powder* (p. 30), RW refers to 'the golden flowers of a Maréchal Niel climbing rose'.

PART FOUR: CISSIE

p. 193 21 Streatham Place.

p. 194 Probably the reactionary Liberty and Property Defence League, founded by the Earl of Wemyss (Lord Elcho) in 1882 with the aim of promulgating individualism as against socialism.

* Shaw's biographer, Michael Holroyd, thinks that this story is likely to be apocryphal.

p. 195 28 Burlington Road, where RW was born.

* Malcolm McHardy, FRCS (1852–1913) was professor of Ophthalmology at King's College, London and consulting surgeon and Vice-President of the Royal Eye Hospital.

p. 197 Joined John Company, i.e. went to India.

p. 198 The Fairfields left Streatham in early 1898, so this passage was written in about the mid-1960s.

p. 199 *friandises* = delicacies, tit-bits.

p. 202 After graduating as one of the top candidates (a considerable achievement for a woman) from the Faculty of Medicine in Edinburgh, Lettie joined the Fabian Society and the WSPU and also read for the Bar. She later became a distinguished medical administrator, working mainly for the LCC, and was widely liked. RW kept up with her but maligned her, often with more passion than shown here, in all versions of her memoirs. Present members of the family think it highly unlikely that the phone conversation described here ever in fact took place. See also intro, p. 5.

p. 204 The hypocrisy of the Dreyfus affair, which RW discusses in detail in *1900*, was a favourite topic in the Fairfield household. The 'Dreyfus case in little' concerns Charles's brother Edward Fairfield, by now assistant under-secretary at the Colonial Office with special responsibility for South Africa. In 1897 Edward was publicly accused of having concealed information about the 1895 Jameson Raid from Joseph Chamberlain, the Colonial Secretary. He died in April of the same year.

p. 206   Probably the meningitis contracted by both Lettie and Winnie in 1897.

p. 209   9 Hermitage Road, Richmond.

*   C.J. Lander exhibited at the Royal Society of British Artists 1895–96.

p. 211   In a longer version of this story RW traces Miss Lysaght's links with an ancestor called Caroline Fairfield.

p. 215   Cousin Jessie's school was Helsington Towers, Bournemouth.

p. 219   The Queen of the Night is required to sing the note F two octaves and a fourth above middle C in each of her two arias.

ॐॐ

APPENDIX: HENRY MAXWELL ANDREWS

p. 223   Presumably some time after Henry's death in 1968.

*   The 'political decision' is RW's refusal, as a young journalist, to endorse Soviet Communism at a time when many writers were joining the Party. She never swerved from this conviction, developing her arguments in *The Meaning of Treason*.

p. 225   To summarize RW's very detailed account of her husband's ancestry:

On the maternal side, Henry's great-grandfather was a Lithuanian called Chavatsky. Henry's grandfather, a civil engineer, became manager of the Hamburg tram system, and married an Irish/Lancastrian, a Miss Chapman, in Manchester Cathedral. Their daughter Mary Chavatsky, Henry's mother, spent her early life in Hamburg, then some time in Lithuania. Mary was thus of Lithuanian/Irish/Lancastrian descent. She married Lewis Andrews when she was 29 and became a British subject.

On the paternal side, RW starts with an Andrews ancestor who emigrated from Scotland to Schleswig-Holstein in the early nineteenth century; later generations dispersed to Scotland, Canada, India. His grandfather Mark, 'mad and bad', ran a fleet of droshkies (a low four-wheeled carriage without a top) in Germany and married a Polish/Jewish/Danish girl. Their son Lewis, Henry's father, was thus Scottish/Danish/Jewish and he too was a British subject.

Lewis and Mary met in Hamburg while he was on a visit to relatives.

*   Sir John Linton Myres (1869–1954), a Lancastrian, was a classical archaeologist who wrote many books on Mediterranean geography, archaeology and anthropology. RW probably has in mind his Frazer lecture reprinted as *Mediterranean Culture* (London, 1943).

p. 226   The Danish baron's visit is not implausible. Scott's novels and poems were extremely popular in Europe and he often entertained admirers at his home in Abbotsford-on-the-Tweed, acquired in 1811–12.

The authenticity of the best-selling epic, *Poems of Ossian*, also widely read abroad, was much disputed. They had been 'discovered' by James Macpherson (1736–96), who described them as translations of a work by a third-century Gaelic poet.

p. 227   RW is probably implying that the three brothers were involved in espionage.

p. 228   'The expense of spirit in a waste of shame/Is lust in action' (Sonnet 129).

* *cloisonnés* = enamels.

* Possibly the Dolder Grand Hotel on the Zürichsberg.

p. 231 In some versions RW names this school as Uppingham.

* Gunter's was an Italian tea-shop on the east side of Berkeley Square, said to have the best ices in London. It was one of the few establishments that a lady could respectably visit unescorted.

p. 235 Mary Baker Eddy (1821–1910), founder of the Christian Science Association in America (1876), a religious movement holding that if faith is unquestioned sickness will be seen as illusory; medicine and drugs were renounced in favour of prayer.

p. 239 In other versions RW names this Cabinet Minister as Arthur Balfour, though he was of course out of office in 1914.

* Harry Hays Morgan (1860–1933), Consul General at many European cities, was at Hamburg 1913–17.

* The rape of Schleswig-Holstein = its annexation by Germany in 1865.

p. 240 Charles Péguy (1873–1914), French poet and socialist who published the republican journal *Les Cahiers de la Quinzaine*.

p. 243 As well as ceding Alsace and most of Lorraine, the French government agreed to an indemnity of five milliard (hundred thousand) francs, reduced from six milliard. It was paid off by September 1873 (Alistair Horne, *The Fall of Paris*, London, 1965). The Imperial War Treasure in the Julius Tower was kept as an emergency war reserve.

EDITORIAL NOTE
AND ACKNOWLEDGEMENTS

At her death in 1983, RW left a great many papers and documents which are now housed at the University of Tulsa. *Family Memories* is based on a draft typescript and xeroxes of the material which related to RW's 'Parental Memoirs', as they were then described, written between the middle 1960s and her death. Unfortunately, none of the material is dated.

The material includes an early typescript, probably written in the early 1970s (labelled A to E); a great many early drafts, some typed and some handwritten, and 32 exercise books (labelled 1–23 with sub-labelling: 13 A, B, etc.) which form the basis of this edition. At different times of her life RW changed the order in which she wanted the material to appear. The section on her husband, for instance, which now appears as an Appendix, was at one time intended as the opening chapter.

RW was a meticulous writer and she tended to make only minor revisions to manuscripts and typescripts. She preferred to start all over again, and some ideas or episodes exist in over twenty different versions. She was working on the 'Memoirs', with her last secretary Diana Stainforth, at the time of her death, and readings of the manuscripts and typescripts and Diana Stainforth's testimony suggest that a considerable body of the manuscript – the chapters on the Campbell Mackenzies and on her husband – had been carefully prepared and polished, as for publication. This probable intention has been respected: in these chapters few cuts have been made, and only gaps and transcription confusions have been attended to.

In the middle section – from Isabella's time in London to the Fairfields' courtship in Australia, written up in the late 1970s and early

1980s — the authorial hold as revealed in the exercise books and typescript was occasionally less firm, the afterthoughts more frequent, and here some further editorial intervention has been necessary. A long section on Mendelssohn and the Judaic-Christian tradition, as told to Isabella Mackenzie by William Heinemann, has been cut.

The history of RW's father Charles Fairfield has also been adapted. This was written and rewritten at great length right up to her death, and a more tractable version has been constructed, based on an early, short account.

The sections dealing with the Fairfields' marriage and the childhood fragments (Part 4), have been compiled from exercise books 13–23. The childhood material was in the main written from the middle 1960s to the early 1970s, and though a typed early draft (Typescript E) provided a basic chronological framework, RW had not incorporated it into the 'Memoirs' by the time of her death. Here much early transcription, sorting, dating and research was carried out by Diana Stainforth at the request of RW's executors.

Straightforward errors (e.g., confusion or misspelling of names or dates) have been silently corrected throughout. Some repetition and 'notes to self' have been cut; transcription errors have been corrected; obvious mistakes (e.g., failure to amend a sentence after a change of heart) have been put right. Chapter divisions, titles and paragraphing have been introduced. Minor cuts have been made wherever illegibility or sense demanded, bearing in mind RW's style and preoccupations as revealed in the body of her published work. It has been decided not to include an index, to avoid conflict with the partly imaginary style of the narration.

During the preparation of this edition, the following people offered advice, information, support or all three: Gwenda David, Monica Evans, Victoria Glendinning, Michael Holroyd, Vida House, Alan Maclean, Marion Macleod, Norman Macleod, Ursula Owen, Jane Parkin, Mollie Robarts, Anne Surma, Raleigh Trevelyan and Martin Wright. Particular thanks go to Rowland Cotterill for his insights into the history of music; to Alison Selford (Macleod) for family documents and a sense of balance; to Diana Stainforth for her valuable work on the papers; to Rosa Stevens and Florence Birmingham for detective work on the Australian chapters; and to Dr John Stokes.

FOR THE BEST IN PAPERBACKS, LOOK FOR THE 🐧

In every corner of the world, on every subject under the sun, Penguin represents quality and variety—the very best in publishing today.

For complete information about books available from Penguin—including Pelicans, Puffins, Peregrines, and Penguin Classics—and how to order them, write to us at the appropriate address below. Please note that for copyright reasons the selection of books varies from country to country.

In the United Kingdom: For a complete list of books available from Penguin in the U.K., please write to *Dept E.P., Penguin Books Ltd, Harmondsworth, Middlesex, UB7 0DA.*

In the United States: For a complete list of books available from Penguin in the U.S., please write to *Dept BA, Penguin,* Box 999, Bergenfield, New Jersey 07621-0999.

In Canada: For a complete list of books available from Penguin in Canada, please write to *Penguin Books Canada Ltd, 2801 John Street, Markham, Ontario L3R 1B4.*

In Australia: For a complete list of books available from Penguin in Australia, please write to the *Marketing Department, Penguin Books Australia Ltd, P.O. Box 257, Ringwood, Victoria 3134.*

In New Zealand: For a complete list of books available from Penguin in New Zealand, please write to the *Marketing Department, Penguin Books (NZ) Ltd, Private Bag, Takapuna, Auckland 9.*

In India: For a complete list of books available from Penguin, please write to *Penguin Overseas Ltd, 706 Eros Apartments, 56 Nehru Place, New Delhi, 110019.*

In Holland: For a complete list of books available from Penguin in Holland, please write to *Penguin Books Nederland B.V., Postbus 195, NL-1380AD Weesp, Netherlands.*

In Germany: For a complete list of books available from Penguin, please write to *Penguin Books Ltd, Friedrichstrasse 10–12, D–6000 Frankfurt Main 1, Federal Republic of Germany.*

In Spain: For a complete list of books available from Penguin in Spain, please write to *Longman Penguin España, Calle San Nicolas 15, E–28013 Madrid, Spain.*

In Japan: For a complete list of books available from Penguin in Japan, please write to *Longman Penguin Japan Co Ltd, Yamaguchi Building, 2-12-9 Kanda Jimbocho, Chiyoda-Ku, Tokyo 101, Japan.*